D1563646

Born to Serve

RACE AND CULTURE IN THE AMERICAN WEST

Quintard Taylor, Series Editor

Born to Serve

A History of
TEXAS SOUTHERN UNIVERSITY

MERLINE PITRE

University of Oklahoma Press : Norman

Publication of this book is made possible through
the generosity of Edith Kinney Gaylord.

Library of Congress Cataloging-in-Publication Data

Names: Pitre, Merline, 1973– author.
Title: Born to serve : a history of Texas Southern University / Merline Pitre. Description:
Norman : University of Oklahoma Press, 2018. | Series: Race and culture in
   the American West ; 14 | Includes bibliographical references and index. Identifiers:
LCCN 2017049021 | ISBN 978-0-8061-6002-3 (hardcover) ISBN 978-0-8061-6890-6 (paper)
Subjects: LCSH: Texas Southern University—History. | African Americans—Education,
   Higher—Texas—History. | BISAC: EDUCATION / History. | HISTORY / United
   States / State & Local / Southwest (AZ, NM, OK, TX). | HISTORY / United States /
   20th Century.
Classification: LCC LC2851.T45 P57 2018 | DDC 378.764/1411—dc23
LC record available at https://lccn.loc.gov/2017049021

Born to Serve: A History of Texas Southern University is Volume 14
in the Race and Culture in the American West series.

The p aper i n t his b ook m eets t he g uidelines f or p ermanence a nd d urability o f t he
Committee on Production Guidelines for Book Longevity of the Council on Library
Resources, Inc. ∞

For

Llayron L. Clarkson and Alvin Wardlaw

Stalwarts of Texas Southern University

Contents

Illustrations

Map

Figures

Preface

Texas Southern University (TSU) is similar to, yet different from, other Historically Black Colleges and Universities (HBCUs). Whereas most HBCUs were established during the Reconstruction and post-Reconstruction eras, Texas Southern University was born during a burgeoning civil rights movement after World War II. Unlike many HBCUs that started as normal schools and later became colleges, TSU sprang full grown with an undergraduate school, a law school, a pharmacy school (one year later), and very little state funding. Created as part of a segregated system, Texas Southern appeared to starve for resources for much of its history and generally lacked the academic facilities, faculty salary pools, and other features found at top universities. In an era when state leaders are frequently talking about degree completion, Texas Southern remains proud of its historic mission, which includes taking students who need remediation before undertaking college-level work and giving them a second chance. In a word, TSU has always done more with less. Yet, after seventy years of its existence as a state supported institution, TSU is without a written comprehensive history. To date, five books have been written on its history. Three of these volumes—Ira Bryant, *Texas Southern University: Its Antecedents, Political Origin and Future*; John Lash, Hortense Dixon, and Thomas Freeman, *Texas Southern University: From Separation to Special Purpose*; and William E. Terry, *The Origin and Development of Texas Southern University*—stop with the administration of the fourth president. E. Bun Lee's *TSU Meets the Press* is an edited version of white newspaper coverage of the university. And the fifth book, the Earl Carl Institute's *Our Story: A History of the Presidents of Texas Southern University*, is a coffee table book that gives only a snapshot view of the presidents. It is, therefore, the purpose of this study to provide a comprehensive history of the university and to place it in its proper perspective among HBCUs, as well other similar institutions.

This book is the culmination of years of reflecting, researching, collecting, and writing. Needless to say, it took longer than I wish to acknowledge. But writing *Born to Serve* was more than an intellectual exercise for me. Not only did I learn more about black men's and women's efforts to advocate for and subsequently to help maintain an institution of higher learning for African Americans, but also I came to appreciate more fully the sacrifices that others made so that I could tell their stories. Their trials and tribulations, successes and failures took on different meanings as I looked at them anew.

During its various stages of development, this book has benefitted from suggestions and criticisms of my many history colleagues, namely, Howard Beeth, Wilma King, and Patricia Prather. My most faithful reader was my former colleague and professor of English, Billy Turner. His assistance was of immeasurable value. He "curry combed" the manuscript, offering extensive comments, correcting facts and notes, and questioning interpretations. I would also like to thank and acknowledge the staff of the manuscript collections at the Lyndon Baines Johnson Library, the Dolph Briscoe History Center at the University of Texas, the University of Houston Library, and The African American Library at the Gregory School, The Houston Metropolitan Research Center, and, of course, the Heartman Collection at Texas Southern. I owe a special thanks to Joyce Thomas and Ruth Blesdsoe, who work in the Heartman Collection where TSU's Presidential Papers are housed. They always greeted me with smiling faces and open arms. Also, it has been wonderful working with Kent Calder, acquisition editor of the University of Oklahoma Press. He and the editorial staff not only offered enthusiastic support and sage advice, but their patience and help made all the difference in the final state of this work.

Finally, I wish to pay tribute to the elders of TSU, Llayron L. Clarkson, Everett O. Bell, and Alvin Wardlaw, who sat down with me on many occasions to discuss "the way it was." Acknowledgment also goes to James M. Douglas, who while president approved a semester sabbatical leave for me to do research for this project. I owe a debt for the typing of this manuscript to Debra Cartwright and the late Marsha Howard. Likewise, I am indebted to Karen Kossie Chernyshev for serving as my photographer, along with Paul Charles. Gratitude is also extended to many of my friends and colleagues for proofreading this manuscript and for their encouragement in this endeavor: Shirley Nealy, Bonnie James, Serbino Sandifer-Walker, Irvine Epps, Shawna Williams, Tomiko Meeks, and Deborah Dirden. As usual, my family provided me with the kind of support that only a family could.

Born to Serve

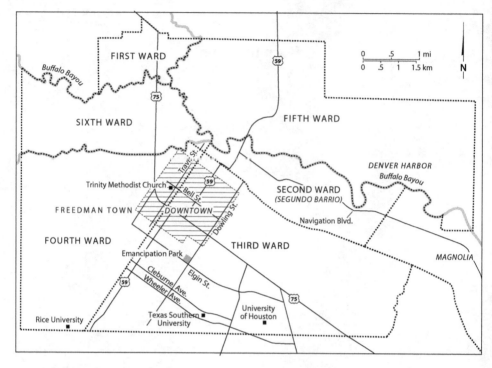

Texas Southern University in relation to Houston's wards, notable landmarks, and other universities. Cartography by Bill Nelson.

1

The Nucleus

Houston Colored Junior College
and Houston College for Negroes, 1927–1947

Established to serve the African American citizens of the state of Texas, Texas Southern University (TSU) was born during the era of Jim Crow in a climate during which white Texans were desperately trying to hold on to a black-proof economic, political, and educational system. Although Houston Colored Junior College, established in 1927, formed the nucleus from which TSU became a state-supported institution in 1947, the call for a separate black university began as early as 1876, with the establishment of the University of Texas (UT). The 1876 Texas Constitution, in making provisions for separate schools, colleges, and universities, explicitly stated that "the Legislature shall also when deem practicable establish and provide for the maintenance of a college branch university for the instruction of colored youths of the state to be located by a voice vote of the people."[1] Almost from the time that this clause was inserted into the constitution, both whites and blacks argued over its implementation. When Prairie View A&M College was established in 1878, the issue became even more complicated. Some individuals took the position to mean that with the establishment of Prairie View, the above-mentioned provision of the constitution had been fulfilled. Others argued that Prairie View was only a normal school and could not be classified as a classical university. Still others felt that if blacks were to receive a liberal arts education, a separate university with a curriculum similar to that of the University of Texas was required.[2]

The chief proponents of a branch university were black legislators and the Colored Teachers Association. In 1888, Robert J. Moore, a black state representative, submitted a resolution that "the Board of Education be requested to make arrangements for a building site for the branch university and for raising funds as it thinks best." Another African American

3

legislator, Nathan H. Haller, introduced a bill in 1893 to establish a branch university for colored youths of Texas. Both bills died in committee. The evidence seems to suggest that from 1878 to 1895, both Democrats and Republicans were dealing more in rhetoric than in substance on this issue.[3] But there appeared to have been a glimmer of hope on the issue in 1896, as blacks and some of their white allies gave support to the cause. In that year, the Texas Colored Teachers Association, one of the most vocal supporters for the branch university, asserted that "now is the time to strive for a colored university. . . . Every teacher and preacher in the state must see the importance and necessity of this school."[4] Robert Lloyd Smith, the lone black in the 1896 Texas legislature, made a motion in support of his white colleague's bill to set aside fifty thousand acres of taxable properties for the creation of a separate branch university.[5] But no sooner had this bill passed than the Texas Supreme Court in the case of *Hogue v. Baker (1898)* nullified the action of the legislature and prohibited the land commissioner A. C. Baker from appropriating more land for educational purposes.[6] It was not until 1915 that the state of Texas decided to take action on the branch university issue. Even so, the amendments that were proposed to provide land and money for black higher education were defeated.

Meanwhile, from the Reconstruction era to two decades into the twentieth century, black higher education in Texas existed through a system of private, church-affiliated liberal arts colleges—since Prairie View did not become a full-fledged normal college until 1924.[7] A paucity of black state institutions of higher learning in Texas not only caused teacher training to be heavily dependent on black private colleges but also hampered the education of black teachers and students. Yet, given the Jim Crow system that existed in the South, if black students were to receive academic, industrial, or manual training, they would have to be taught by black professionals.

Despite the shortage of teachers during Reconstruction and post-Reconstruction, African Americans exhibited an insatiable appetite for knowledge. The illiteracy rate declined not only among the masses but among black Texans as well. In Texas, that rate declined from 53.2 percent in 1890 to 35.5 percent in 1920. A similar decline was also seen in Houston, which because of economic opportunities was well on its way to becoming the largest city in the state during the 1920s. Two decades earlier, oil was discovered in a well at Spindletop, located in Beaumont. This discovery had a tremendous effect on the southeastern part of Texas, including Houston. It transposed Houston into a boomtown and catalyzed a population explosion. And as the total population grew, so did the number of blacks. As

Jack Yates High School (later, Ryan Junior High, now Baylor High School for the Science Professions) is the site that housed the Houston Colored Junior College and Houston College for Negroes, 1926–1947. Courtesy of Merline Pitre.

such, Houston boasted of having the largest black middle-class population of any southern city. As this socioeconomic trend continued, blacks pushed for more schools and more teachers. For example, in 1900 Houston had one black high school (Old Colored High), but by 1911 there was a need to add a night school component to it. By 1926, another school was needed and added, namely, Jack Yates High.[8]

In-service institutes and extension classes offered by private black colleges were used as a means to ease the shortage of teachers in Houston, as well as throughout other cities in the South. While both programs were used to improve the quality of teacher preparation, the in-service institutes posed a special problem because they did not lead to the bachelor's degree. On the other hand, the extension class movement, which swept across the South in the 1920s, led to certification and the awarding of a bachelor's degree. Wiley College, located in Marshall, Texas, and considered by many at the time as the best historically black college west of the Mississippi River, took the lead in offering one of the first extension class programs in the Lone Star State.[9] Wiley opened its first extension class operations in Dallas in 1924 and made a similar move in Houston in 1925. At that time, there were only 175 black teachers in the Houston Independent School District (HISD), and of that number, only 16 held bachelor degrees. So, on September 11, 1925, at the request from a group of Houston teachers, Robert R. Davenport of Wiley College came to Trinity Methodist Church, which was then located on Travis Street at Bell Avenue in the Third Ward area of Houston, with a two-fold purpose in mind: to set up extension class operations and to register students. For the 1925–26 school year, extension classes were held at Old Colored High on San Felipe Street and included the following subjects: child psychology, French, rhetoric and composition, history, and government. These afternoon and evening classes were so popular during the academic year that the Prairie View alumni demanded that their alma mater participate in the extension school program. The demands for the classes became so great that during the second year (1926–27), additional faculty and building spaces were required. Jack Yates High, located on Elgin Street, was secured, but enrollment trends dictated that plans should be made for the future. Consequently, a visionary group of black citizens that included Ernest Ollington Smith, B. H. Watson, W. J. Smith, Helen Lafond, Mary E. Ben Isaacs, W. Leonard Davis, and Jacob T. (J. T.) Fox met with L. T. Cunningham, assistant superintendent of HISD, early in 1927 and requested the establishment of a colored junior college.[10]

The citizen committee was very perceptive. Its members were keenly aware that at the time Wiley College began its extension class experience in Dallas in 1924, Houston Independent School District had just hired a new superintendent, Edison Ellsworth Oberholtzer. Oberholtzer was not only concerned with filling the void of qualified teachers via in-service institutes, but he also was in the vanguard of the junior college movement that was sweeping the state. His position was of special interest to black teachers because many of them did not and could not attend Prairie View's in-service institute and had to travel to other sections of the country to become certified.[11]

Prior to African Americans meeting with Cunningham, a group of white high school graduating seniors met with Superintendent Oberholtzer in November 1926 to discuss what they called "an urgent matter." They were concerned with furthering their education but could not afford to go out of the city to do so; nor could they afford the tuition or meet admission standards at Rice Institute, the only institution of higher learning in the city. As Oberholtzer listened to their testimonies, he became more and more convinced of the need for a junior college system (for blacks and whites) in Houston. There were those who were of the opinion that Oberholtzer came to Houston with the idea of starting a junior college there inasmuch as the junior college movement had become a trend in Texas in the mid-1920s.[12] Time would prove them right. Amid cries from the citizens of Houston, Oberholtzer moved to establish a junior college system. He asked Rice Institute's board of trustees to help in the preparation for this two-year college system. After being rebuffed by Rice because of financial reasons, Oberholtzer turned to his own board of education, the Houston School Board (now HISD).

When Oberholtzer made a presentation before the board of education, he made it clear that a junior college system would be established with the provision that it would be self-sustaining and would not create a debt for the Houston Independent School District. Such a proposal aroused a number of critics; chief among them were the ones who said "it would not only be unwise, but impossible to operate these institutions on a self-sustaining basis." Many of the school board trustees, although supportive, questioned whether such a system could be successful without a tax base. Oberholtzer responded with a proposed budget: a tuition fee of $150 per thirty semester hours, or $6 per hour for a part-time student. He also proposed that the board of education open a bank account of $2,000 to cover any advance cost. This amount would be repaid to the board at the end of the first year.[13]

Oberholtzer also had plans for the physical plant, the staff, the faculty, and the issue of accreditation. During its hours of operation in the evening, the white junior college would use Sam Houston High, and the black junior college would use Jack Yates High School. By using these facilities, the colleges would not have to worry about maintenance, utilities, and janitorial services. The administrative staff would operate on what Superintendent Oberholtzer called the "Two-Hat Tier." Most HISD administrators simply donned another hat when they left for their respective junior college. The faculty was drawn from the ranks of senior instructors in Houston's public schools and would be paid a modest salary collected both from tuition and other income generated by the school district. Full-time members of the faculty would receive salaries ranging from $66.60 to $166.66 per month depending on their qualifications. Accreditation was also a major issue that had to be resolved before the Houston School Board would buy into the idea of a junior college. To this end, Oberholtzer proposed that both the white and Negro colleges partner with an established institution of higher education. As part of a binding agreement, the University of Texas and Sam Houston State would accept credits from the white junior college, while Wiley and Prairie View would accept credits from the colored college, thus giving continuous assurances that the new junior colleges were being operated in accordance with standards of the department of education and the Texas Association of Colleges.[14]

After listening to Oberholtzer's plan, HISD passed a joint resolution on March 7, 1927, which cleared the way for the establishment of a junior college for white students and made provisions for summer school for colored teachers. African Americans then had reason to hope that a colored junior college was in the offing. The enrollment of three hundred students that summer far exceeded the expectations of the administration and bolstered African Americans' efforts to continue to push for the formal establishment of a junior college. Black Houstonians' dream came true on September 14, 1927, when the board acted affirmatively as the superintendent "presented a petition signed by a large number of colored citizens to authorize the establishment of a junior college for colored people."[15]

Houston Colored Junior College

The Colored Junior College grew out of the need for a college to serve African Americans of Houston, especially for those whose only hope for higher education was by simultaneously working and studying. The purpose of the Colored Junior College was twofold: to make two years of upper-level education available to many who might not otherwise have the advantages of college training, and to enable teachers already in service to secure or to extend certification or to make up professional deficiencies. Similar to the white junior college, the Colored Junior College was established under the supervision of the Houston School Board with Edison E. Oberholtzer as both president and superintendent of public schools. Also included were L. T. Cunningham, who as assistant superintendent served as financial and academic director, and Jacob T. (J. T.) Fox, dean of the college. Fox was charged with running the day-to-day operations of the college.[16]

At the time that the Houston Colored Junior College was established, Houston was experiencing both economic prosperity and troubling race relations. Spindletop, the site of the discovery of oil in the surrounding area in the Gulf Coast region of Texas, had not only placed Houston on the map, but it brought newcomers to the city from the countryside, from small rural towns, and from many other cities and states. Moreover, this was a time when black Houstonians were waging a legal battle against the white Democratic primary statute that held that "only white males" and no others could vote in primary elections. The full impact of this statute cannot be grasped unless it is understood that Texas was a one-party state. Winning in the Democratic primary was thus tantamount to winning in the general election. To be excluded from the Democratic primary was in effect to be disenfranchised. Because blacks perceived this action by the state in a negative light, they were determined to alleviate their plight. In the early 1920s they defined their problem as being twofold: the need for political freedom and the need to extend economic and educational opportunities. In their minds, their plight in Houston could only improve with a junior college in the midst.[17]

On September 14, 1927, Houston Colored Junior College opened its doors amid joy, jubilation, hopes, and doubts.[18] For those who were in charge, their uncertainty stemmed from the fact that the fall enrollment would not be as good as the summer's, since a large percentage of the summer students were teachers who had to return to their respective jobs, thereby leaving the college to rely on high school graduates. The opening of the college also was contingent on the number of students enrolled. The magic number needed for fall 1927 was 50 students able to pay tuition. Inasmuch as the college was self-sustaining, without having the requisite number of students meant that the professors had little or no assurance of receiving their salaries. Determined not to close the college, Fox came up with a plan to pay the teachers in the event that his recruitment efforts fell short of 50 students. The plan stated that at the end of the first month, one ninth of whatever money had been collected would be divided among the teachers; at the end of the second month, one eighth, and so on. As it turned out, the funds came in better than expected because three weeks after the opening date, Fox announced that he had 88 students. Perfecting its recruitment efforts, the college enrolled 103 students in the spring of 1928.[19]

The Houston Colored Junior College made tremendous strides during J. T. Fox's administration. During his tenure, academic departments increased from eight to ten. They included science, education, English, history, mathematics, sociology, music, home economics, vocational education, and philosophy. The increase in the number of departments of necessity required an increase in faculty; and an increase in faculty brought a broader perspective to the students. In recognition of the rapid increase in enrollment and the quality of its work, Houston Colored Junior College received a first-class rating from the state department of education in 1927. In 1931, it became a member of the Southern Association of Colleges and Schools (SACS), the accrediting agency for educational institutions in the South.[20] Upon the death of Fox, the board moved quickly to get a replacement. It selected William Lucky D. Johnson as dean. No doubt Johnson was selected as acting dean for his administrative skills. He had served as principal of Blackshear Elementary and as former principal of Adult High School at Old Colored High (which is now Booker T. Washington).[21]

Following Johnson's one-year tenure, the board selected North Carolina native Raphael O'Hara Lanier as dean. Lanier had earned a bachelor's degree in English from Lincoln University in Pennsylvania and a master's

degree from Leland Stanford University in California. Prior to coming to
Texas, he had served as an instructor of history at Tuskegee Institute from
1923 to 1925. He moved to Florida A&M College in 1925, where he held many
positions: director of the Extension School for Teaching, 1925–27; dean and
registrar, 1927–28; dean of the Division of Arts and Sciences, 1928–32; and
director of summer school from 1925–33.[22]

Given his experiences, Lanier seemed to be exactly what the doctor
ordered for the Houston Colored Junior College. He brought new life and
ideas to the college, and his impact on the institution and community was
immediate and far reaching. Lanier also played a major role in advocating
for vocational education and explaining how vital it was to the economy of
the black community of Houston. This latter position supported his belief
that the economic suppression of the black community was largely due to
the lack of training and that this lack of training was a direct product of segregation. Other actions taken by Lanier during his tenure included reorga-
nizing the junior college, lengthening the summer school to twelve weeks,
increasing personnel and library equipment, and proposing and submitting
a ten-point plan for the Negro junior and senior colleges to the board of
education. His plan included the following: (1) the purchase of twenty-five
to thirty acres as a future site for the junior and senior colleges; (2) the construction of a building and municipal auditorium with a seating capacity of
two thousand; (3) an African American Museum; (4) a practice cottage for
home economics; (5) a theatre; (6) an adult education center; (7) a library
of fifteen thousand volumes; (8) a board of visitors whose function was to
serve as liaison between the colleges and the community; (9) a service program that would include lectures and forums for African Americans; and
(10) classes to be held during the day since all college classes had previously
been held in the evening.[23]

Lanier was disappointed when the board of education did not approve
his program, but all was not lost. In October 1933, Governor Miriam A.
Ferguson signed House Bill 194, which made the White Junior College eligible to become a four-year institution, with the Colored Junior College as
a branch thereof. On April 30, 1934, the HISD Board adopted a resolution
accepting House Bill 194. Consequently, the White Junior College became
the University of Houston, and the Colored Junior College's name would be
changed to Houston College for Negroes, contingent on its moving to four-
year status. That is, during the academic school year 1934–35, the Colored
Junior College would offer junior-level work in education, political science,
and social sciences. Senior-level work would be added during the summer
of 1935. Thus, the first four-year graduating class received degrees at the

close of the regular session in 1935–1936. There were sixty-three members in this class, most of whom were teachers in the Houston Independent School District.[24]

Houston College for Negroes

Under Lanier's administration, the college experienced phenomenal growth in student numbers, in faculty programs, and in prestige within the city and throughout the state of Texas. The faculty and students also became involved in many local, state, and national projects. Most notable among these was the establishment of a student chapter of the NAACP. This chapter worked along with black Houstonians and black Texans to eliminate the white Democratic primary—a state statute allowing only white males to vote in the white Democratic primary. In fact, it was the student chapter, under the leadership of Roy Lee Hopkins, that helped revise the senior chapter that had lain dormant for many years.[25] Additionally, a number of student clubs and organizations were established, all of which helped prepare students for the workforce. Without a doubt, Lanier put the Houston College for Negroes on the map; therefore, many were surprised when Lanier tendered his resignation as dean in the summer of 1938. His action was predicated on an invitation from Mary McLeod Bethune, director of Negro Affairs of the National Youth Administration, to become her assistant. After serving with Bethune for two years, Lanier moved on to become dean of Hampton Institute in Hampton, Virginia, in September 1940. Within three years, he was promoted from dean to acting president, thus achieving the honor of being the first of his race to serve as president of that institution. Lanier moved from Hampton in 1946 when he was appointed as United States minister to Liberia.[26]

Upon Lanier's initial departure in 1938, the board of trustees appointed John D. Bowles, a part-time college instructor and science teacher at Harper Junior High, as acting dean of the college. Bowles served in that capacity for three years before volunteering for military service when the United States entered World War II. Since Bowles had given the trustees ample notice of his impending resignation in 1942, the board named a permanent dean, Allen E. Norton, a part-time instructor at the college and chairman of the social studies department at Phyllis Wheatley High School.[27]

Houston College for Negroes made significant progress during the administration of Dean Norton. During the summer of 1943, several professors from the University of Houston were employed to teach masters-level courses in education. Moreover, the curriculum now included five divisions: Language and Literature, Natural Sciences, Applied Arts and Sciences, Social Sciences, and Community Services. The Community Services Division was considered by many to be very innovative in that it offered cultural programs, special lectures, institutes, and practicum training courses for the teacher training program. In conjunction with the Applied Arts and Sciences Division, the college also offered courses in tailoring, cleaning and pressing, food chemistry, applied physics, photography, public health, and nursing. No doubt, the Community Services Division impacted and influenced the opening of the Houston College Vocational School at 1127 Dart Street in 1944. This vocational school marked a new phase in the development of the institution. It provided opportunities for World War II veterans to receive instructions in trades notwithstanding their grade and college levels—elementary, high school, and undergraduate level.[28]

The expansion of the college, both in enrollment and in curricula during the war years, forced the administration to take a hard look at its physical facilities and to assess its ability to accommodate the influx of veterans as well as students from outside the city and state. In a letter to Edwin R. Embree, president of the Julius Rosenwald Foundation, asking for assistance for a building program, Dean Norton wrote, "The College has been progressive . . . but has been handicapped by a lack of its own physical plant." Norton went on to say that "the first step toward the college owning its own plant was taken when we purchased fifty-three acres of land with our tuition funds. [Please help]."[29]

Despite its many years of existence, Houston College for Negroes did not have a single building. As of 1943 it was still holding classes at Jack Yates High. It should be noted, however, that both Houston College for Negroes and the University of Houston were established as self-sustaining institutions. But while the University of Houston received generous donations from wealthy white citizens, such was not the case for Houston College for Negroes. Because of the great need for a building to accommodate increases in enrollment, Edison E. Oberholtzer, superintendent of HISD and president of the University of Houston, W. W. Kemmerer, comptroller and vice president of the same, and Allen E. Norton, dean of Houston College for Negroes, asked the board of education to construct a building for Houston College for Negroes on the fifty-three-acre site that had already been purchased. Approving this plan was not a problem. The concern was where to find the money for the construction of the building. A committee of distinguished African Americans answered the call in 1945 via a fundraiser.

Headed by John W. Davis and Charles W. Pemberton, the committee solicited funds from philanthropists, businesses, individuals, black schools, churches, and civic and social organizations in the city. African Americans even purchased bricks (some did so one brick at a time) for the cause. With the cooperation of the aforementioned groups and individuals, the committee raised $110,000. The largest donors to the drive were Thornton McNair Fairchild and his wife, Mamie. For their generous donation, they received the distinction of having a building named in their honor—the Thornton McNair Fairchild Memorial Building. Although this drive was a success, the construction of the first building could not have occurred without the support of Hugh Roy Cullen, a wealthy oil tycoon, who not only matched the money raised by the African American committee but gave more than that amount. Construction of the Fairchild Building began in the spring of 1945 but was not completed until April 1947.[30]

By 1945, HISD had begun to experience problems with the administration of the University of Houston and its branch, Houston College for Negroes. The University of Houston had grown too large and complex for HISD to oversee, and Houston College for Negroes had begun to experience a downward spiral in its enrollment. So, HISD went before the Texas legislature and asked to separate itself from this private college and its branch. The legislature responded in kind. On March 12, 1945, Senate Bill 207 was signed into law, thereby removing HISD from control of the University of Houston and its branch, and placing both of them in the hands of a board of directors. After the completion of the Fairchild Building, Houston College for Negroes moved from Jack Yates High School to its present location in the Third Ward area of the city.[31]

One year prior to the passage of Senate Bill 207, the Supreme Court in *Smith v. Allwright* (1944) declared the Texas White Democratic Primary, which barred blacks from voting, unconstitutional. At that time Houston was a base of operations for a burgeoning civil rights movement, and the ruling in *Smith v. Allwright* not only allowed blacks to vote in the Democratic primary but also opened the door for an impending attack on the white educational citadel that barred blacks from graduate and professional training throughout the South. Since blacks could now vote in any primary they chose, poll taxes notwithstanding, they now had the political clout needed to challenge segregated educational institutions. In 1945 the NAACP, having used Texas as a proving ground in *Smith v. Allwright*, decided that its next move would be to launch a frontal attack on segregation in higher education in Texas. By this time, black Texans had begun to express concern not only about a branch university and about equal opportunities in general, but also

The Thornton M. Fairchild Building, the first permanent building on TSU's campus. Upon completion in 1947, it housed administrative offices, classrooms, the library, and a medical clinic. Courtesy of *TSU Yearbook*, 1948.

about the lack of graduate and professional training institutions for people of color. In the entire South, graduate and professional schools existed only at a few privately supported black institutions. The general feeling among African Americans was that each state should provide advanced training for its black as well as its white citizens.[32]

A most significant step toward providing graduate and professional training for African Americans in the South had been the Supreme Court's decision in *Missouri ex rel. Gaines v. Canada* (1938). This case involved twenty-four-year-old Lloyd Gaines, who had applied for admission to the University of Missouri Law School. Except for his skin color, Gaines would have been admitted. The state of Missouri asked him to accept tuition to study in a nearby out-of-state institution offering legal training for blacks. Gaines refused and took his case all the way to the Supreme Court, which held that it was the duty of each state to provide education for all of its citizens, that this provision must be made within the state, and that payment of tuition fees in another state does not remove discrimination.[33]

The *Gaines* case caused immediate consternation in Texas. For one thing, the state of Texas did not provide graduate and professional training or pay out-of-state tuition for African Americans. Further, the state conference of branches of the NAACP had made it clear in 1937 that one of its major goals was to challenge the dual system of education in Texas. Thus, shortly after the *Gaines* decision, the NAACP arranged for George L. Allen, a black business executive from Dallas, to register in a business course at the University of Texas in the hopes that a court action would force the legislature to provide out-of-state scholarships for blacks. "The only wrench in the whole machine," said Allen, "was that they admitted me." When Allen arrived on the UT campus in October 1938, he presented himself for admission and was allowed to register and attend classes. Unintentionally, the university's tradition of segregation had been broken, but not for long. After attending classes for ten days, Allen was called in by university officials and asked to withdraw from the university. When he refused to do so, his classes were cancelled. The NAACP's strategy of enrolling Allen had paid off. However, within nine months after Allen's departure, the state legislature passed a law that provided for out-of-state tuition for blacks seeking graduate-level education.[34]

By the mid-1940s, many Texans had begun to see the inadequacies of the scholarship program. Not only did it fail to compensate for black students attending out-of-state universities, but the funds were insufficient to provide for all qualified blacks who applied. As Lulu B. White, executive secretary of the Houston branch of the NAACP, put it, "The travel money was not enough to pay for the student's railroad fares, and the distances that separated them from their loved ones created hardships." These scholarships could not stand up under litigation and were rendered obsolete by the court's ruling in the *Gaines* case.[35]

In June 1945, the NAACP announced that it would challenge segregated public professional education in Texas. The state government's immediate response to this challenge was the passage of Senate Bill 228, which changed the name of Prairie View State Normal and Industrial College to Prairie View State University. Additionally, the measure authorized the Texas A&M Board of Regents to provide at Prairie View upon demand training in law, medicine, engineering, pharmacy, and journalism, as well as any other courses taught at UT. The legislature's action initially baffled many blacks. Why would the legislature make Prairie View a university without rewarding its white counterpart, Texas A&M, equal status? Soon, however, it became clear that the purpose was to prevent integration at UT.[36]

About the same time that the NAACP decided to test the dual system of education in the state, another black group was organized. At its inception, the Southern Negro Conference for Equalization of Education (SNCEE), founded by Carter Wesley, editor of the *Houston Informer*, denounced the South's dual school system but said nothing about integration. This stance implied that integration could not act as a panacea for the problems blacks faced in education.

When Wesley formed the Southern Negro Conference for Equaliza-tion of Education in 1945, he resolved to work for equalization of education at all levels. Still, he was opposed to making a frontal attack on segrega-tion—a method used by the NAACP. Rather, his emphasis was on the man-ner of obtaining civil rights. While he saw the need to pursue equality in the courts, he believed, idealistically or naively, that true equality could be accomplished under the "separate but equal" doctrine. [37]

However wise Wesley's tactics may have been, Lulu B. White, executive secretary of the Houston Branch of the NAACP, did not concur with Wes-ley's views. She sharply rebuked his organization for its failure to confront the segregation question. She challenged the "separate but equal" alterna-tive that proposed bringing black schools up to parity with white ones while keeping them separate. The fact that segregation was a violation of the Con-stitution made it awkward, in her mind, to pursue true equality in sepa-rate-but-equal schools. Wesley and White further differed in that Wesley demanded equal opportunity under the current segregation laws as stated in the Texas Constitution, whereas White could see no equality in segrega-tion. This feud would continue for many years, with a number of blacks tak-ing one side or the other.[38]

Meanwhile, in October 1945, Lulu White wrote to Thurgood Mar-shall, "I think I have a plaintiff for the Education Case." The individual was Heman Marion Sweatt, a thirty-three-year-old Houstonian with a bache-lor of science degree from Wiley College, who was employed full-time by the post office and part-time by the *Houston Informer*. Sweatt earlier had given some thought to attending UT, but he did not make this known until he heard Lulu White speak at a meeting and appeal to the audience for a volunteer to serve as plaintiff in a lawsuit against the University of Texas. While calling it a "brash decision," Sweatt's willingness to become a plain-tiff had a great deal to do with the discrimination that he had experienced and with his acquaintance with Lulu White. Before Sweatt could have sec-ond thoughts, A. Maceo Smith, director of state branches of the NAACP, and William J. Durham, resident counsel for the Texas NAACP, encouraged him to file an application immediately for admission to the UT Law School. Sweatt told them that he could not do so until he had consulted with his

Heman Marion Sweatt, the plaintiff in the case *Sweatt v. Painter*, which led to the establishment of Texas State University for Negroes. Courtesy of *TSU Archives*.

employer, Carter Wesley. Wesley approved the idea, assuring Sweatt that his job would be waiting for him despite his appearance in court.[39]

Urged on by the NAACP and accompanied by Lulu White and other supporters, Heman Sweatt attempted to register at UT in Austin on February 26, 1946. After a discussion with President Theophilus Painter and other university officials, Sweatt left his application at the campus and returned to Houston, hoping for a quick answer. During his stay on campus, Sweatt made no mention of his intention to file a lawsuit; but given the wide publicity previously accorded the NAACP's plans, university officials realized that one was in the making. It is not surprising, then, that Painter wrote to Texas Attorney General Grover Sellers, asking for an opinion on Sweatt's application. "This is to be a test case on the question of admission of Negro students in higher education of the state. . . . This applicant is duly qualified for admission to the Law School, save and except for the fact that he is a Negro. [Please advise]." Sellers's ruling did not come until March 16, at which time he upheld Texas law, which read, "No African or persons of African descent should be admitted to the University of Texas." Adding insult to injury, Sellers noted that Sweatt could apply for legal training at Prairie View, since in 1945 Senate Bill 228 had made it (on paper) a university.[40]

Sellers's opinion set events in motion, signaling the beginning of a concerted campaign to end segregated education in Texas. Conversely, it stimulated the thinking of some blacks who wanted a separate but equal university. Shortly after Sellers issued his opinion, A. Maceo Smith wrote to Wesley that Sweatt's case should be pursued although "realism dictates that a special university is about all we are going to get [and] . . . the Texas

Council of Negro Organizations is the appropriate agency that should prepare for negotiation when the time arises." Wesley countered that "mule"
caution should guide blacks in accepting such an alternative. "The seeming
advantage," he reasoned, "that we might have in putting them on the spot
might trap us." Wesley was very perceptive. Sweatt's registration attempt
mobilized the political establishment to press for a black statutory university.[41]

Refused admittance, Sweatt commenced legal proceedings against the
University of Texas in March 1946; he asked the court for a writ of mandamus that would compel the University of Texas to admit him. After Sweatt
sued university officials on May 16, 1946, for denying him admission, Dudley K. Woodward Jr., chair of the UT Board of Regents, began to talk about
making provisions for a black university. He took the lead in advancing the
cause of a black university not for humanitarian reasons but to ensure that
"a branch university for colored youths," required by the state constitution, would not threaten UT's permanent university fund. In Woodward's
opinion, having a black university share the endowment would "entail con-
sequences of [the] most destructive character," but creating another black
university by statute would avoid this possibility since a state law mandated
that only UT and Texas A&M be benefactors of the permanent university
fund. "It is of great importance," Woodward wrote, "that the [constitutional
option] be effectually destroyed."[42]

On June 17, 1946, Judge Roy C. Archer made public his decision to post-
pone issuing a writ of mandamus to compel UT to admit Sweatt. This decision not only delayed Sweatt's action but also allowed the Texas legislature
enough time to create a statutory black university that would be substantially "equal to white." Subsequent to Archer's ruling, which set December
17, 1946, as the date for final execution of the judgment, officials from UT
and Texas A&M College, charged in 1945 with studying Negro education,
held a joint meeting to address the issue. In essence, this joint committee on
Negro Education recommended that a black statutory institution of higher
education be established, and that Prairie View provide agricultural and
mechanical training for blacks on the same order that Texas A&M provided
for whites. This group also recommended that the governor appoint a biracial committee to study its report and recommend to the governor proposals that could be presented to the legislature as soon as possible. When Lulu
White heard about this group, she warned Thurgood Marshall that state
officials were planning to establish a separate black university. She wrote,
"There is a possibility that the present Houston College for Negroes will be
used as the nucleus around which the Negro University will be built."[43]

On July 25, 1946, the biracial committee met in Austin and approved the recommendations of the Joint Committee on Negro Education. The biracial committee also decided to hold a similar gathering with blacks on August 8, 1946, to discuss their concerns regarding an institution of higher learning. Realizing that such a meeting might be a fiasco unless blacks reached a consensus beforehand, A. Maceo Smith called a meeting of ninety-six black leaders from throughout the state, to take place on August 3, 1946. Eighty-three of the leaders agreed that they should base any actions on Article 7, Section 14, of the Texas Constitution, which reads, "The Legislature shall also, when deemed practical, establish and provide for the maintenance of a college branch university for the instruction of colored youths of the state." Blacks interpreted Section 14 to mean that such a university would share in UT's endowment fund and would not exclude blacks from attending classes at the main UT campus. At the conclusion of this meeting, Carter Wesley and Joseph J. Rhoads, president of Bishop College in Marshall, Texas, were selected to present the views of the black leadership to the biracial committee.[44]

When Wesley and Rhoads made their presentation on August 8, 1946, their demands went a little farther than Governor Coke Stevenson and his cohorts had expected. Blacks had agreed to support the NAACP in the *Sweatt* case but also had demanded the establishment of a black university that would share equally with UT in an endowment fund. Further, they made it clear that they were not interested in a legislative arrangement by which a makeshift university would be established.[45]

Responding to this group, UT's president Theophilus Painter asserted that a black statutory university would be established. In an effort to head off integration of other professional areas, Painter told his audience that this university should be located in Houston, not only because the state of Texas would purchase Houston College for Negroes for this purpose, but also because the city's two black hospitals would enable the black university to establish its own medical school. In a heated debate, Lulu White attacked Painter's statement as an insult to black people. She pointed out that the hospitals referred to were separate and unequal; one of them, Jefferson Davis, had refused to treat black patients. Painter's suggestion, she charged, was simply a ploy to prevent blacks from attending UT.[46]

Meanwhile during the interim between Judge Archer's initial ruling in June 1946 and his decision in December to deny Sweatt admission to UT, the state decided to apply Senate Bill 228 to the creation of a law school at 409½ Milam Street in the Odd Fellows Temple in Houston under the auspices of Prairie View. The Odd Fellows Temple (the place that housed the

Law School) had three rooms with desks and chairs, and two local attorneys who would be responsible for instruction. When no qualified black applicants sought admission and Sweatt ignored it, the school was permanently closed in February 1947. The Texas legislature then took further steps to counter Sweatt's challenge. On February 28, 1947, a black law school was established in the basement of a petroleum firm building at 104 East 13th Street in downtown Austin by the UT Board of Regents. This school had a dean, a registrar, and a makeshift library. It appears that the only thing lacking were students. When the school opened in March 1947, several students made inquiries, but only one expressed real interest, Henry Doyle. Dissuaded by the NAACP and other blacks, he decided not to enroll at the new school. Consistent in his action, Sweatt refused to apply on the grounds that this law school was unequal to that of any white school.[47]

Going back to the drawing board, the state came up with its final offer to keep Sweatt out of UT. On March 3, 1947, the Texas legislature passed Senate Bill 140, providing for "the establishment of a three-million dollar Negro University, including a law school to be located in Houston." The passage of this bill was made easier by the fact that Houston College for Negroes at the time was under the supervision of the University of Houston and was experiencing financial problems. So, when the state of Texas made an offer to purchase Houston College for Negroes, those in charge responded affirmatively. With the passage of Senate Bill 140 and House Bill 780, which allowed the state to purchase a fifty-three-acre site from the University of Houston, Texas State University for Negroes (TSUN), later called Texas Southern University, became a state-chartered institution of higher learning. Houston was chosen not only because of location but also because Houston College for Negroes provided a ready-made faculty, student body, and at least one building. Thus, with the acquisition of Houston College for Negroes, the state had taken the cheapest way out, had gotten a new university off the ground, and had managed, at least for a while, to hold on to a black-proof educational system.[48]

2

The Emergency University and the Lanier Era, 1947–1955

After the passage of Senate Bill 140, the 50th Texas Legislature moved rapidly in coming to grips with the awkward situation of establishing a university for the "special purpose of providing at once similar courses for Negro citizens as were offered to white students at the University of Texas"—courses that were found in arts and sciences, literature, law, medicine, pharmacy, journalism, and other professions.[1] With this act, the state not only declared and recognized an actual emergency to create a separate black university before the Supreme Court's ruling in *Sweatt v. Painter* (1950) but also accepted this as its obligation to its black citizens. Because the state deemed it impractical to establish a branch of the University of Texas for the instruction of colored people, it established an entirely separate and (at least on paper) equivalent university of the first class for the same purpose. Yet the problems inherent in the establishment, operation, and maintenance of Texas State University for Negroes (TSUN) were awesome. "To begin the operation of a first-class institution in a hurry will and did entail not only expense, but problems not commonly found in the path of normalcy."[2]

Since Texas State University for Negroes was established to satisfy an emergency in education and since the university had to qualify as first-class in a hurry, there were a number of items that the state had to handle very rapidly in order to prepare for the opening of the university in September 1947. First was the arrangement for the transfer of properties from Houston College for Negroes (HCN) to Texas State University for Negroes. In addition to the task of negotiating a satisfactory contract with the University of Houston, arrangements had to be made for a complete audit of the financial statements of Houston College for Negroes by a certified public accountant. Accounting procedures and methods of operating the institution had to be changed almost overnight from methods used by private educational institutions to those used in state institutions. In this regard, a completely new system of accounting was established, and under the direction of the state auditor's office, a manual of accounting and purchasing procedures was prepared.[3]

Administrators, faculty, and staff had to be transferred from HCN, and every academic unit had to qualify at once to meet the standards of accreditation. In order to effect the above, a board of directors was appointed by the governor on April 1, 1947, but it was not sworn in until May 7, 1947. Meanwhile, during the interim between the establishment of TSUN and the swearing-in of board members, Attorney General Price Daniel served as temporary chairman of the university. As the board members were selected, Daniel told them that it was their duty to sell the university to blacks, to convince them that the state, via the establishment of TSUN, had fulfilled its obligation to provide graduate and professional training.[4] Not all blacks took kindly to that suggestion. Those who were active in the NAACP scoffed at the idea. Others were concerned with the composition of the board and requested an all-black board or at least a majority of black members. The latter request was denied, as the governor appointed five whites—J. K. Brim of Sulfur Springs, J. R. N. Score of Georgetown, Craig F. Cullinan of Houston, Major T. Bell of Beaumont, and Charles Devall of Kilgore—and four blacks, namely, Isaac B. Loud of San Antonio, Martin L. Edwards of Hawkins, Ben Morgan of Corsicana, and Willette R. Banks, former president of Prairie View College. Governor Beauford Jester said that his selection was made with two things in mind—that there should be black board members who would ensure the growth of the university, and that the chairman would be a person of note. His selection of Craig Cullinan, son of an oil tycoon whose family was noted for philanthropy, was well accepted in the black community. On the other hand, the other whites were not well known outside of their communities.[5] The same could be said of the black members. Only Willette R. Banks was widely known throughout the state, but his selection was not well accepted in the black community. Blacks had mixed feelings about Banks for a number reasons: (1) Banks was generally regarded as a conservative on civil rights; (2) many felt that as a former president of Prairie View, he would now have to give directions to a rival institution; and (3) Banks, many opined, would have a great deal of influence on personnel matters of the new university. There were reasons to believe that a number of regulations that came out of the board directives at the inception of the university were due to the influence of Banks. For example, "no teaching professor or employee could be transferred from Prairie View to Texas State

University for Negroes without spending a year elsewhere." Also there were several unexplained policies that were enforced at the new institution that were attributable to Banks, such as whatever amenities Prairie View did not have, TSUN would not get. One such item was air conditioning in newly constructed buildings.[6]

In keeping with the state and board directives, the faculty, staff, administrators, and other employees of Houston Colored College had to transfer to TSUN effective September 1, 1947. Ordinarily, a faculty is selected in keeping with the normal appetite of an institution's growth, but this was not the case. The great majority of the faculty did not have the necessary credentials to meet the needs of the new university. Those who did not have a master's degree had three years to get one. Those who wanted better salaries had to acquire additional college credit hours. There were concerns as to whether the new university would pay its faculty of equal rank the same as UT, but this was not the case. Yet, it was logical for the faculty at TSUN to expect the same salaries as their white counterparts, not only because the enabling act implied equality, but also because Texas black public-school teachers had just won a salary equalization case.[7] But this did not happen. Rather, on August 8, 1947, the board proceeded to appoint as acting president Allen E. Norton, dean of Houston College of Negroes. One month later, on September 8, 1947, TSU opened its doors for registration and began classes on September 14 with an enrollment of 2,303 students in the College of Arts and Sciences, the College of Industrial and Vocational Education, the School of Law, and the Graduate School. At that time, the College of Arts and Sciences had five divisions, which consisted of a total of fourteen departments: (1) the Division of Humanities consisted of the Department of English and the Department of Foreign Languages and Literature; (2) the Division of Fine Arts comprised the Department of Drama and Speech and the Department of Art and Music; (3) the Division of Natural Sciences and Mathematics contained the Departments of Biology, Chemistry, Mathematics, and Physics; (4) the Division of Social Sciences and Education held the Department of History and Government, the Department of Sociology, the Department of Philosophy, the Department of Education, and the Department of Physical Education and Health; and (5) the Division of Commerce and Technical Services, which held the Department of Commerce and Technical Services.[8]

An enrollment of 2,303 students taxed the institution's facilities. When the university opened its doors, it had available for use the following buildings: the Thornton M. Fairchild classroom building; one large corrugated metal automobile shop building; five shop buildings that had been built by the vocational department of Houston College for Negroes; and twelve buildings that had been moved from Camp Wallace by arrangement with the University of Houston. During the first semester, arrangements were made with the Federal Housing Administration for immediate erection of four high-rise apartments for housing married veteran students. A majority of these students were taking advantage of the GI Bill, which paid their tuition. Others included mature teachers anxious to improve their professional status and ambitious youths who were planning careers for their futures.[9]

The university was located on a fifty-three-acre site in southeast Houston, and many of the streets that led to it were impossible to navigate. The only bus that ran to the university was the one that ran from Milam to Cleburne. Because the bus did not accommodate black students, and because the state of Texas was trying to make "separate equal" via the establishment of TSUN, Superintendent Oberholtzer wrote Mayor Oscar Holcombe and asked him to improve the streets so that a bus could transport students to the "Negro College." Oberholtzer "thought that it would be unwise to let a condition arise which might cause difficulty between the students of the two races." So, when TSUN opened, at least one bus was running down Cleburne Street.[10]

In regard to its programs, Senate Bill 140 was designed to transform TSUN from an emergency university to one of first class, but several elements in the state and in the university mitigated against this. For one thing, building a segregated first-class university was expensive, and the state would not and did not commit sufficient dollars. Equally important was the part of the bill that called for providing courses "on demand for any and all Negro students of the State of Texas." This charge placed the university in a precarious position. It worked both for and against the university. For example, various departments added courses without long-range planning; and instead of a school or college being scientifically developed, it might have been better to say they simply came into existence. In the beginning, not only did departments create courses on the basis of the slightest demands, but new programs were put into the catalog, which many times showed unnecessary duplication. In a few cases, departments were developed as independent units rather than as part of the College of Arts and Sciences. For example, the School of Pharmacy had its origin in the College of Arts and Sciences as a department in the Division of Natural Sciences and Mathematics, but it became a school as a result of the demand from six students.

Raphael O'Hara Lanier, 1948–1955. Courtesy of *TSU Archives.*

First President, First Year

The culmination of the search for a new president coincided with the resignation of A. E. Norton as acting president on February 24, 1948. On March 1, 1948, the board announced the selection of Raphael O'Hara Lanier as the first president of TSUN, effective July 21, 1948. But until that time, the university was in need of leadership; therefore, the board asked William A. Bell to serve at the helm, but Bell felt that the responsibility for the operation would be better implemented by a committee. With the board's approval, that committee consisted of William A. Bell, chairman, B. E. Taylor, Lloyd Isaacs, and E. W. Stewart. These individuals held the university together until Lanier arrived on campus in July.[11]

If it appeared to some that it took a long time to select a president, choosing a president for TSUN was almost as chaotic as was establishing the university itself. The state felt it necessary to find someone who had a national stature in the black community, who had experience in higher education, and who had popularity among the rank-and-file in Houston and Texas in order to effect a smooth transition for its "colored statutory university." But more important, the state wanted to hurriedly find someone to foil Sweatt's attempt to enter the University of Texas. Lanier fell into all of these categories. Lanier was no stranger to blacks either in Houston or in the Southwest for that matter. As previously stated, not only had Lanier been a former dean at Houston College for Negroes from 1933 to 1938, and a former acting president at Hampton Institute, but he also had served as United States minister to Liberia before resigning to accept this current post.[12]

The announcement of Lanier as president was met with mixed reactions from the faculty, the general public, and the various factions who were either for or against the establishment of Texas State University. While there was great joy and satisfaction among rank-and-file Houstonians, many faculty members did not appear impressed by Lanier's credentials since he did not hold a terminal degree—something they felt was needed for a first-class university. Members of the NAACP and other black liberal groups in the community who knew of Lanier's temperament and of his advocacy for the equality of blacks felt that he had become the board's choice in an attempt to put down the opposition to a segregated institution.

Lanier was not unmindful that he had a daunting task before him. In his first presentation to the board, he thanked the members for the confidence that they had shown in him and informed them that he had met with the following audiences: the administration committee, the academic committee, the graduate council, students, and the faculty. Most important, he wanted to let the board know about the questions that he had received from people in the community. Upon his arrival the following questions were posted: (1) What is the present status of the Law School? (2) How soon will the vocational unit on campus be removed? (3) Should the president take orders from John H. Robertson, the white executive assistant to the university board? (4) Why does the institution have to carry the label "for Negroes"? (5) What provision is to be made for medicine, pharmacy, and dentistry? (6) What is to be the status of students who had done their work under the auspices of Houston College? Of the above questions, the ones that were most troubling for Lanier were those involving vocational and industrial education and the proposed medical school.[13]

At the beginning of his administration, Lanier had to decide whether to move forward with the four academic units that were part of the Houston College for Negroes—Arts and Sciences, the Graduate School, the Law School, and the Vocational and Industrial Education School—or whether to exclude the latter. Many individuals were of the opinion that if TSUN were to become a first-class university, the vocational unit should be removed. During the transitional period, black intellectuals protested its move to the new university. As the verbal war intensified, Lanier not only asked the commissioner of education for a decision on this issue but also suggested that the vocational unit be transferred to Prairie View. Board member Willette R. Banks objected, arguing that the transfer would in effect place Prairie View under TSUN. In a haste to get the university off the ground, the commissioner sided with Banks. Lanier was now in a quandary. He knew firsthand the long, arduous fight that he and other blacks had waged for a vocational school in Texas when he was dean of HCN. Academically, vocational and industrial education does not belong in a first-class institution; therefore, it should have been placed at Prairie View just as the War Training Program had been placed at Texas A&M. But on this issue Lanier acceded to his superiors. He simply accepted the commissioner's position and allowed the unit to remain as part of the university's programs.[14]

Meanwhile, Lanier was focused on his first priority—to build a first-class university by hiring individuals with terminal degrees and by meeting accreditation standards. To that end, he immediately went out and hired eight individuals with terminal degrees (PhDs) and then moved toward accreditation. But accreditation was expensive, and the university needed monies if the above goals were to be achieved. So Lanier wrote the state board of education and asked it to reconsider TSU's biennial appropriation over and beyond that of the state formula that determined higher education funding. "Our institution is an emergency case, just one year old—not being in a position to properly request the funds necessary for adequate development of a first-class institution, the university is required by law to offer courses on demand which places it in a position of always trying to anticipate future demands," said Lanier.[15] Cognizant of the fact that accreditation also required the university to have adequate buildings to accompany programs and students' needs, Lanier requested that the legislature give consideration to the following: a science building, a men's dormitory, a women's dormitory, a Law School building, a gymnasium, an athletic field, a library building, a fine arts and music building, a medical administration building for a medical school, and a medical laboratory (although money had not yet been appropriated for a medical school).[16] Lanier's request did not fall on deaf ears. On June 29, 1949, Craig F. Cullinan (board chairman) thanked Governor Beauford Jester for signing Senate Bill 253, which provided $400,000 in emergency appropriations for TSUN.[17]

With the above funds, the university moved forward with its plan for a site visit from the Southern Association of Colleges and Schools. Before Lanier arrived on campus and before Senate Bill 253 was finalized, the board had designated Dean Wesley J. Lyda to prepare a self-study for the College of Arts and Sciences for approval by SACS. After a site visit, SACS reported that the institution had met the minimum requirements in most areas but had failed in others. The university was sharply criticized for the inadequacy of its library, the condition of the registrar's office, and for insufficient equipment in scientific laboratories.[18]

The library was located in the Fairchild Building adjacent to a noisy entrance hall and next to a restroom. At the beginning of the 1948–49 school year, there were approximately 3,139 volumes of books, periodicals, pamphlets, documents, and other reading materials in the library. These included materials donated on September 14, 1948, by Charles Fred Heartman, a former resident of Biloxi, Mississippi, and one of the county's best-known bibliographers. The collection contained eleven thousand items on African Americans and was valued in excess of $50,000. Yet the major problem with the library was a lack of staff, insufficient card trays, inaccurate cataloging, and a lack of monies to fix these problems.[19]

The board moved quickly to allay the fear that the college would not be approved by its accrediting agency by telling the visiting team that the board would provide the necessary monies to purchase books and equipment. While the committee was pleased to hear of the board's commitment, it was nevertheless concerned about the registrar's records. Dean Lyda, who had worked diligently on the self-study, told the SACS team that the board would take corrective action and that he would report to the board weekly on the progress made on correcting the registrar's records.

Though many thought that the college was on the right track to get accredited, Lanier complained to the visiting team about John H. Robertson, executive assistant to the board. Following the policy adopted by the administrations of several public HCBU, the board appointed a white man as executive assistant to the board. This individual had an office on campus and was to perform duties as assigned to him by the board. This person also played a role in hiring faculty and had oversight of the finances at the new university. Although Robertson was hired and given a job description before Lanier arrived on campus, Lanier told the visiting team that Robertson's function interfered with his duties as president. Lanier was fearful that if SACS would grant the university approval under its present administrative set up, nothing would be done by the board about making further improvements. Despite Lanier's action, the college was approved by SACS, and only time would tell if Lanier was correct in his assessment of Robertson's position.[20]

Following the accreditation of the College of Arts and Sciences, the university then focused its attention on the Law School, which had been moved to TSUN in Houston in June 1948 by statutory rule. Since accreditation was expected to satisfy Sweatt, as well as foil his attempt for admission to the University of Texas, the Law School quickly became a favorite of the board of directors. The board, then, moved quickly to initiate a search for the dean of the Law School. Ozie Harold Johnson was recommended, but he was not approved by the board until a month after Lanier's arrival. Almost as soon as he arrived in the fall 1948, Johnson started to make application for approval by the Texas State Board of Law Examiners and the American Bar Association. Pleased with Johnson's interest, efforts, and attempts to get approval from the aforementioned accrediting agencies, Governor Beauford Jester summoned Johnson to his office and asked him if anything needed to be done that required action by the legislature before it convened in January (1949). According to Johnson, this was the first time that the governor had intimated that the school would be maintained as a state institution regardless of the outcome of the *Sweatt* case.[21]

When Johnson made inquiries to the American Bar Association (ABA) about TSU's application, the ABA sent Lanier a letter requesting certain information. First, it wanted to know whether there were any other professional schools or colleges in the university. John E. Henry, president of the American Bar Association, stated that his reason for making the inquiry was that "where the Law School is the only . . . professional school within a university, there develops a tendency to treat the law school simply as a department without sufficient recognition of its professional status."[22] Second, he wanted to know whether or not the law school library was part of an all-university library. A tertiary concern was whether the president followed the recommendations of the dean in hiring faculty and if the dean of the Law School had control of the faculty. To Lanier, the most disturbing aspect of this letter was the part that said that "if the law school is the only professional school within the university then . . . it should have recognition and autonomy accorded to professional schools." The writer further stated that "only in those universities and colleges in which recognition is given to the professional status of the law school . . . are the law schools approved by the American Bar Association."[23]

Upon reviewing the ABA letter, Lanier called Johnson into his office to discuss this matter. Lanier's first impression of the letter was that autonomy would create a school within a school. His experience in higher education dictated that the president had the power to hire and fire and that he had control over the budget, that sometimes he made decisions in consultation with his subordinates, and that at other times he did not. To settle this matter and in accordance with ABA policy, the board passed a resolution giving the dean authority over the faculty, the budget, facilities, and equipment. Meanwhile, Johnson appeared unfazed by the meeting with the president and proceeded to work on an accreditation application that was to be submitted to the ABA in February 1949. But before Johnson submitted the application, an event occurred that further clouded the issue. Clifford Pemberton, a native Houstonian who had worked for several years in the Illinois State Attorney General's Office, applied for a teaching position at the TSUN Law School. Carter Wesley, editor of the *Houston Informer,* had told Pemberton about the job and had urged him to apply. Pemberton had received the endorsement of many prominent citizens in the community and had even spoken to President Lanier about the position. Lanier called Johnson and asked his opinion of Pemberton. Johnson was reluctant to hire Pemberton because he was recommended by Carter Wesley, a newspaper editor who often criticized the board and attempted on many occasions to exert his influence on board decisions. Johnson told Lanier that the board would not approve Pemberton, but the president insisted that he take Pemberton's name to the chairman of the Academic Committee of the Board, Major T. Bell.[24]

After interviewing Pemberton, Bell advised Johnson to submit Pemberton's name along with those of several other applicants to the advisor of the ABA for his opinion. The ABA's reply was that Pemberton should not be hired because the school (university) where he had received his legal training was not approved by the ABA. The dean and the law faculty agreed, but Wesley and Pemberton's supporters would not take no for an answer. They continued to pressure the president. Never one to submit to subordinates, Lanier submitted Pemberton's name to the board anyway. When the board convened, before the president could make his report, Major T. Bell addressed the hiring of Pemberton. He reported his interview with Pemberton, pointed to the letter the board had received from the ABA, and cited Dean Johnson's negative recommendation. Despite these facts, when Lanier was asked for his recommendation to fill the vacancy in the Law School, he indicated that he was in favor of Pemberton. The board was incensed by Lanier's actions, and the chairman reminded him of the negative factors surrounding the hiring of Pemberton. One board member even suggested that Lanier be fired at the next board meeting, and Dean Johnson became so angry he submitted his resignation to the board effective March 1, 1949.[25] When the board heard of Johnson's decision, its members pleaded with him to stay on, and bowing to that pressure, Johnson continued to work on accreditation. In October 1949, the Law School was approved by the Texas State Board of Law Examiners. Similarly, the Law School was granted provisional approval by the American Bar Association in September 1949 with the ABA stipulation to make periodic inspections each year. The school was supposed to go up for accreditation in 1950, but the executive committee of the ABA postponed the hearing on the application until after a decision was rendered in the *Sweatt* case.[26]

Meanwhile, as Lanier dealt with the Law School, he was also pressured to do something about the promise the state had made for a medical school. When the legislature decided to create TSUN as a bulwark against integration, it paid little more than lip service to creating a medical school for African Americans. UT's president Theophilus Painter was given an estimated budget of $192,000 for the first two years of operation of the "colored" medical school. Prospective black students made inquiries immediately when they heard of the legislature's action, and two of them actually applied for medical school when TSUN opened in September 1947. Others sought the advice of black board member Willette R. Banks, president emeritus of Prairie View. Rather than work behind the scenes to help establish this medical school, Banks told Painter that these students did not want to embarrass the state, so he suggested that they attend Meharry Medical College in Nashville, Tennessee.[27]

Not only did members of the NAACP vigorously protest Banks's stance, but they also continued to remind the state of the need to train blacks in the medical profession. Under continued pressure to provide blacks with equal medical training, early in 1948, Painter announced that he would support establishing a regional black medical school. The NAACP refused to accept this alternative. While intimating that the reason TSUN did not have a medical school was that its board had not pushed for it, Painter early in 1948 predicted that if the state of Texas "does not make adequate provisions for a medical school before September, we are going to have a hard time keeping Negroes out of Medical and Dental schools."[28]

In July 1949, Painter's prophecy came true when Herman Barnett applied for medical school. The state legislature then belatedly appropriated $175,000 for a medical school at TSUN. The state's action was regarded as suspect, however. If the basement law school had proven unsuccessful, why should anyone expect a medical school, which was more expensive and required more expertise, to be different? Responding as it had when Sweatt applied to the UT Law School, the state asked UT to contract with TSUN to provide the necessary professional training in medicine for blacks. Under this plan, Barnett would register at TSUN but take classes along with white students at University of Texas Medical Branch at Galveston, but only until the state had time to provide medical training at TSUN. As it turned out, the medical school, contingent to a certain extent on the *Sweatt* case, never materialized, and Barnett received his medical degree from UTMB in 1953.[29]

The Sweatt *Case*

The Supreme Court announced its findings in *Sweatt v. Painter* on June 5, 1950. In a unanimous decision, the court ordered Sweatt admitted to UT. Speaking for the majority of the court, Chief Justice Fred Vinson asserted that there was no comparison between the two law schools Texas State University for Negroes and the University of Texas. TSUN had 23 students compared to UT's 880. TSUN had less than one-third the number of full-time instructors, and its library was one-fourth the size of UT's. Unlike TSUN, UT published a law journal and had moot court facilities, scholarships, and many alumni.[30] The impact of the *Sweatt* case was stunning. This decision not only required admission of blacks to graduate and professional schools in the state, but it also established precedents for *Brown v. Board of Education.* In the *Sweatt* case the court implied that the doctrine of separate but equal was unconstitutional. In *Brown*, the doctrine was declared null and void. Striking a major blow at the separate but equal doctrine, the *Sweatt* case had a far-reaching implication for the state of Texas. It meant that *de jure* Jim Crow was on the descent and that segregation was not only costly, but would become increasingly so over the years. Its overall impact was generally interpreted not only as ordering Sweatt's matriculation at the University of Texas but also as nullifying the racial restrictions written into the legislation establishing Texas State University for Negroes. In effect, this decision said that UT could no longer be for whites only nor could TSUN be for Negroes only. This decision then had the prodigious effect of eliminating the legal support for racial segregation in American higher education.[31]

Obviously, the months that followed the *Sweatt* decision were critical for TSUN. The state of Texas had made an investment, albeit not a preemptive one, in TSUN. Whatever the motive the state had for establishing TSUN, the court declared such a motive illegal. If the state's official interest in the promulgation of the new institution was indeed confined to the preservation of racial segregation in public colleges and universities, a question to be faced immediately was the future of the institution that was the state's main tool for the implementation of a position now legally discredited.

Although an official reaction to the *Sweatt* case in legislative terms was expected soon, it did not come until the legislature convened in 1951. At that time, the state demonstrated its commitment to TSUN in a rather strange way. It slashed TSUN's appropriations from $1,570,000 to $958,672. But the budget was not the only issue involving the new university. TSUN students seized the moment, held a demonstration at the capitol, and noted that the racial phrase "for Negroes" in the official designation of their institution was no longer valid. They suggested that the name be officially changed to Texas Southern University. This demonstration also caught the attention of officials from the University of Texas who objected to the designation "Texas State University" because of what they perceived as confusion that may arise from both institutions having "Texas" and "University" in their names. The 52nd Texas Legislature then struck a balance between the two. Noting the fact that the present name, Texas State University for Negroes, did not properly designate the new institution, the legislature passed an act changing the name of the institution (via an amendment to the original name bill) to Texas Southern University, effective on June 1, 1951.[32]

The official name of the institution at the time of its establishment strongly implied a second-class status. But if one believed that the action of the legislature in changing the name of the university removed whatever onus may have been attached to the original name, one was sadly mistaken. It is noteworthy, however, that the legislation that changed the name specifically reiterated the commitment of the state to the applicable purpose and objectives of the original institution. While the university could not, of course, operate exclusively for blacks, the legislation preserved intact "applicable laws and appropriation heretofore and hereafter . . . relating to Texas State University for Negroes as applicable and relating to Texas Southern University."[33] Here, then, was a legislative confirmation of the State's expectation of developing a first-class institution in Houston.

Even after the legislature had verified the continued existence of the university in 1951, there were those Texans who interpreted the action of the legislature as a hopeful effort to divert what might well have been a large influx of black students into previously all-white colleges into what was now permissively a university of their own. Though there was nothing in the 1951 legislation to suggest such a strategy, it is true that some state officials—among them Governor Allan Shivers, who had assumed office upon the death of Beauford Jester—publicly declared a renewed intention to make the university so attractive that it would be the institution of first preference for its prospective, presumably black students.[34] At the time, one could only speculate about what attraction Texas Southern would have in regard to the relevance and excellence of its academic and service programs, its institutional ability to address the real needs and problems of its several clienteles, and the quality of the institutional staff that was steadily growing in size and in experiential expertise.

Lanier's Accomplishments—1948–1953

Despite the various problems that the Lanier administration encountered along the way, one could see improvements in the curricula, in the library, and in the quality of the university's programs, as well as a steady increase in enrollment. During the five-year period of Lanier's era (1948–1953), the university experienced a 16 percent increase in enrollment. In the early years, the student body was composed mainly of veterans, but as the years passed, veteran students were replaced by nonveteran students. In the first semester the university was open (September 1947), 65 percent of the students enrolled were veterans. By September 1951, the percentage had dropped to 42 percent. The university's veteran enrollment had dropped from 1,494 in 1947 to 897 in 1951. While the university's veteran enrollment was falling, its nonveteran enrollment was increasing, from 809 in 1947 to 1,725 in 1952. Many of these students were part-timers, but this too would change over the years with more and more becoming full-time students and being drawn not only from Houston but from other parts of the state and the South. This meant that the influence of the university was being felt outside Texas.[35]

The Lanier administration made a concerted effort to improve the curricula in various colleges and schools. In the College of Arts and Sciences, very few curricular changes were permitted in the catalog, but two divisions witnessed structural changes. The Division of Education, which had continuously endeavored to change its structure to meet the demand of the students, was reduced from six departments to three: the Departments of Elementary Education, Secondary Education, and Psychology. The Department of Child Development in the Division of Home Economics was firmly established with a first-class nursery school and a laboratory unit accommodating twenty-four children.[36]

In regards to the professional schools, the School of Pharmacy started out with six students in 1948 but had sixty-three students in 1952. At that time, the school also received accreditation as well as membership in the American Association of Colleges of Pharmacy. The Law School, which was moved to Houston via a statutory directive in June 1948, had two students enrolled that year. In September 1949, the faculty consisted of a dean, four professors, and a librarian. In 1951 an additional full-time member was added to the faculty, making a total of seven. The loss of two full-time faculty members in September 1951 caused the school to hire five part-time instructors to carry out the teaching load. As noted previously, the school was approved by the Texas State Board of Law Examiners in 1949 and by the ABA in 1951.[37]

The story of the Graduate Program over the course of these five years was also one of change. The dominant philosophy of graduate work as strongly education centered changed to an approach whereby one could receive master's and doctoral degrees in other areas; the program also witnessed a change in the number of graduate students—from 863 during the academic year 1947–48 to 2,563 in academic year 1952–53. This latter change was due largely to the fact that prior to the *Sweatt* case, blacks were prohibited from attending graduate school in white universities in the South, and moreover, the offerings were limited in black private colleges.[38]

As with the Graduate School, one saw visible signs of change in the School of Vocational and Industrial Education, namely, a decline in enrollment. Programs in the school involved two types of curriculum—a certificate program and a degree-granting program. The majority (627) of the students enrolled in the certificate programs were veterans in 1948–49, but by 1952–53 the number had declined to 149. With this decline in veterans' enrollment in the certificate program came simultaneous increases in the number of students majoring in the degree-granting programs.[39] It should be noted that at the time that TSU experienced a decline in the veteran population, the university was asked to become administratively responsible for the Jefferson County Vocational Extension Program located in Beaumont, Texas. TSU accepted this responsibility for one year, which was deemed long enough for veterans enrolled there to complete their training in auto mechanics, carpentry, electrical appliances, radio servicing, and tailoring. Following the tradition of many black private colleges in the past, TSU also became involved in the Extension Class Workshop movement. The purpose of the extension school was to provide services to the people on and off campus. Starting in the summer of 1948, teachers could come to the university and could take six hours toward a master's degree. Likewise, the university sponsored many workshops for teachers in Texarkana, Dallas, and Waco.[40]

The university library also saw considerable growth from 1948 to 1953. In 1948, the library was located near a restroom in a noisy environment in Fairchild Building and had a seating capacity of only 120 students. In 1951, it was relocated to the administration building and had a seating capacity of 260. As for resources, the library grew from approximately twenty-one thousand books to over sixty-three thousand at the close of the 1952–53 school year. This was an increase of over forty-two thousand books and

Completed in 1950, Hannah Hall served as the administrative and classroom building. It housed the president's office, the School of Law, the Graduate School, the bookstore and classrooms. Courtesy of *TSU Yearbook*, 1952.

periodicals, or an average of eighty-five hundred items per year. Similarly, the library grew in its circulation service. Approximately thirty-two thousand books were circulated in the 1948–49 school year, while sixty-five thousand were circulated in the school year 1952–53. The library also grew in personnel. From a staff of six people in 1947–48, it grew to seventeen persons in 1952–53. Although it was not yet a first-class library, it had improved.[41]

Despite Lanier's efforts and commitment to building a university of the first class, he had his share of detractors, within and outside the university; neither whites nor blacks were excepted. Challenges came as soon as he was selected to run a first-class institution without himself having a terminal degree. The problems continued as his silence gave approval, for whatever reasons, to maintain the School of Vocational and Industrial Education on campus. Those challenges were exacerbated as Lanier feuded with the Law School dean over the rules and regulations of the American Bar Association, which gave autonomy to the dean of that unit. Lanier looked with suspicion at the white executive director of the board, and this attitude did not enhance his relationship with the board. Also, some white conservatives labeled him as racist and others as a communist. But some of his strongest opposition came from a small group of faculty, who through the news media claimed that Lanier was an incompetent administrator and was causing confusion and unrest among the faculty.

Most of the opposition to Lanier was funneled through the news media; the most vicious attack on the president came from the *Houston Chronicle*, the *Houston Labor News*, and the *Houston Defender*. Before each board meeting, these newspapers would publish something negative against the president; therefore, much of the time at each meeting was devoted to responding to these accusations. Arguably, much of Lanier's opposition came from the Law School and spread to other faculty areas. This group of faculty included professors with PhD degrees whom Lanier had recruited in an effort to build a first-class university. The situation intensified to such a degree that board members began to look at Lanier in an unfavorable light, with at least one board member calling for his resignation. This disagreement was aided and abetted by the *Houston Chronicle*'s rumors that Lanier was dropped from the budget salary schedule (although he got paid) several months in 1949. As the differences between the president and opposing faculty became more pronounced, the black community became divided over the issues. One group who voiced opposition to Lanier was Herman Rochelle and Post 827 of the American Legion. As its members listened to and read accusations and allegations against Lanier, its president called for a special investigation of the university president. This group believed that the university had failed to meet the ideals established in Senate Bill 140 and that this failure was the cause of student unrest on campus. The action of this group was countered by supporters for Lanier via student rallies and letters written on his behalf to the governor by the student body president, the Business and Professional Men's Club, the Harris County Council of Organizations, and TSUN alumni groups. In a direct response to the American Legion's letter, the alumni wrote, "We do not question the rights of groups and individuals . . . to ask for an investigation, but we do question the basis on which groups and individuals make their request." The letter went on to say that "at no time did the [American Legion] make a positive contribution to any development of the university and that the attempts to discredit the present administration are jeopardizing the educational opportunities of a group of Texans."[42]

Citizens of the community wanted to know about the status of the university vis-à-vis the University of Texas. Was its continued existence certain? Was the president given full support by the board? Would it be wise to continue to send black youths to TSU, given the turmoil that existed? The issues surrounding the president got so bad in 1953 that the board issued a press release denying the following allegations: that Lanier was barred from some meetings; that the executive assistant to the board was the de facto head of the institution; and that the business manager ignored the president.[43]

Because of the negative publicity and the accusations made against the president, the board of directors established a citizen committee to "make a study of the university." The committee was charged with presenting its findings to the governor and to the general public. The committee agreed to investigate several charges against the president as they appeared in the newspapers from 1948–1952: (1) noncooperation with the Law School; (2) employing unprepared staff personnel; (3) shortages in the fiscal offices; (4) unrest among faculty and students; and (5) the firing of seventy-five faculty and staff. The purpose of this study was to ascertain the facts via data gathered from files of the university and from reports, letters, and interviews with teachers and students.[44]

In its report, the committee pointed out the unusual circumstances under which the university was established and the accomplishments of Lanier's five years. The committee also took into consideration the fact that in the black community; there was a group that favored the creation of TSU and one that opposed it; and those groups allied with other like groups in expressing their views of Lanier, both pro and con. When the committee presented its findings, it reported that the university had progressed under Lanier. In scholastic standing it received the following: accreditation recognized as a Class A institution by the Texas Education Agency; recognition as a Class A institution by the Southern Association of Colleges and Schools; membership in the American Association of Colleges for Teacher Education; accreditation of the School of Law from the Texas State Board of Law Examiners and the American Bar Association. The School of Pharmacy was likewise accredited by the American Council on Pharmaceutical Education as a Y-2 class institution. In athletics, the football team won the conference championship in 1952, while the track team placed second. TSU was also one of the founding members of the national Intramurals Recreational Sports. Moreover, the debate team had not lost a debate to a Texas college or university in three years, and the enrollment increased in both graduate and undergraduate programs.[45]

While acknowledging the above accomplishments and after listening to and investigating complaints from all sides, the committee was concerned with four alleged problems: (1) that seventy-five faculty members had been fired, resigned, or demoted during the Lanier era; (2) that Lanier was responsible for fake professors being added to the staff; (3) that the university administration had failed to keep adequate fiscal records; and (4) that there were turmoil and unrest on campus. As to the first charge, the committee found that the accusations were not supported by evidence. Only eight teaching positions had been eliminated, and eleven faculty members had resigned. Likewise, the evidence did not verify the second charge. On the other hand, the committee did find problems with the fiscal affairs of the university. There were problems with requisitioning, purchasing, inter-departmental vouchers, and paying and collecting debts on time. In looking at the fiscal affairs of the university, the committee discovered that the university was in a system of dual control. The president was in charge of the academic side of the university, whereas John Robertson, the executive assistant, was in charge of the fiscal side of the university. The committee was of the opinion that as long as this dual system existed, there would be conflict between the two administrative heads. It is noteworthy that when the state audit was released, of the eight charges made, only two were against the president. The other six were related to the function of the business affairs office. The committee's visit to the campus did not reveal the extent of the turmoil being propagated by the newspapers.[46]

According to those who knew Lanier and worked with him, he showed a zealous determination in establishing a university of the first class; however, he did not have an entirely free rein in handling the university's affairs, since there was a board-designated white presence in the business office. When the investigation was completed on August 12, 1953, the *Houston Informer*'s headline read, "There Is No Unrest at TSU. Board Clears Dr. Lanier." After the committee's findings were published, the board announced the resignations of John Robertson, executive assistant to the board, and French Stone, university comptroller. Contrary to the board's announcement, John Robertson did not leave the university until 1956, and "the small areas of friction that existed had [not] been cleared up." This announcement implied that Lanier would now be allowed to run the school. But this was only the calm before the storm. The die had been cast, and many people in the university, city, and state had already formed negative opinions of Lanier. No matter how many favorable reports Lanier received, his days were numbered.[47]

Early in 1955, rumors were rife that Lanier would be leaving the university. On June 8, 1955, he tendered his resignation, albeit a forced one. After the board meeting on that same day, Lanier was told that he was not to go back to the president's office for any reason and that whatever personal items he had left, the university would return them. He was given a definite time period to vacate the president's house and was told not to come back on campus. Since he did not have a contract, no severance pay was offered and none was given.[48]

By the time the Lanier era had ended, TSU, unlike her sister state colleges and universities, had grown up in the midst of a large number of abnormal and irregular circumstances. The law out of which it became a state institution provided that it should not only become a university of the first class, but that it should do so in a hurry. Less than four years after TSU's establishment, the Supreme Court's ruling in the *Sweatt* case transformed it from an emergency university to a fledging institution with minimal state support. Although the court's ruling was not followed by a change in the law that created the university, it was followed by a change in attitude toward the infant institution in that its financial support became influenced more by the court's decision than by the legislation creating it. Through it all, Lanier served the university in its darkest hours and brought about a general acceptance of the university by the general public and the university community. For all intents and purposes, with the end of the *Sweatt* case and Lanier's departure, the emergency was over. What was needed now was a strong leader who would make a serious effort to develop the kind of institution described in Senate Bill 140, obstacles notwithstanding.

3

Building despite the Odds

The Nabrit Era, 1955–1966

Raphael O'Hara Lanier's departure from the university in June 1955 fueled fears and speculations regarding who would become the second president. But this anxiety did not last long. After one month, the search committee recommended and the board of directors approved as president Samuel Milton Nabrit, distinguished biologist and dean of the Graduate School at Atlanta University, effective September 1, 1955. Nabrit was no stranger to academia; he was from a family that was well known in the black community. One of eight children born to James M. Nabrit and Margaret Perry Nabrit of Macon, Georgia (all of whom received one or more college degrees), Nabrit received his bachelor's degree from Morehouse College in 1925, and he served as an instructor at his alma mater from 1925 to 1928. During the summers of those years, he studied at the University of Chicago and at the Marine Biological Laboratory at Woods Hole, Massachusetts. He received his masters and PhD degrees in biology from Brown University in 1929 and 1932, respectively. Nabrit joined the Atlanta University faculty in 1932, became the chairman of the biology department in 1937, and ten years later was made dean of the Graduate School.[1]

At the time of his appointment to TSU, Nabrit was one of two black members of a select corporation of scientists who were invited to do research at the Marine Biological Laboratory at Woods Hole, Massachusetts. A member of various scientific and educational societies, he was known for his research on basic facts in embryology. Additionally, Nabrit was a supporter of the civil rights movement and freely discussed the race issue. It is noteworthy that he was the brother of James M. Nabrit Jr., who worked with Thurgood Marshall and prepared research briefs for the plaintiff in the

Samuel M. Nabrit, 1955–1966. Courtesy of *TSU Archives.*

Smith v. Allwright case, as well as in lawsuits filed by the NAACP that led to the Supreme Court's ruling in *Brown v. The Board of Education* in 1954.

Nabrit took a cut in pay to come to Texas Southern when he accepted the $18,000 presidential salary. He came because he felt that it was a challenge, and indeed it was. This was at the beginning of the modern civil rights movement, when the winds of change were blowing in the direction of desegregation as opposed to segregation. It was also a time when Texas Southern was operating on a shoestring budget and was suffering from a shortage of money. In common vernacular, TSU was financially poor and would likely continue to remain so, barring some windfall from the legislature or from private philanthropies. Either source would have been welcomed, but few if any were in sight. For all intents and purposes the "emergency" was not over. Moreover, Nabrit was coming into a situation in which the TSU board had little or no confidence in the previous administration, and where the faculty and president were more often than not in a combative mode. The challenges facing Nabrit were awesome, and if he were going to turn TSU into a first-class institution, he would have to do so despite the odds.[2]

When Nabrit came to TSU in the fall of 1955, he brought with him courage, efficiency, experience, and character—ingredients sorely needed for building a great university. Speaking before the Business and Professional Men's Club luncheon two weeks after his arrival, he laid out three qualifications for a great university. They included an informed and creative faculty, sufficient numbers of students, and sustained financial support. The new president made it clear that it was his purpose and aim to build TSU into a first-class university. Created as an emergency measure, Nabrit argued that TSU's growth up to this point had been more or less fluid. He, therefore, saw it as his duty to steer the university in the right direction. Reflecting on the past administration from a comparative perspective, Carter Wesley said, "Nabrit has brains [and] character and will make a good president if the board will let him and stay out of the administration." Fortunately for Nabrit, he had both the confidence of the board and of the black community. Speaking as a voice of the black community, Wesley wrote, "I do not believe that he would sell the race cheap because he has sufficient training and standing in the black community to get another job, if things don't work out."[3]

Aware of the need to change the course of the university, Nabrit's first priority was to deal with the shortage of money that the university faced. Nabrit quickly realized that from its inception TSU had been strapped by state regulations. Among these was a 1923 bill that prevented the state from allotting money to state colleges for auxiliary buildings such as dormitories, cafeterias, student unions, or gymnasiums. Even though tuition could be used for the normal expansion of the physical plant, the $200,000 collected from tuition each year was not enough. Immediately, TSU needed $2.5 million to build a science building and a library. Nabrit, therefore, entered into a compromise with the state. Since TSU did not have enough money for both buildings, Nabrit proposed the construction of a science building (which was a must) and one floor of the library at a later date.[4]

Problems in the business office, coupled with regulations governing the allotment of money to pay faculty, also restricted the university in making broad educational plans. In fact, on Nabrit's first day on the job, Willette R. Banks said to Nabrit, "Sam, everybody knows your qualifications, but be forewarned, if you cannot control the business office, you cannot stay here."[5] At that time, all requisitions and business transactions had to get approval not from the president but from John H. Robertson, the executive assistant to the board. Although the board had indicated it was going to abolish this position, that did not happen. Nabrit was then forced to deal with Robertson. Yet the business manager's only experience in fiscal affairs had come from managing the athletes at Florida A&M University; and he was expected to help Nabrit clear a $50,000 deficit that resulted from dormitories, bookstores, and food services. When Nabrit confronted the business manager about the $50,000 deficit, Robertson said that the problem would work itself out within a year. But this idea was impossible because the budget for the dormitories was based on an anticipated 730-bed revenue, whereas an examination of the said revenue revealed that only 300 beds had been purchased.[6]

The bookstore and food services also created fiscal nightmares for Nabrit. There was no rule regulating when a professor could change a book order. The result was that many professors changed their book orders at will, and the bookstore was left with books they could not sell. Concomitant with the problem of the bookstore was that of food service. The student newspaper ran editorials that said that "day after day, it's the same old thing, poor food, poor service and often unpleasant attitudes exhibited by the cafeteria personnel." To remedy this situation, Nabrit removed the highly paid chef who had formerly worked at the Shamrock Hilton and replaced her with another individual who was equally skilled in the culinary arts but was willing to work at a cheaper rate. Similarly, he removed individuals who were hired as cashiers and who had professional degrees and replaced them with individuals whose education did not require such salaries.[7]

Campus finances appeared to foreshadow most of the problems that Nabrit encountered during his first year; and the problem with the fiscal manager John Robertson was front and center. Early in 1956, Nabrit moved to resolve this situation when the Southern Association of Colleges and Schools (SACS) was in the process of admitting black colleges to its membership. At that time, Fort Valley State College was scheduled to go up for accreditation, but because TSU was stronger (on paper) than Fort Valley, SACS invited TSU to make application too. Nabrit accepted the invitation but told SACS that in matters dealing with finance, the president was being forced to take orders from a subordinate, a white man in the business office, a duty that Nabrit deemed to be in conflict with the office of the president. Nabrit felt that if SACS would grant accreditation under the existing conditions, the TSU board would never take corrective action. Taking Nabit's concern into consideration, SACS responded affirmatively: "Until the situation changes, we will not admit TSU." Nabrit discussed the response of SACS with the board and asked for Robertson's resignation. Robertson was allowed to remain in his job four months in order to complete his eleven-year tenure, which would make him eligible to draw his pension. While Nabrit thought he had resolved the situation, by the end of the year, Robertson returned to TSU as a state auditor.[8]

Having gained control of the fiscal office and having gained the confidence of the board, Nabrit next turned to the area of academics, where he was most comfortable. He operated from the premise that every child should have a right to education and that everyone should have the opportunity to learn. In his opinion, the teacher played a major role in student development; therefore, he began to push for the hiring of more faculty members with terminal degrees. He also implemented a policy that said "once in every three summers, an individual without a terminal degree should go back to college [to work toward one]." The student newspaper supported Nabrit's efforts by calling for "a quality faculty necessary to develop a student body which will be representative of the founding purpose of the university," namely, to become a first-class institution. Nabrit developed open communications with faculty and administrators, telling them that teaching was a twenty-four-hour job and that "what you do speaks louder than what you say." Nabrit's philosophy of education and his idea of a great university would become more pronounced in his inaugural address on March 18, 1956.[9]

Toward a "First-Class" University

In an impressive inaugural ceremony witnessed by approximately 1,800 persons, including 154 visiting delegates and dignitaries from various states, as well as members of the distinguished Nabrit family, Samuel Milton Nabrit was formally invested as president of TSU on Sunday, March 18, 1956, by Texas governor Allan Shivers. On July 1, 1951, Governor Shivers unexpectedly rose to the state's highest office upon the death of Governor Beauford Jester. By 1952, Shivers had become extremely powerful and popular within the state. Hence, he continually planned and schemed to get his conservative programs into bills and resolutions to the state legislature and his influence into decisions of the state courts. His election in 1954 brought a new twist to Texas politics, as he threw his power and support to Republican presidential candidate Dwight Davis Eisenhower. Speaking on the issue of segregation during his campaign, Shivers declared that "we are going to keep the system that we know is best." Further, he declared that integration would not take place in Texas while he was governor. As titular head of the state of Texas, he had come to the inauguration of Nabrit to execute his duty.[10]

Although Nabrit had no problems with the governor executing his duty, several people in the black community in Houston and throughout the state had concerns. When Governor Shivers, accompanied by Judge Spurgeon Bell, arrived at Nabrit's inaugural ceremonies, they were met by NAACP picket signs that read, "Hypocrisy, the Main Speaker. We want integration, Not Interposition. Shivers you send your boy to an integrated school, why not us?"[11] There were pros and cons as to whether there should have been picket signs at the inauguration of the second president. Some felt this was not the time nor the place and that it was an embarrassment to President Nabrit. Others felt that the NAACP had every right to protest because of the state's past action regarding the establishment of TSU. Carter Wesley, being a bit more objective, admitted that except for Shivers's pronouncements on race during the 1954 campaign, he "was not a bad governor" insofar as he kept some balance on the TSU board and gave TSU a black chairman. Conversely, on the invitation to speak at the inauguration, Wesley stated that "it is not human nature to expect Negroes who have suffered so much at the governor's hand to be enthusiastic about him." Visibly shaken by the public and aware of blacks' feelings toward him, Shivers called for tolerance: "If we claim tolerance from others as a mark of our freedom, we should be tolerant of their views."[12]

Following Shivers's speech, in a highly professional address Nabrit outlined a blueprint for the university, which included its students, faculty, the physical plant, and academic standards. It was Nabrit's belief that education not only transmits social heritage but also transforms it. Education, he said, "was a means of shortening the time necessary for one to become acquainted with the best of the experiences of mankind; to improve one's skills and abilities; to develop appreciation and social responsibility; and to gain competence for a livelihood."[13] In his pursuit to build a first-class institution, Nabrit called for high academic standards at TSU, financial assistance from the business community, and competitive faculty salaries. Appealing for financial help in the pursuit to build a first-class university, Nabrit said that "the University shall have to enlist the aid of private businesses, individuals and foundations in order to keep pace with the demands made upon us." Nabrit also made it clear that salaries of the faculty were important and even essential for attracting and holding qualified persons. "We need better prepared teachers and need to provide a broad set of educational experiences for our children to be more competitive."[14] He further pointed out that 8.6 percent of the college-age Negro youths in Texas were attending college, and that TSU serviced 46 percent of that number. Nabrit made it clear that TSU was presently operating at a minimum $300 per capita student cost for the undergraduates, $1,000 for law students, and $750 for pharmacy students. Without resources for enriching the university's programs, the institution was doomed to failure; yet Nabrit argued that if TSU were given the needed facilities, faculty, and administrators, it could become a first-class university.[15]

At the heart of Nabrit's academic concerns were the students. When

Nabrit arrived on campus in 1955, the majority of TSU's students were studying to become teachers. This fact troubled the president for a number of reasons. For one thing, he was a strong believer in a liberal-arts education that required a general comprehensive learning prior to specialization. He argued that the "university has an obligation to develop educated men and women rather than prematurely skilled artisans." Thus, he was concerned with whether teachers were adequately prepared and whether the students' backgrounds had prepared them for college work. In Nabrit's own words, "Many students are entering programs because of somebody they knew, [but they are entering] without any knowledge of whether they can master it or find employment in it." So, at the School Administrators' Conference held at TSU on February 4, 1956, Nabrit used this opportunity to discuss the issue. The School Administrators' Conference, established in the early 1950s, was designed to upgrade the performances among Negro school children in the Houston area. Discussions for the 1956 conference included the following topics: using test results for improving instruction; the administration assuming responsibility for improving instruction; and revisions in instruction.[16]

Subsequently, the findings of this conference revealed that the university should do the following: reevaluate the achievements and competencies of the students so as to "ascertain whether their levels of growth were up to college standards"; determine if teacher-education needed to be carefully scrutinized and the requirements in skills and abilities raised; and determine whether the School of Education should become a part of the College of Arts and Sciences in order to provide an education based in the liberal arts.[17] After the conference, Nabrit and his faculty began to brainstorm over how to help the underprepared student. They came to the conclusion that the majority of TSU's students were working students who were in need of academic and financial assistance. For two years, Nabrit mulled over this issue. In 1958, he was invited by Ira Bryant, principal of Kashmere High School, to give the 1958 commencement address. After his presentation, Nabrit sat quietly while Bryant and the philanthropist Evan Worthing presented scholarships to deserving students. Worthing is reported to have leaned over and whispered to Nabrit, "These students are getting scholarships now, but half of them won't be in school at the end of the year." Nabrit conceded that nothing could be done for the summer of 1958, but that something had to be done in subsequent years.[18]

For the time being, Nabrit recommended strengthening the guidance program whereby faculty would volunteer to work in the dormitories. Prior to 1951, there were no dormitory accommodations available; therefore, TSU functioned as a day school even though most of its classes were offered at night. With the opening of its first two residence halls in the fall of 1951, the university assumed a new role in higher education. It combined the task of developing its students academically and socially. In the opinion of the administration, the faculty and staff felt that one of the best ways of accomplishing this task was to combine the counseling program and the tutorial program in the dormitory. Faculty members were then asked to set aside one hour per day for this task. Experiencing success with the above effort and being concerned with the recruitment and retention of students, the university in the summer of 1959 invited high school students to come to TSU for an enrichment program designed to prepare them to do college work in reading, English (writing), and mathematics free of charge. An assessment of this first summer program indicated great success among those who returned to their respective schools, as well as among those who went on to institutions of higher learning, including TSU. While the program was a recruiting mechanism for the university, there was no requirement that the students attend TSU after participating in the program.[19]

Amid praises and accolades, this enrichment program continued during the summer of 1960. In that year, twelve students from Yale University came to the campus with the intention of helping TSU students in the civil rights struggle. According to Nabrit, he told these students that "Yale needs more civil rights than TSU, but if you really want to help the university, you can join the tutorial program and help high school students who are enrolled in our summer programs." These students accepted the president's offer, lived in the dormitories, tutored students, and worked with them in understanding the lectures given by their professors. They also taught them how to take notes.[20]

For his success in remediating students and in raising standards among faculty and students, the TSU board gave President Nabrit a commendation for five years of outstanding leadership in 1960. According to the resolution, "under [Nabrit's] guidance, educational standards have been raised and scholastic achievement on the part of both students and faculty has been stressed to the end that good learning is flourishing on the campus and respect for the institution in the educational community is growing."[21] In 1960, a board statement reiterated the university's commitment to the development of a university of the first class. This resolution was undergirded by the university's commitment to engage in a continuous program of self-evaluation, improvement, and expansion of its curricula, faculty, and facilities. In the process of examining "the self," it became clear that TSU had developed certain remedial and compensatory educational programs for students who came to the university from social and educational backgrounds that were often ill-fitted for first-class university work.[22]

The university was able to accomplish its goal of remediation because it was privy to state funds allocated for that purpose. But in 1962 the state ended such funding. Recognizing that many of the students entering the university needed additional help, Nabrit sought private and federal funds to continue as well as to expand remedial offerings. To his credit, Nabrit brought to his office a certain prestige and pattern of educational accomplishments that made possible important connections for the university in the total academic community, especially in grantsmanship. Consequently, grants to the university from government and from private foundations began to accumulate in increasing amounts. For example, on September 17, 1963, Nabrit announced to the board that TSU was being recommended for two Ford Foundation grants totaling $900,000—one for retaining and upgrading faculty, the other to help remediate underprepared students. Enrichments for faculty included a faculty exchange program with the University of Wisconsin at Madison; two $1,000 faculty recognition awards to be granted annually to faculty members who showed special initiative, imagination, and conscientiousness in their responsibilities to students; and a faculty creativity fund that would enhance research into educational problems faced by blacks at the local and regional levels. For remediation, funds were allocated to establish a college remedial studies program and to provide faculty with released time to do research on developmental work.[23]

In the summer of 1964, with the support grants from the Ford Foundation, three hundred high school graduates were brought to campus for an intensive four-week program designed to prepare them for college work. The next summer that number increased to six hundred. In 1965, all potential freshmen who wished to matriculate at TSU were required to participate in the program. For a continuation of the grant, Nabrit relied heavily on the feedback from high school teachers.[24]

It is noteworthy, instructive, and informative that Nabrit played an instrumental role in the solicitation of financial support not only from Ford, but from other private foundations—Carnegie, Duke, and the Houston Endowment, to name a few. In 1964, Nabrit also thought that it would be wise to tap into funds from the Southern Association of Colleges and Schools (SACS), funds designed to aid underprivileged children. In a cooperative effort with Rice University, the University of Houston (UH), and the Houston Independent School District, TSU (as principal investigator) submitted to the executive director of SACS a proposal titled "An Experimental Program in Cultural and Educational Improvement among Youths of Houston, Texas." The unfunded proposal was designed to upgrade incoming students, to retool high school teachers, and to break their cultural lag. In March 1965, the Carnegie Foundation boosted TSU's operation in seeking potentially talented youths from among the underprivileged in order to motivate and to prepare them for college. Funds from Carnegie were supplemented by the U.S. Office of Economic Opportunity (OEO), which provided Texas Southern University with a grant of $127,194. This grant was part of OEO's new program called "Upward Bound," which was given to seventeen participating colleges. Along with TSU, other HBCUs involved in this project were Fisk, Howard, and Morehouse College.[25]

Arguably, the Upward Bound Program and Title III came out of a TSU initiative that, aided by the Ford Foundation, brought talented, underprivileged high school students to campus for summer enrichment prior to their matriculation. President Nabrit was part of a "think tank" group that conceptualized, experimented with, and implemented (with the support of Carnegie Foundation) a precollege youth program that became a model for the national Upward Bound Program. Likewise, it was TSU in partnership with North Carolina A&T College, North Carolina State College, and the Extension Division of the University of Wisconsin at Madison that helped give impetus to what is now called Title III in the Higher Education Acts of 1965. At its inception, this act provided set-aside monies for Historically Black Colleges and Universities.[26]

It should be noted that seeking funds for education was not difficult in the 1960s, a decade marked by many movements, including the civil rights movement, and educational fervor on many college campuses. During that decade, poverty and discrimination, as well as the general socioeconomic and educational status of blacks, were brought glaringly to the public's attention. As a result of its introspection, the nation passed legislation that attempted to right past wrongs—civil rights acts, voter rights acts, economic opportunity acts, and job training programs. Coupled with the above were the establishments of Head Start, Upward Bound, Work Study, Title III of the Higher Education Act, and various titles of the Elementary and Secondary Education Act. The actions of these agencies, as well as the grants awarded by various philanthropic organizations, were all attempts in one way or another to provide better educational opportunities for the various disadvantaged social and economic minority groups.

The real meaning of the awards granted to TSU lay in the fact that appreciable private support had been extended to underwrite the costs of exploratory but extensive retooling and upgrading of a public black institution that catered primarily to a black clientele so as to receive substantial grants from national philanthropies. These grants were an objective recognition of the potential of the overall Texas Southern University program as well as the administrative leadership that was trying to move in the direction of a first-class university. In the words of John Lash, executive assistant to President Nabrit, "The availability of this private support was critical to the University, not only because the grant funds underwrote certain programs which did not receive State support, but also because presumably there had to be outside evaluation of the university's existence and potential capabilities for growth in educational stature before the grants were approved."[27]

Nabrit was elated over the previously mentioned grants, but he was equally concerned about the teachers and the university's programs. It was his opinion that "TSU's faculty should be teachers first, but that they should remain intellectually alive; they must have some time for independent research work."[28] In his last appearance before the Legislative Budget Committee in 1966, Nabrit told the members that TSU was becoming competitive for teachers, and they needed lower teaching loads and better retirement benefits to really compete. At that time, he was also able to point to the fact that TSU's student quality had improved as a result of past efforts, and that both the enrollment and the number of students graduating were up. The Legislative Budget Committee gave TSU a glowing report. In the minds of many, TSU was well on its way to becoming a first-class university. But still there were roadblocks in the way.[29]

The Merger of Professional Schools

The talk of merger began almost as soon as the Supreme Court ordered an African American law student admitted to the University of Texas. In 1956, the Texas legislature created the Texas Commission of Higher Education (TCHE) and passed a law which stated that the commission shall order consolidation or elimination of programs where such action is in the best interest of the institutions themselves and of the general requirements of the state of Texas.[30] Six years after its creation (1962), the commission ordered a feasibility study done on TSU's law and pharmacy schools to determine if they should be merged with the University of Houston. Motivated by the student-teacher ratio, as well as the costs to maintain these programs, the commission's study revealed that the University of Houston's Law School had 350 students, whereas TSU's Law School had only 30 students. Yet the costs for educating TSU students were five times higher than the costs at the University of Texas and nearly four times as high as the costs at the University of Houston.[31] The TSU board chairman became very nervous when he read a newspaper clipping about a possible merger; and he sent the same to other board members, pointing out that "this talk of merger is serious business which we ought to inquire into to see just what really is in the minds of the proponents thereof. I think that we all have lived long enough to know that Texas Southern could be adversely affected."[32]

According to the news report, the TCHE moved to consider the merger of the two schools after some of its members made reference to the fact that the University of Houston would soon become a state-supported institution and that the state could not afford to have two law and pharmacy schools so close together. The commissioner from Houston thought that "a phasing out of the schools at TSU and UH would be advisable."[33] In a prepared statement, the TSU administration launched a counterattack. The president said that no steps should be taken to reduce the number of Negroes trained for legal and pharmaceutical professions in the state; that TSU produced 93 percent of the non-Anglo practicing pharmacists in the state despite the fact that the University of Texas had admitted blacks for a number of years and had far greater resources. Nabrit went on to point out that supporting two professional schools in one city was not without precedent. This same scenario existed in North Carolina and Louisiana, and in each case the minority race law schools were smaller than TSU.[34]

Despite the plea from President Nabrit, in 1964 by a vote of 11–12 the Texas Commission of Higher Education agreed to phase out the law school beginning in the fall of 1966, while giving the Pharmacy School a reprieve. Nabrit then made another special plea before the commission in October 1965 to keep the Law School open; and the Law School dean Kenneth Tollette wrote a letter to the commission asking for a reprieve and pointing to the commission's obvious, profound misunderstanding of the role race played in the legal profession.[35] But neither Nabrit nor Tollette gained any traction. So this time Nabrit would have to solicit support from Governor John Connally. When Nabrit went in to see Connally, he not only pointed to the reason and purpose for a black law school, but he also pointed out a technicality. The TCHE could not close a university. It could only make recommendations of its finding to the board of directors who would then inform the president. The TCHE had made its announcement on the closing of the two professional schools without following its own rule. When Nabrit presented his case, Governor Connelly assured him that nothing would happen to TSU's law school if Nabrit would not align himself with one of the small schools in east Texas that was trying to get a PhD program. Nabrit agreed, and nothing happened to the Law School at TSU. For the rest of Nabrit's tenure, which ended in 1966, he could breathe a sigh of relief.[36]

Student Activism and Desegregation in Houston

It is not too much to say that the eyes of Texas, if not the nation, were indeed on the fledgling school during the civil rights movement of the 1950s and '60s. The *Sweatt* case had signaled the beginning of the end of racial segregation in professional areas of Texas and throughout the South. It inevitably led to a reevaluation of both the legality and appropriate roles of public higher educational institutions restructured for members of one racial group or another. Two years after the *Sweatt* case, several white students attempted to test TSU's admissions policy but were denied. Although the university's staff had been integrated since 1953, it was not until 1956 that this restrictive admissions policy was lifted. After going through extensive discussions on this issue, and two years after the University of Texas admitted undergraduate black students, the TSU board voted five to one to drop the "race designation in its admissions policy.[37] The dissenting member said he opposed the resolution because it would hurt TSU's funding. Yet one would be hard pressed to believe that there would be a floodgate of whites seeking to enter TSU. When asked about his opinion on the board's action, Nabrit said, "It would be untenable for our students to seek admission at their schools while [denying admission] of others at ours."[38]

In a distinct way, TSU moved toward an inclusive community. During the early '60s, the university served as an agency for revolution and the resolution of distinctive and unique social problems and prospects. Nowhere was this notion more evident than in student protests and demonstrations in the city of Houston during the Nabrit era. The student sit-in demonstrations that galvanized the civil rights movement and provided a new tactic for mass movement began on February 1, 1960, when four black students from North Carolina A&T University in Greensboro sat down at an "all-white" lunch counter, requested service, and were refused. The students came back on the next day in larger numbers, and occupied every seat at the lunch counter, effectively shutting down the business. This sit-in tactic caught on immediately and within weeks had spread to fifty-four cities in nine Southern states, including Texas. That TSU students would join the

TSU students staging a sit-in demonstration at Weingarten lunch counter, March 4, 1960. Courtesy of Houston Public Library, Houston Metropolitan Research.

movement did not come as a surprise to the faculty or to the larger black community. In the words of Nabrit, "If all of the other students in the South were fighting segregation as unjust and morally wrong, then there would have to have been something wrong with our teaching if our students thought otherwise."[39]

For one month, TSU students paid close attention to the sit-in demonstrations throughout the South. At the time that they were planning their strategy, they were catapulted into the movement by remarks made by then-senator Lyndon Baines Johnson. According to Holly Hogrobrooks, Johnson had allegedly said that "[TSU students] were too complacent to engage in public protest." After a series of discussions on that topic, a student movement was formed by Holly Hogrobrooks, Ted Hogrobrooks, Eddie Rigby, Jesse Purve, and Eldrewey Stearns, and a sit-in demonstration was planned for March 4, 1960, at a Weingarten grocery store. Ironically, the above date was also TSU's charter day, and the student meeting place was the flagpole in front of Hannah Hall. So, on March 4, the students marched from TSU to the Weingarten grocery store on Almeda Street, not far from the campus. Since that store catered mainly to a black clientele, the students felt that it would be most vulnerable to the pressure to integrate its lunch counter.[40]

When the sit-in demonstration started, no one knew how long it would last, how many students would be involved, what reception they would receive from the store owner, or what disciplinary actions if any the TSU administration would take. What is known is that the march to Weingarten's started out with thirteen students, but by the time they arrived at their destination there were approximately seventy-two students. The students were fearful of the possibility of violence, but they were determined to stay the course. Within minutes of their arrival, the manager closed the counter and policemen arrived. But as was the case in Greensboro, the students continued to sit there for nearly four hours, in effect shutting down business. The students left without incident but returned the next day and put Mading Drugstore on notice that it would be next. On the following Monday, March 7, the students made their appearance at Heinke and Pilot Supermarket and then moved to Mading Drugstore and later to Walgreen's Drugs.[41]

While the demonstrations caught many white Houstonians by surprise, a large number of blacks supported the movement surreptitiously or by indirection. Black patrons boycotted many of the stores while some black businessmen stood by to bail students out of jail. On March 8, 1960, a white banker on the TSU board, Ralph Lee, told the press that the sit-ins were going too smoothly, that Nabrit must have engineered them, and thus he demanded that Nabrit put an end to the demonstrations. Lee was very perceptive. When the demonstration occurred on March 4, 1960, President Nabrit was attending a meeting of the Council of Presidents of Southern Colleges and Universities. But while Nabrit did not orchestrate the sit-in, he was aware of it. Before Nabrit left to go out of town, Dean of Students Ina A. Bolton told him that she had heard that TSU students were ready to begin a sit-in demonstration and that she wished for instructions on what to do. Nabrit's response was that if Bolton "could not join a revolution and help shape it, she should get out of the way so that it would not run over her." When Nabrit returned home, the press asked him to respond to the allegations, but he refused.[42]

On Monday following the sit-in, Nabrit called Mack Hannah, chairman of TSU's Board of Regents, to discuss the students' activities. Hannah informed Nabrit that he had spoken to Governor Price Daniel regarding the situation each day. After the meeting, Hannah called several members of the board of directors and Carl Shuptrine, the Houston chief of police, to inform them that TSU administrators had no role in the protest and would cooperate to prevent any bloodshed or property damage. With this assurance, Shuptrine called Nabrit and assured him that if students called him before each demonstration, behaved properly, and had broken no laws, they would be protected.[43] At the time Shuptrine was under the impression that the demonstrations would end soon. But this did not happen. When it became clear that the sit-in movement was not going to stop, Mayor Lewis Cutrer, along with a group of merchants and businesses, increased the pressure on

Nabrit to put an end to it. The president then arranged a meeting between Cutrer and the students. Cutrer came to campus on Monday, March 14, in an effort to dissuade the students from continuing their protest activities. In the words of Nabrit, Cutrer came "with a police patrol, honking horns and everything else to indicate power."[44] The students were under the impression that they would discuss a compromise with the mayor; instead they received a threat that if they did not vacate certain property when told to do so, they would be arrested. The meeting came to naught, and the students vowed to continue the protest.

On the next day, Nabrit convened a general assembly of students and faculty to make his views known about the sit-in demonstrations. Nabrit began by saying that he was not afraid of his job and that he viewed the issue of demonstration as one of citizenship and not academic policy. As to the laws regarding sit-ins, Nabrit stated, "I have reviewed the laws of the city and state and find that the students are not violating any laws by their activities." Additionally, Nabrit argued that the students were not in violation of regulations at Texas Southern and that "as long as they attend their scheduled classes, we shall take no disciplinary actions." While many black presidents at other HBCUs capitulated to the white power structure, Nabrit stood firm on his position that as citizens of the country the students had a right to protest. "Our view then is that it is the democratic right of students to seek remedial measures for social injustices within the framework of the law. We stand with our students," said Nabrit.[45]

It is interesting to note that the print media did not carry Nabrit's speech as an endorsement of the movement. Rather, the speech was couched in language such as "the students have demonstrated and now it is the time for negotiation." When Nabrit gave his speech, he was keenly aware that TSU was a state-supported institution and that keeping it open was paramount. He therefore called the leaders of the movement to his office and told them that he supported their cause and would not expel any of them if they would plan their protest activities off campus.[46] Following his advice, the students took their demonstration to the nearby YMCA Building on Wheeler Avenue.

By mid-March most of the lunch counters in the city had closed and the sit-in demonstrations appeared to have ceased, but the movement was not over. Student activists then organized the Progressive Youth Association (PYA) to continue the struggle. This group, led by Eldrewey Stearns, a TSU law student, forged alliances with students from the Erma Hughes Business College and Rice University. Together they decided to attack the following retail businesses in downtown Houston—Foley's, Grant's, Kress, Walgreen's, and Woolworth's. Afterward, they picketed City Hall, entered the Municipal Building, and requested service at the cafeteria. Subsequently, they were served, and they hailed this as a major victory. It is interesting to note that the white media did not publish anything about the integration of the City Hall cafeteria because they felt that it would draw attention to the students' cause and that the sit-in would probably create a scene at City Hall while Argentina's ambassador was visiting the city.

The action taken by the students to integrate City Hall had a great impact on the Retail Merchants Association. By this time, members of this group had come to the realization that they could not stop the forces behind integration and that segregation was not worth the dollar. As this group dialogued with the mayor about this issue, Mayor Cutrer moved toward creating a Biracial Committee to study race relations in Houston and to advise him accordingly. TSU students had earlier proposed such a committee to the mayor, but he rejected it. Now that he had begun to see the proverbial handwriting on the wall, he changed his mind. On April 17, he named a forty-one-person committee, which included President Samuel Nabrit.[47]

From the outset, the committee, which was strictly advisory, was divided into two groups—the pro-integrationists and the anti-integrationists. The first group called for integration in all municipal offices and selected Aloysius Martin Wickliff of the Harris County Council of Organizations as their leader. The second group, led by the Retail Merchant Association and Leon Jaworski, president of the Houston Chamber of Commerce, was opposed to integration. At the first meeting, Jaworski, who thought that the student demonstrations were tarnishing the image of a progressive city, asked the committee to vote on a statement condemning the sit-ins on the grounds that participants were trespassing on private properties. He was stunned when the majority voted against it. Deanna Lott Burrell, who represented the students and who sided with Wickliff, told the committee that blacks expected to be treated in the same manner as whites in every respect. Jaworski, somewhat puzzled, called for a vote on Wickcliff's motion for municipal desegregation. When this majority voted with Wickliff, Jaworski swore the committee to secrecy until he had talked to Mayor Cutrer. More importantly, Jaworski did not want the press to know of the committee's vote for integration. Whatever transpired between Cutrer and Jaworski, the committee's vote was never announced to the public.[48]

While the Biracial Committee held deliberations from April through June, the students' sit-in activities were suspended. This was due in part to the fact that the students wanted to give the committee time to come up with an acceptable solution, and also perhaps because this occurred at the end of the semester when students needed time to prepare for their final examinations. But if merchants thought that they could return to business as usual after the students left, they were sadly mistaken. The students started a second wave of protests on August 2, when they staged a protest in the Garden Room at Joske's Department Store. On September 18, the Progressive Youth Association (PYA) expanded its demands to include integrating the staff of drugstores, filling stations, and banks in black districts. And as if this was not enough, a third wave of protests came in January 1961 when the PYA staged a sit-in at the Houston Police Station's cafeteria on Riesner Street. In February of that same year, students protested at movie theatres and at Houston's Union Station. By the summer and fall of 1961, students had achieved the goal of integrating many public facilities in the Bayou city. For a brief period of time afterward, there appeared to have been a decline in the sit-in activities, but the students nevertheless continued to push for equal treatment and equal rights as citizens of the United States. For example, on June 1, 1963, TSU law students picketed City Hall for its slow pace in integration. Also, the National School Board's meeting held in Houston in April 1964 was picketed by TSU students for its members' stance on maintaining segregation.[49]

Nabrit stood tall regarding his conviction of equality for all. Not only did he support the student demonstrations, but when eight TSU student athletes decided not to run in a championship track meet at the University of Houston on June 1, 1961, because the fans were required to sit in segregated seating, Nabrit acknowledged their efforts by calling a university-wide assembly and announcing to a thunderous standing ovation, "We did not run today, but we walked out with dignity."[50] It is both instructive and informative that, contrary to the wishes of and pressure from powerful whites of the city who wanted Nabrit to discipline the students and who had a great deal of influence in the Texas legislature, Nabrit did a balancing act. He supported the constitutional rights of students to protest while sitting at the table with the mayor, the board, and the businessmen to come up with a solution to the race problem, a solution that helped change the political landscape of Houston.

Departure

In June 1966, President Lyndon Baines Johnson appointed Nabrit to a four-year term on the Atomic Energy Commission, the first black to be named to this post. Nabrit was a personal friend of Johnson and had dined at the White House on several occasions, but he had never been asked to serve the nation. Johnson was not the first president to utilize the services of Nabrit. John F. Kennedy utilized Nabrit's service in 1963 when Secretary of State Dean Rusk named Nabrit as one of ten Americans chosen to attend a United Nations' conference in Geneva, Switzerland, titled "Assistance to Under-Developed Nations." President Eisenhower appointed Nabrit in 1956 to the National Science Board and in 1959 to the National Advisory Committee to assist the Office of Education with a program to improve modern foreign language instruction. So, upon hearing of his Senate confirmation to a position on the Atomic Energy Commission, Nabrit requested a leave of absence from the university for one year. The request was granted, but doubts prevailed in local academic circles that Nabrit would return after a year.[51]

The Houston community expressed a great deal of pride that the TSU president was receiving such honors. Fittingly, a reception was held for Nabrit at the Rice Hotel, where two hundred civic, business, and educational leaders heaped praise on him. Dignitaries included the mayor of Houston, the president of the Houston Chamber of Commerce, and the faculty and staff members of TSU. But just as some people had speculated, in March 1967, Nabrit tendered his resignation as president. When asked by a reporter if TSU had achieved the goals that he had set for it when he took over the leadership, Nabrit answered, "I would say we are moving in the right direction rather than that we had achieved our goals."[52]

Nabrit changed the academic and physical landscapes at TSU. Under his leadership, TSU more than tripled the number of its faculty having PhD degrees, increased its enrollment by 50 percent, increased graduation rates, and balanced the budget. Additionally, the faculty and staff were enlarged and became racially integrated to an unprecedented extent, at one point reaching approximately 35 percent of nonblacks on the instructional side. Long before there were black studies programs on white campuses, TSU had courses in African and African American history and eventually started a consortium with Rice University and the University of Houston for an African American studies program, an effort which gave rise to the Black Studies Program at the University of Houston. These efforts were complemented by construction of new buildings, by extracurricular activities, and by the solicitation of grants. In a ten-year span, TSU constructed a new science building, a library, two dormitories, and a home economics lab. In regards to extracurricular activities, it is of special significance that the debate team, coached by Thomas Freeman, defeated Harvard University in a forensic competition, while the TSU basketball team was runner up in NIAA in 1956. Equally as important was the fact that at one point during the Nabrit era, TSU had thirteen federally funded programs ranging from Operation Head Start to training teachers and school administrators in the problems and challenges involved in school desegregation. It seems safe to say that the university had reached the "end of its beginning" under Nabrit and had moved from an emergency university to a nationally known HBCU.

4

The So-Called TSU Riot

Joseph A. Pierce and the Committee of Three, 1966–1968

It was a general consensus from both supporters and detractors of Texas Southern that Samuel M. Nabrit had taken the university to a new level in higher education. Upon his departure, the question that was uppermost in everybody's mind was who would succeed him. For two years, however, the university was run by Joseph Alphonso Pierce and a "Committee of Three." A native of Waycross, Georgia, Pierce received his early education from the public schools of Georgia and later earned a bachelor's degree in business and sociology from Atlanta University. Pierce started his professional career as an assistant football coach at Texas College in Tyler, where he discovered that he would be required to teach mathematics. Pierce soon fell in love with the subject matter, and after four years of teaching went on to receive both his masters and doctorate in mathematics from the University of Michigan. In 1938, he became professor of mathematics at Atlanta University; and in 1948 he left Atlanta to become professor and chairman of the Mathematics Department at Texas State University for Negroes (TSUN). Two years later, he took on added responsibility—becoming chairman of the division of natural and physical sciences (1950) and then dean of the graduate school (1952). Motivated by the fact that blacks had been denied admission to graduate schools at major southern universities, Pierce was determined to build a strong graduate program at TSU. He recruited senior professors from nearby universities to assist with the demand for graduate courses. As a result of his efforts, the graduate student enrollment increased—from 95 in 1946 to 304 in 1958. With this track record and at sixty-four years of age, Pierce was asked to serve as acting president in 1966. After his departure from office, he was named the third president of the university.[1]

Joseph Alphonso Pierce, 1966–1967.
Courtesy of *TSU Archives*.

When Pierce assumed the office of president in 1966, there had been a shift in tactics and location in the civil rights movement, as well as a great deal of unrest on college campuses. The use of nonviolent methods to achieve equality in public spaces in both rural and urban locations no longer took center stage. There was a shift in geographic locations to include the North and the West. A shift in tactics involved a more militant approach to eradicating segregation while at the same time concentrating on surrounding communities, on poverty, and on education. Prior to 1964, the collective demands of college students had found voice in a national, student-led civil rights group, the Student Non-Violent Coordinating Committee (SNCC), which advocated nonviolence. After 1964, students began to commit themselves to larger civic and societal issues of inequality. College students who once had left their respective campuses to protest Jim Crow policies and practices downtown were now returning to their own campuses to effect changes. They were looking introspectively at their own history and culture. Like other black youths, they had by this time begun to listen more closely to Malcolm X than to Martin Luther King Jr.

In 1965, while civil rights activists were debating issues, tactics, and locations, James Meredith, the first black to attend the University of Mississippi, decided to stage a march from Memphis, Tennessee, to Jackson, Mississippi, in order to register blacks to vote and to show that they were not afraid to march. On the second day of the march, he was shot. Almost immediately, most of the national civil rights leaders converged on Memphis and vowed to continue to march. This group included the new chairman of SNCC, Stokely Carmichael, who had replaced John Lewis, a disciple of Martin L. King's nonviolent approach. Each night after a long march, the participants set up tents and held rallies. There, Martin L. King Jr. preached nonviolence; but when his organizational members attempted to sing "We Shall Overcome," militants would respond "We Shall Overrun." When the crowd reached Greenville, Mississippi, Carmichael violated police orders prohibiting him from putting up a tent at a black school. He was arrested and placed in jail. Upon his release, Carmichael held a rally and vowed that he was not going to jail anymore, and in his own words said, "The only way we were going to stop them white men from whipping us is to take over. Now we are going to start saying Black Power." The "Black Power" slogan was considered a turning point in the black liberation struggle. "Everything that happened afterward was a response to it." In the age of television, all blacks were exposed and affected by those words, including TSU students.[2]

TSU students had been actively involved in protest activities since the early 1960s, but after Carmichael's speech, they, like many other students, began more and more to embrace black consciousness, black pride, and black power. Also, many of them became more receptive to the teachings of Malcolm X and Stokely Carmichael than to those of Martin L. King Jr. They began to take an active part in their communities and were invigorated by the emergence of new leaders and a groundswell of new activism. As such, a group of TSU students came together in the fall of 1966 and formed an organization known as the Friends of SNCC. This group was led by Reverend Frederick Douglass (F. D) Kirkpatrick, a TSU sociology graduate student; Millard Lowe, a local coordinator of SNCC; Franklin Alexander, the national president of the W. E. B. DuBois Club; and Lee Otis Johnson, a TSU student who some described as a brother you would take with you to a fight. The Friends of SNCC were concerned with uplifting the black community politically and economically, as well as with opposing police brutality.

Although the Friends of SNCC was not a duly recognized campus organization, it was permitted to use the Religion Center on campus for its regular meetings and had a great deal of influence on some TSU students. On October 26, 1966, James Farmer Jr., former president of the Congress of Racial Equality (CORE), spoke to TSU students on "Black Power as Political Power." From that point on, the leaders of the Friends of SNCC began to discuss with the students the meaning of black power. The first real influence of SNCC on TSU students became evident in December 1966 when a group of students demonstrated against Mayor Louie Welch when he came to campus. This meeting between Mayor Welch and the students had begun in the early 1960s during sit-in demonstrations and was designed to provide a question-and-answer forum in order to keep the mayor abreast of current race relations in the city and to get firsthand knowledge of the students' concerns. When the mayor arrived on campus that week, he was greeted with the chant "We want freedom" and with protest signs that read, "The mayor is white power, we need black power." This behavior on the part of the students created fear and anxiety for the TSU administration and for the white community.[3]

Dean of Students James B. Jones, who was somewhat troubled by the Friends of SNCC, became even more so when the organization sought official recognition as a campus organization on January 7, 1967. At that time, Jones told the local leaders Reverend Frederick Douglass Kirkpatrick, Millard Lowe, Franklin Alexander, and Lee Otis Johnson that in order for the Friends to qualify, they had to present a copy of a proposed constitution that specified requirements for membership; the amount of dues (if any were to be paid); the dates of regularly scheduled meetings; a list of officers; and a faculty sponsor.[4] The students' choice for advisor was assistant professor Mack H. Jones. Jones had completed his BA degree in political science at TSU after being suspended for his involvement in sit-ins and other civil rights demonstrations at Southern University in Baton Rouge. Upon graduation, he pursued the MA and PhD degrees at the University of Illinois. After completing all of his course work for the terminal degree, Jones was hired at TSU by Henry Bullock, chairman of the Social Sciences Division, over the objection of the political science chairman. Jones, along with three other young scholars from the Woodrow Wilson Foundation, interacted with students on several issues and saw the world through lens different from some older, more conservative professors. It was not surprising, then, that the TSU administration would single out Jones along with the leaders of Friends of SNCC as potential trouble makers.[5]

On March 8, 1967, the Friends issued a call for a mass meeting to be held near the TSU campus at the YMCA on Wheeler Avenue. According to the memorandum that announced the meeting, one of the items on the agenda was titled "Police Brutality Throughout the State of Texas." The issue of police brutality as stated in this memo was exacerbated by the print media, which alleged that a state highway patrolman had beaten four gospel singers and that during the incident a state trooper had remarked that "he killed one nigger and was dying to kill two more niggers."[6] In an attempt to galvanize the students, the Friends countered with a statement by saying,

"Every day hundreds of our own black brothers and children are drafted to fight in a war thousands of miles from home. . . . Another form of violence is perpetuated by white America [and the police against Negro people]." [7] Some considered this memo to be inflammatory, but long before the Friends had come on the scene, black residents were openly critical of the police department for the discriminatory ways it enforced the law and for its lack of protection of black people. Moreover, the students were demanding that Wheeler Street, which ran through the middle of the campus, be closed to city traffic.

Although the Friends of SNCC was never officially recognized as a campus organization, Dean James B. Jones sent the leaders a letter on March 11, 1967, and asked if they and their advisor Mack Jones could meet for lunch to discuss the upcoming rally. No doubt, the result of the meeting was predetermined. No sooner had the group assembled than Dean Jones informed the group that it was banned from using university facilities.[8] At this time, the fear surrounding the group was unwarranted because the group did not have a massive following. Yet, the issues raised by this group impacted the black community, and some students felt that the administration's actions toward the Friends seemed to push the university further away from the community of which it was a part. They also believed that their destiny linked them to the larger community. To add insult to injury, on March 15, 1967, in an effort to avoid future problems with the Friends, the TSU administrators fired its faculty advisor, Mack Jones, citing budget reductions and the hiring of too many political scientists with international relations specialties. Responding facetiously to the chairman of the Division of Social Sciences, Mack Jones said, "I am sure that my association with the campus-based Friends of SNCC had nothing to do with my firing." More seriously, he said, "After all, Texas Southern is committed to the emancipation of the Negro. And we do not bow and scrape simply to please powerful persons external to the University." According to Mack Jones, the administration "tried to hold [the faculty] responsible for what the students did . . . I could not control them and more importantly I would not have anyway."[9]

The suspension of the Friends from TSU's campus and the firing of Mack Jones created a strained relationship among the students, faculty, and administration. Faculty and students, who had been relatively quiet for most of the year, now questioned the administration's action. The faculty circulated a flyer that read: "A faculty member's service has been terminated due to participation in the civil rights movement. The administration of TSU has trampled on the faculty's rights for too long without anything being done about it." At a meeting on March 30, 1967, a faculty committee headed by John Biggers, chairman of the Art Department, offered a resolution, which the faculty assembly passed, demanding a review of Jones's dismissal. Students who galvanized around this issue began making demands on the administration and threatening to boycott classes. The students' demands included the closing of Wheeler Street, where motorists traveling at high speed put students and faculty in harm's way; placing more African American literature in the library; improving cafeteria food; extending curfew hours; establishing a student court with authority equal to the dean of students; and allowing student organizations to bring to campus speakers of their choice. The administration ignored both the threats of the students and the demands of the faculty. And to make matters worse, the police placed the Friends of SNCC under surveillance, arguably with the approval of the university president.[10]

Upon the university's refusal to recognize the Friends, a student demonstration ensued, temporarily disrupting classes and halting traffic on Wheeler Street on March 28, 1967. The students moved away from Wheeler Street after they were warned by Dean James B. Jones that they were violating the law and were subjecting themselves to possible arrest.[11] The next day, the boycott continued, but not everyone participated because the plan called for disrupting midterm examinations. Lee Otis Johnson, a student activist who had been suspended earlier for climbing onto two tables in the cafeteria to make his voice heard among his fellow students, told the protesting students that the purpose of the boycott was to demonstrate student power so that they could be heard on social and racial issues such as police brutality, a black studies curriculum, poverty, and the antiwar movement. Another member of Friends plucked away at a guitar as students chanted "One, two three, four, Uncle Tom must go!"[12]

The proposed student boycott was slated to last a few days, but tension eased somewhat when leaders of the Friends of SNCC acceded to the administration's demand for the group's recognition from the parent organization by asking the officials at the Friends' headquarters in Atlanta to send the university a letter to that effect. In return, the Friends would give the university a week to respond to their demands. Within one week, when none of the demands had been met, student demonstrations resumed. The three main entrances to Hannah Hall were chained and padlocked, and a human blockade was formed to halt traffic on Wheeler Avenue, which ran through campus. When a white foreign language instructor, Mary Kimbrough, attempted to break the picket line, she was knocked to the ground by Lee Otis Johnson. Newspapers throughout the country captured this scene. One newspaper editorial stated that "had the attacking nut been white, there would [have been a] hue and cry to awaken the dead for the troublemaker."[13]

Nervous about what such demonstrations portended for the future of TSU, university administrators in cooperation with the police urged arrests of the leaders of Friends, namely, Reverend Frederick Douglass Kirkpatrick, Franklin Alexander, and Lee Otis Johnson. Kirkpatrick and Alexander were first taken into custody. The next day, students met with President Pierce to demand that charges be dropped against the duo. When the president was noncommittal, Lee Otis Johnson proposed another demonstration and asked TSU students to solicit support of students from the University of Houston (UH). Two days later Johnson was arrested when he led approximately 750 activists in a march on the Harris County Jail to protest the arrest of Kirkpatrick and Alexander.[14] Shortly thereafter, TSU's administration was informed of an increased police presence of undercover and plainclothes officers on the campus. As Reverend William "Bill" Lawson, pastor of Wheeler Avenue Baptist Church, put it, "This action by the police was designed to control and deter the students, but it only made matters worse."[15] Students would continue to throw rocks at passing motorists as they drove through the campus on Wheeler Street.

Meanwhile, a court hearing was held for the three leaders to determine if they would remain in jail or be released under $25,000 bonds. According to the newspaper accounts, President Pierce was not willing to drop the charges, but he agreed to lower the bonds to an amount the students could pay. After the hearing and when the students had been released on $1,000 bonds, Pierce sent out a memo to the TSU student body and personally asked representatives of each student organization, including the Friends of SNCC, "to discuss with him any grievance that they may have had."[16] By this time, this olive-branch gesture was a little too late. The die had been cast. Lee Otis Johnson argued that he and other black nationalists had accomplished what they had set out to do on campus—to create black awareness on campus. In his own words, "This is liberation of the black mind." Johnson was right in his assessment. This was a movement that reached all across the nation, a movement of black consciousness, a movement of black power that embraced the idea that one should and could take control of one's community. This idea was reinforced by Stokely Carmichael when he spoke at TSU on April 13, 1967, and told the students that "black folks had been letting white folks play God too long, but the play period was now over."[17]

While the demonstrations on campus subsided for a few weeks after the arrests of Johnson, Kirkpatrick, and Alexander, the idea of redressing the community's social and economic injustices did not die. Two incidents happened on May 16 and 17, 1967, that invigorated the students even more. The first occurred in northeast Houston at Northwood Junior High School. After a fight broke out between white and black students, the whites were readmitted to school while the blacks were not. Frustrated over this incident, black citizens picketed the school for two days and were joined by TSU students on the second day, when twenty individuals were placed under arrest.[18] The second incident involved a garbage dumpsite near Sunnyside, which claimed the life of an eleven-year-old black boy. Shortly afterwards, a mass rally was held to close the Holmes Road dumpsite. The leaders of the protest vowed to go to jail and stay there until their voices were heard. When TSU students arrived on the scene, they circulated a flyer which read, "Brothers and sisters, we need your help. Let us stick together and have student power. Let's back those dump trucks up to the mayor's house."[19] In the heat of the moment, students and other citizens blocked the street at one location and continued to protest at the other. At the end of the two days, fifty persons were arrested—twenty in northeast Houston and thirty at Sunnyside. Demonstrators who were not arrested vowed to continue the struggle. They returned to their respective homes to enlist more participants and to raise funds to bail out those who were in jail.[20]

Nervous about these demonstrations and what they portended for the future, city leaders became concerned about the possibility of a riot. For some reason, Houston police focused on the easily identified concentration of blacks at Texas Southern University. Tough talk by student leaders on racial issues, and students' unhappiness over streets being closed on the University of Houston campus while an open thoroughfare ran in the middle of TSU's campus, were causes for concern. But more than this, there was the fear that male students were hoarding guns in the dormitories. This notion led to intense paranoia that a riot was eminent; and Mayor Louie Welch and Police Chief Herman Short were determined to do whatever they could to keep this from happening. Police presence on campus was reinforced, although some had been there for over two months. Officer Robert Blaylock boasted that he had spent more time on the TSU campus in the past two months than at his home. Still, the political "powers-that-be" felt that this was not enough. On May 16, Houston police officers stationed themselves on the periphery of the campus in a show of force. Heavy weapons, squad cars, police dogs, and police riot gear with helmets were evident near the campus at Jeppesen Stadium on Scott Street.[21]

On the night of May 16, a student rally was held to garner recruits and

Houston policemen and patrol cars at TSU during the "riot." Bill Thompson, *Houston Post.* Courtesy of *Houston Chronicle.*

to support a demonstration in opposition to the Holmes Road dump site. The police kept close watch over this rally. One of their focal points of interest was Charles E. Freeman Jr., an articulate twenty-year-old student leader from Port Arthur, Texas. During that rally, another TSU student, Douglas Wayne Waller, threw a watermelon rind at an officer patrolling on Wheeler Avenue. He was subsequently taken to jail, but when he was arrested, the police found a small semiautomatic pistol in a shoulder holster. Waller's arrest was tantamount to pouring fuel on a fire, and the students threw rocks at motorists passing through the campus. When Blaylock, the arresting officer, returned to campus at about 10:00 p.m., someone at Lanier Hall for Men fired gunshots at a couple of carloads of intelligence officers and plainclothes sergeants. Blaylock, already on the ground, crouched behind one of the police vehicles and was hit in the leg by a ricocheting bullet fired from the dorm. He called for help. It was at this point that Mayor Welch gave the order to do whatever it took to stop the disturbance.[22] Over five hundred policemen rushed the TSU campus to confront whoever was doing the shooting. Welch then called Reverend William Lawson, who had been one of the arrested protestors at Sunnyside and who had just been released from jail. As Lawson rushed onto campus, he was told that a riot was building up, and he was asked to help prevent it. But when he arrived, it was too late. The city police had already assembled a show of riot force by blocking Wheeler Avenue with helmeted officers who were aiming guns at the dormitories. Shortly thereafter, the chief gave the order to charge.[23] According to Lawson's account, police officers seemed to have been in a state of confusion. "Over six hundred policemen ran down the street firing over 5,000 rounds of ammunition. They were in each other's way. Young rookies who had never seen real action fired wildly [and] one policeman shot another."[24] It was in this state of confusion that Louis R. Kuba, a rookie on the police force, was hit in the forehead by a bullet that ricocheted from a fellow policeman's gun. Kuba died immediately

Finally, at about 2 a.m., the volley stopped. The police dashed forcefully into the men's dorm. They used fire axes and pistol butts to break down doors to students' rooms. "We were hit and beat and dragged out of our room, not even given time to put on proper clothing,"[25] said one student. Such police behavior caused another student to say, "Until then, I didn't know what police brutality was. . . . The police intentionally allowed the dogs to bite me. When I kicked the dog, the policeman told me, 'Get up Nigger and get downstairs,' and when I reached the outside door, he hit me [again]."[26] White and foreign students were not exempt from this ordeal. These nonblack students were beaten and called nigger lovers. A Puerto Rican student was struck on the head because he couldn't understand English very well and was not sure what the cops were saying to him.[27] When the TSU students were asked how they were treated when they got to jail, one student said, "They rushed us into cells, cursed at us and called us names."[28] While looking at many of the students who were taken into custody in their undergarments, one police officer asked another, "What are we going to book them on?" The second officer replied, "indecent exposure."[29]

For a while during the melee, the men's dormitories looked like a war zone. There was physical and personal property damage everywhere, and broken glass was scattered all over the place. Bullet holes in the doors and windows sills stood out like sore thumbs. The second floor of the Lanier men's dormitory was demolished from within. After wading through debris an inch deep in his room, one student cried out, "This is a portrait of living hell." Other students had their televisions, radios, and other instruments broken or shattered. Moreover, some had their clothes ripped apart and had the locks shot off their closet doors. There was an estimated $15,000 to $30,000 in damages.[30] At the end of this melee, one police officer had been

The Houston police forced students from the men's dormitories and ordered them on the ground during the TSU "riot." *Houston Chronicle* photo courtesy of *TSU Archives*.

Students arrested during the "riot," waiting in the Harris County Jail chapel to be processed and fingerprinted. Owens Johnson, *Houston Post*. Courtesy of *Houston Chronicle*.

killed. Three officers and more than twenty students had been injured, and 486 male students were arrested and placed in jail. While city officers and mainstream newspapers focused attention on the killing of a police officer, many parents, faculty, and students went to the jail to provide food, clothing, and transportation for students who were released the next day.

No doubt, the TSU administration had a great deal to do with the aftermath of the riot. In addition to holding classes, the university had to assess damages and provide a place for students to stay to take their final exams, which were coming up soon. The day after the riot, the board agreed to support the president in whatever disciplinary action he would take against students involved and urged him to rid the university of the "undesirables." President Pierce then expelled twenty-five students, including the five believed to have incited the riot. The announcement that the students had been expelled caused a great deal of consternation on campus. Many argued that the end of the semester was the only thing that saved the administration from the wrath of the students angered by this decision, since no findings, studies, or investigations had been done. At this point, after withstanding a barrage of criticism for his decision and for what some called lax discipline toward activist students, Pierce told the press that he had met with the FBI, Texas Rangers, and city police, and that he was told to go light on the students. In June 1967, Pierce submitted his resignation, effective August 31, 1967, as did James B. Jones, dean of students.[31]

Reactions to the "Riot"

While the president, faculty, and students tried to adjust to the infamous riot day of May 17, 1967, reactions from whites and blacks were swift. Whites' reactions included feelings of disgust and repulsion. They suggested severing all federal and state aid to the black institution and blamed President Lyndon Baines Johnson for the riot. Some expressed a desire to merge TSU with the University of Houston. One white man wrote Governor John B. Connally that TSU should be closed immediately. He argued that "at any time, it should be determined that there is enough of those young savages who sincerely desire a college education to justify continuation of TSU, then it should be moved from Houston to East Texas."[32] This man further posited, "Another reason for moving TSU is because students at the University of Houston are participating with those from TSU."[33] Another individual writing Governor Connally placed the blame on President Johnson, saying that "Lyndon Johnson has told these Negroes to take to the streets to protest injustice for his political reasons."[34] Calling on the governor to recommend merger, one woman told the governor, "We simply do not believe that Texas Southern is under the control of persons able or willing to provide anyone with anything resembling worthwhile knowledge."[35] Containing more forceful language, another letter written to the governor said, "The decisive action on your part will be reflected at the polls. . . . This school is a hot bed of turmoil, and citizens of Houston are not proud of it." [36]

For blacks, the situation was different. Responding to those who wanted to merge TSU with UH, and especially to a television editorial from Channel 11 espousing such an idea, TSU professor Jesse E. Gloster wrote, "Your editorial about the university was inaccurate in its accusations of the TSU administration and highly inflammatory. While the death of Louis Kuba was unfortunate, this should not be a reason to close an institution of higher learning in the State of Texas." Gloster went on to say that "two percent of the student body should not be in a position to cast aspersions over the entire student body, faculty, alumni and many good friends of the university." [37] One student at TSU wrote to the governor and asked him to "use an open mind, whether [his] heart was that way or not. The responsibility for the disturbance lies with the police department's mishandling of a potentially explosive situation."[38] In even more forceful language, another black man wrote the governor, saying that "the Negro was not about to become frightened over what authorities say or do. We know the truth and we have witnessed foul play in the pretense of carrying out the law. We will not be intimidated."[39] Reverend Bill Lawson was most critical in his attack against the mayor and police force: "It has been called a riot, but most of the ingredients of a riot were absent. There was no evidence of widespread resistance to arrest even though brutality by police was painfully obvious."[40]

The United Ministries staff of the university, which consisted of five clergymen appointed by their respective churches—Catholic, Episcopal, Lutheran, Methodist, and Presbyterian—tried to get at the real reason for the riot by issuing a statement on June 5, 1967, which said, "It is our contention that an impartial, dispassionate investigation of this vicious incident is imperative." According to the United Ministries, "the official account of the melee on TSU's campus, circulated via all the local mass media . . . was white washed on the part of the city administration and the police."[41] As such, some members of the University Presbyterian Church circulated a petition to have the records, including fingerprints and photographs of all individuals involved, expunged from the police files and destroyed immediately. This petition was sent to the governor, the mayor, the district attorney, the police chief, and the chairman of the board of regents.

Reverend Granville V. Peaks Jr., rector of St. Luke's Episcopal Church, wrote a similar letter to Governor Connally on behalf of the group. In it he laid out the reason for the riot, as well as recommendations for coping with the aftermath of this event. As Peaks put it, "The issue of the riot is not now and never was the traffic flow on Wheeler Street or even the presence of SNCC on campus . . . the issue has an ugly name for an ugly fact, racism." With this letter, the minister also submitted several recommendations for action: (1) that a course in Minority Relations be instituted in the Police Academy and that all active law enforcement personnel be required to take the course; (2) that a policy be established for defining and handling potential riot situations; (3) that an impartial investigation of post-riot charges of excessive property damage be held; (4) that the records of the innocents in this incident be purged; and (5) that TSU be merged with UH. The explanation given by the rector for the last recommendation was that "so long as the Negro University exists, so long will racism [exist] and fear will stalk the campus and the community." Nothing immediately came from these recommendations.[42]

Although a number of letters called for action on the part of the governor, he did not take any action because he believed the city of Houston's police department had everything under control. What is not so well known is that Governor Connally had signed a proclamation to "call and order into the active service such part of the Active Militia as [was] necessary to protect life and property, maintain peace and order in said city."[43]

The Committee of Three

When President Pierce left office on August 31, 1967, he was then succeeded by a Committee of Three—Herbert (H.) Hadley Hartshorn, dean of Arts and Sciences; Augustus Palmer, business manager; and Everett O. Bell, assistant to the president. As chairman of that committee, Hartshorn's first order of business was to deal with a lawsuit filed by students who had been suspended or expelled on September 8, 1967. In their lawsuit, they alleged that they had been denied readmission to the university in violation of their constitutional rights. They were suspended at the end of the spring term for their participation in several peaceful assemblies and so were protected by the First Amendment. Moreover, they argued that they were not given a hearing relative to this suspension. In response, the judge issued a restraining order instructing TSU to permit them to register until a hearing was held. At the end of the case hearing on September 13, 1967, the judge issued a summary judgment for the university and against the defendants, stating that some of the students were scholastically ineligible for readmission, while others were dismissed for violation of the campus curfew. Still others had blocked the entrance way to a campus building so as to prevent entry by the faculty and students.[44]

Before the students' lawsuit against TSU was resolved, five of them (Charles Freeman Jr., Douglass Wayne Waller, John Parker, Floyd Nicholas, and Trazawell Franklin) were charged with inciting the riot, the murder of one policeman, and the attempted murder of two others in June 1967. It is not known whether the grand jury had information to the effect that it was a ricochet bullet that killed Louis R. Kuba. The position of District Attorney Carol Vance was that when "one engages in any riot whereby an illegal act is committed, [he or she] shall be deemed guilty of the offense of riot according to the character and degree of such offense." The grand jury foreman supported this statement by saying that the jury found that "our law enforcement officers acted with due restraint." After the indictment, the judge denied the bond. It took two weeks before the NAACP lawyers were able to convince the judge to set bond and a trial date. The trial was set for July but was postponed until the fall of 1967 because of protest by the black community.[45]

The reactions to the indictment were swift. According to many students who were on the campus at the time, the charges leveled against these individuals were not accurate because on the night of the incident, Douglass Wayne Waller was in jail. Trazawell Franklin Jr. was at home. John Parker and Floyd Nicholas were away visiting relatives, and Charles Freeman Jr. was under surveillance. A lady from Nashville, Tennessee, called on Governor John Connally to intervene on behalf of those five students: "I am writing to protest the arrest and indictment of these students. The responsibility lies with the police mishandling of a potentially explosive situation." "These young men represent me and millions of other youths who are courageously standing up against racism," said Harold R. Fray of Pittsburgh, Pennsylvania. From Newton, Massachusetts, Ed Botzt protested the singling out of these young men to stand trial. It is noteworthy that Charles Freeman was first tried in Victoria, Texas, on assault charges for the shooting of Officer Robert Blaylock but was acquitted. Charges against the students for inciting a riot were dismissed November 4, 1967, because the jury could not reach a unanimous decision for conviction.[46]

Meanwhile, the United States Senate Permanent Sub-Committee on Riots began an investigation in October 1967. Among those appearing before this investigating committee, along with H. Hadley Hartshorn and James B. Jones of TSU, were Mayor Louie Welch; Samuel Price of the Harris County Community Action Association; Blair Justice, aide to Mayor Louie Welch; Walter H. Richter, southwest regional director of the Office of Economic Opportunity; Lt. M. L. Singleton, head of the intelligence division of the Houston Police Department; Houston police officer C. F. Howard; and patrolmen in the intelligence division. All of the above, except Hartshorn, placed the blame for the riot on the students. Dean H. Hadley Hartshorn told the committee that the action of the police appeared to be legalized vandalism.[47]

The students' accounts of what happened on May 17, 1967, were different, and their request to appear before the committee was at first denied. Mayor Welch also was opposed to student participation, stating that it would only open up wounds. The students did not sit idly by. Elvis Eaglin, president of the student body, called a press conference and stated that the investigative committee was grossly unjust to TSU students inasmuch as the committee permitted testimonies only of the mayor of Houston, his aide, members of the police department, and the administration of TSU. Eaglin therefore solicited the help of the NAACP and fifteen other colleges and universities.[48] Before the aforementioned groups could extend a helping hand, the TSU liaison faculty committee, headed by John Biggers of the Art Department, sent a telegram to Senator John L. McClellan, chair of the U.S. Senate Permanent Subcommittee, asking for a balanced investigation and warning the committee that "whitewashing (police) indiscretion constituted frustration in the Negro community and ultimately could precipitate further unrest." Dean Kenneth S. Tollette of the TSU Law School wrote McClellan with a similar view: "I cannot believe you are incredibly credulous as to believe that the Texas Southern students destroyed their own television sets, radios, musical instruments and valuable property as Lt. Singleton testified before the committee." As a result of these and other communications, the students were eventually called before the committee.[49]

After a year of study, the subcommittee concluded that the riot was caused by a series of racial incidents precipitated by police action, protest activities, previous disorder in the city, and the lack of administration of justice. The report further stated that with a preexisting reservoir of underlying grievances, frustration and tension grew with each such incident until at some point a final instance occurred that was followed almost immediately by violence. The subcommittee cited Houston as a typical example of alleged discrimination in the administration of justice. It is interesting to note that whereas the McClellan subcommittee called the incident at TSU a "major riot," the commission appointed by President Lyndon Johnson to study this incident referred to it as a "serious disorder."[50]

Although the Committee of Three was consumed by dealing with the riot and its aftermath, its members continued to hold the university together until a new president was selected, notwithstanding a firebomb thrown in the home of H. Hadley Hartshorn. Because of the volatile situation on campus, Marvin Griffin, chairman of the board of directors at TSU, promised that the selection of a new president would be expedited because of campus unrest. Specific criteria would be someone under fifty years of age who had a PhD degree and academic experience. Although selected in March 1968, the new president would not start his tenure until July of that year.[51]

Just as the riot had causes, it also had results. One of the results of the riot was that it served as an impetus in the eventual closing of Wheeler Avenue some years later. It caused TSU to become a total community. More importantly, it caused the university to come to the hard realization that the educational process at the collegiate level dictated that it had to modify its traditional and conventional postures to meet the current needs of society. As a result of that riot, TSU would no longer be a place where students would come only to discuss or theorize about civic affairs. Rather, it would also be a place where students could come to engage practically in solving societal issues.

5

Carving a Niche

The Special Purpose University and the Sawyer Era, 1968–1979

Granville M. Sawyer, who had formerly served as executive assistant to President Walter S. Davis of Tennessee A&I University and later as chairman of the University's Interim Executive Committee, became the fourth president of Texas Southern University on July 12, 1968. Having been named in March 1968, Sawyer had the dubious distinction of serving as acting president of one institution and president-elect of another at the same time. A native of Alabama, the forty-nine-year-old educator received his early education in Mobile, Alabama, and earned his AB degree from Tennessee A&I in 1947. Between the years 1947 and 1950, he served as assistant professor of English and speech and as director of student recruitment at Samuel Huston College in Austin, Texas. From 1952 to 1955, he attended graduate school, and he subsequently earned the MA and PhD degrees in speech science from the University of Southern California. Upon graduation, he returned to his alma mater, Tennessee A&I, where at various times he served as professor of speech and drama, director of communications and public relations, and director of institutional research.[1]

Between the naming of Sawyer as TSU's president-elect on March 1, 1968, and the time that he actually assumed office in July 1968, several dramatic events occurred that impacted most people, not only at the university but also throughout the nation. For example, some of the staunchest supporters and advocates of the civil rights movement passed from the scene. Martin Luther King Jr. was assassinated in Memphis, Tennessee, on April 4, 1968, and President Lyndon Baines Johnson, a native Texan and an influential spokesman for civil rights, withdrew his name from consideration as the Democratic Party's presidential nominee for a second term. To make matters worse, Robert F. Kennedy, another strong supporter of civil rights

Granville M. Sawyer, 1968–1978.
Courtesy of *TSU Archives*.

and a possible Democratic presidential nominee, was assassinated in California in June 1968.

The Sawyer years at Texas Southern began at a time of uneasy quietude at the university, as well as on many American college and university campuses. On the national scene, there was concern as to why the United States was engaged in the Vietnam War, and this sentiment was juxtaposed with the peace movement and civil rights demonstrations. Subsequently, on many college campuses, there were confrontations pitting some students against both institutional and civic authorities. Closer to home was the aftermath of the so-called TSU riot. As a result of this incident, there were backlashes, doubts, and fears about students' concerns, the university's future, and faculty morale.

While the above events played a major role in the selection of a new president, of equal importance was the fact that within the circle of black higher education, student unrest had to be addressed within the larger context of the future of historically black colleges and universities. Of particular interest were new roles for these institutions in relationship to the general academic community, to the burgeoning civil rights movement, and to the nation's commitment to cultural pluralism. Inherent in these concerns were periodic speculations about HBCUs regarding the quality of their educational programs, their financial sovereignty, and their declining student populations, which could lead to elimination or merger with other institutions.

Sawyer's response to the above concerns came on April 4, 1968, when he made his first formal presentation to the TSU family—the board of directors, administrators, faculty and student representatives, alumni officials, and community leaders. In a speech titled "Challenge of the Negro University," Sawyer told his audience, "We are called upon to prepare and encourage our students to react to a great variety of issues that dog our day-to-day existence. . . . [But yet] we must make more than a reasonable attempt to fulfill the special requirement of a community of scholars."[2] While not making specific reference to TSU, Sawyer made it clear that black institutions were similar to yet different from their white counterparts. "The Negro university has all of the woes of colleges and universities everywhere and in addition, it has to deal with the special implications of race and poverty as no other such institutions."[3] To be sure, the challenge confronting the leadership of HBCUs was daunting. Cognizant of the time during which he came to the university (after the riot), Sawyer made it clear to the board that he wanted TSU to become a student-centered university.[4]

Upon his arrival on campus in July 1968, Sawyer began a series of briefings with administrative officers and faculty members to determine "where TSU was and where it was headed." In spirited discussion sessions day after day, he learned a great deal about the university's fiscal operations, academic programs, student personnel services, campus organizations, the university's self-study, student activities, athletics, and student government. After this series of discussions, Sawyer set forth his priorities for the academic school year 1968–1969. These included establishing a student-centered university, completing the university's self-study, moving the faculty manual from a working document to an actual document approved by the board of directors, and establishing the position of assistant to the president for community relations.[5]

In the order of priority, Sawyer first turned his attention to the students. Expressing sensitivities to students' concerns, Sawyer argued that "the university has an obligation to the young, strong, aggressive students who are on our campus. . . . All of them will not defy authority to a point of being dismissed. Many will remain within the boundaries of campus regulations." In Sawyer's opinion, understanding the students required a flexible approach: having the patience to let them vent about some of the problems, having a tolerance for their personal freedom, and having a resolve to provide them with social and constructive programing.[6] This approach would form the basis of Sawyer's "Student-Centered Initiative." The president publicly declared himself as always being available to meet with students. He favored an open-door policy with respect to listening to students' complaints, and more often than not, he made extra efforts to accommodate them. This policy was tested over and over during his tenure. It was a policy that caused some to complain that the president was unduly soft and yield-

President Granville Sawyer talks with students and tries to ease tensions after the "riot." Courtesy of *TSU Yearbook*, 1969.

ing on matters involving students. Ironically, Sawyer saw this policy as a turning point for meeting students' demands, especially those of activists and militants.[7]

One of the first things Sawyer did to empower students was to alter the administrative organization so as to allow for student membership on the University Council. To ensure the best possible participation by students in decision making at the university, Sawyer held a retreat for student leaders in August 1968 to acquaint students with the legal and administrative frameworks within which the university operated. This retreat set the stage for student participation on major committees, with particular reference to student advisory committees in each department. Further, three students were added to the steering committee of the university's self-study. Under the leadership of James Race, dean of students, a committee consisting of students, faculty, and administrators was established to study ways and means of improving the communication between them.[8]

While expressing concerns for student support and participation in university matters, Sawyer cautioned the students regarding the slogan or meaning of black unity in a speech given at the 1968 fall convocation. "To me," said Sawyer, "your concern for black unity is a manifestation of your search . . . for identity. . . . You have a strong need growing out of contemporary experiences to seek racial identity. The search for group pride is not inconsistent with the basic purpose of the university." Yet, Sawyer cautioned the students not to exploit this slogan and turn it into reverse racism. The militant and activist students did not respond well to this speech. Instead, they provoked confrontations of sorts with university administrators and also called for a boycott of classes. This behavior, coupled with the fact that Wheeler Street was still not closed to through traffic one year after the TSU riot, did not make for a good or ideal situation. In point of fact, the Organization of Black Student Unity, established in 1967, was in the vanguard of the student movement for civil rights, students' rights, and for relevancy regarding the college curricula on campus; and its members were not yet ready to compromise their position.[9]

TSU students were not shy in testing the president's student-centered initiative. In March 1969, members of both the student council and the Organization of Black Student Unity made the following demands of the president: that he fire an administrative officer, an academic counselor, and a security officer; that he put an end to compulsory class attendance and improve administrative services; that he increase the availability of staff and faculty personnel for student conferences; and that he initiate a development of a black studies curriculum. In the end, Sawyer was able to convince the students that some of their demands could not be met because they had their roots in the fact that black colleges did not have the same kind of resources as did their white counterparts. Concerning the security officer, Sawyer told the group that the board had authorized the employment of a well-qualified security administrator and that he was expanding the force to five.[10] Sawyer agreed with the students on compulsory class attendance. It was the students' position that a student's grade should not be tied to class attendance, but rather to academic performance. The students got their wish when the university decided to end the compulsory class attendance policy on December 19, 1969.[11] For the problems associated with counseling, the president proposed reorganization. To those who were concerned with a black studies department, he suggested that the students take this matter up with their advisors, John T. Biggers and Ali K. Bakiri. For one of the most pressing problems, the closing of Wheeler Street, Sawyer told the students he would take up the issue with city officials. When his efforts fell on deaf ears, he appealed to the state legislators, but a positive answer did not come until 1971. Also, Sawyer recommended that a student/faculty committee begin studying ways to increase fiscal support for the *TSU Herald*, the student newspaper.[12]

Just as Sawyer thought he had resolved some of the major concerns of the students in December 1969, a series of shooting incidents occurred intermittently on campus, and the Organization of Black Student Unity (OBSU) was allegedly involved. Responding to the charge that the OBSU should be banned from the campus as a result of these incidents, Sawyer said, "This attitude was taken because guns were found in their headquarters, but I refuse to indict the whole organization because of the action of the few." It was Sawyer's position that extreme caution should be taken in weeding out the students in the OBSU who showed a propensity for violence. "If we over-react in this transitional stage," said Sawyer, "we may find ourselves using approaches where we too will become ineffective."[13]

Concomitant with student concerns was Sawyer's concern with the overall health and direction of the university. One year prior to the shootings on campus, Sawyer decided to call a mid-winter planning conference, the first in a series extending over a period of five years. The purpose of this conference was to review and evaluate objectives of the university's programs and services, as well as its commitments to and projection of appropriate, new, and updated institutional activities. The conference was also to discuss other important issues relating to student concerns. But the most immediate concern of this first conference was to deal with two basic student issues—personal identity and curricula relevancy. In short, the students wanted to know if their education at the university would address their history while at the same time equip them with skills for a career. As John Lash, an English professor, put it, "It would have been easy to dismiss the students' behavior [and concerns], but to do this would be a failure to come to grips with real problems, real challenges and real opportunities at the university." So, from December 26th through the 28th, 1968, in Galveston, Texas, forty individuals—members of the board of directors, university officials, faculty, student representatives, community leaders, and alumni—came together to take a hard look at and to update the goals and objectives of the university. Discussions at the 1968 conference ranged from student unrest and faculty dissatisfaction to university goals, objectives, and projections for the future. While there were some faculty members who aired personal gripes, for the most part, the conference participants expressed

realistic concerns relative to student protests, to the faculty's lack of participation in university governance, and to a failure on the part of the university to communicate its goals and objectives to several of its clienteles.[14]

Out of this conference came a statement of goals (short, immediate,
and long-range) that later served as the preliminary institutional blueprint
for Sawyer's administration and for the university's involvement in urban
affairs. The short-range goals focused on finding solutions to some existing university problems: retaining the Law School, which was then under
a phase-out mandate from the coordinating board; responding to students'
calls for a more active role in university governance; and the closing of
Wheeler Street.[15] The immediate and long-range goals called for both philosophical and programmatic changes that would add another dimension to
the university's overall mission. These goals were coupled with two institutional objectives: (1) "An involvement in the community life of Houston
and of Texas for the purpose of preparing large numbers of black citizens
for greater participation in the democratic processes through increased economic independence and self-determination; and (2) the continuation of
programs and services which exemplify how majority and minority groups
may teach, learn and live together in a mutually satisfactory and enriching
way. Sawyer stressed that the welfare of students ought to be paramount and
thus superior to any other group's concern at the university."[16]

The deliberations at the planning conference resulted in refining the
short and immediate goals for the rest of the 1968–69 school year. These
included allowing a meaningful involvement of students in administrative
governance via committees, the implementation of an educational program
that took into consideration the personal and intellectual needs of minority
students who have suffered cultural and educational deprivation, and the
sponsorship of faculty workshops designed to guide the faculty toward the
practical interpretation of relevance. After the conference, all academic and
support units were instructed to begin planning for the implementation of
the goals and objectives developed in Galveston.[17]

In planning for the future, it became necessary for the university to
take a hard look at its programs and resources. In 1968, several curricula
of the university were offered through programs of six schools and colleges: Arts and Sciences, Law, Business, Pharmacy, Vocational and Industrial Education, and the Graduate School. The College of Arts and Sciences
housed the largest number of departments and included training programs
that were then most relevant to the postbaccalaureate employment expectations of minority students. Equally as important were the facts that several
areas of instruction, most notably in the Schools of Pharmacy and Business,

had already secured important recognition via accreditation and had demonstrated strength and growth potential. In part because of these and other program offerings, the 1968 Self-Study Committee recommended, and President Sawyer accepted, a plan for administrative reorganization. This plan called for the identification of a senior-level instructional office that would monitor and coordinate the operations of the existing schools and colleges in order to respond to the needs of curricula and programmatic activities.[18] Thus, H. Hadley Hartshorn, a member of the 1968 Interim Administrative Committee, who previously had served as dean of the College of Arts and Sciences and as acting dean of the Graduate School in 1967–68, was selected for this new post. After one year, Hartshorn was transferred to staff vice president. The role of the chief instructional officer was then filled by the new dean of faculty, Lamont J. Carter. The position itself was the result of an evolving process of responding to programmatic needs in the 1970s. The title of this position was changed to that of the vice president for academic affairs when Robert J. Terry, former head of the Department of Biology and later dean of the College of Arts and Sciences, assumed the new post as chief academic officer, a post he held throughout the decade of the 1970s.[19]

A thorough examination of university personnel, resources, physical plants, and other pressing problems led Sawyer to conclude that TSU, like many historically black colleges and universities, needed reorganization, whether as a physical entity or in terms of its programmatic functions. So, in May 1969, he issued an interpretive statement titled "Goals for Texas Southern: Discussion and Design," in which he argued that the university had reached a point wherein it had "to make assessment and evaluation of its present overall status." In his opinion, now was the time "to give serious thoughts to future projection of a viable [urban thrust] for its administrative, academic, personnel, and physical structures."[20] Thus, between 1969 and 1971, the university would spend an inordinate amount of time incorporating relevancy into the programmatic units of the university while focusing on the urban thrust.[21]

Toward an Urban University

When the 1969–70 school year began, Sawyer instructed all units at the university to incorporate relevancy into their operations. That is, they were "to make sure the educational experience that TSU provides for its students was more meaningful as it relates to the problems and issues of contemporary society." This mandate included, among other things, the updating of curricular offerings and the university's involvement in the community life of Houston and Texas. It is not surprising, then, that when the mid-winter planning retreat was held in January 1970, the theme "Goals in Action" had, to some extent, been played out. These goals were undergirded by the following activities: (1) the establishment of the School of Education; (2) the strengthening of a more viable College of Arts and Sciences; (3) an effort to gain accreditation for the MBA in the School of Business; and (4) a decision to separate the area of professional education from the College of Arts and Sciences and to locate it in a newly created School of Education. The necessary approval for the School of Education had been obtained from the coordinating board in 1970, and it began its independent operation in September 1971. Earl W. Rand, the head of the Division of Education and dean of the Graduate School, became the first dean of the School of Education. The School of Business, as planned, received accreditation for the MBA program, and the Law School escaped a merger and phaseout with a generous grant from the Ford Foundation.[22]

Between 1969 and 1971, the university made great strides toward incorporating relevancy in its programmatic structures. The university's posture in this regard was affected to a large extent by the community in which it was located, namely Houston's Third Ward. In 1970, the city of Houston had been identified and had accepted funding for an experimental "model city" project under the aegis of the Department of Housing and Urban Development, in accordance with the Provisions, Title and Comprehensive Cities Demonstration Program. It soon became apparent that municipalities accepting "model city" funding were required to have appropriate ethnic and minority representation and to be involved in the planning and implementation of acceptable programs and activities. Houston had no problems in meeting the guidelines since it was populated by a large percentage of blacks and Hispanics, and TSU was located in a black neighborhood. No one was surprised when Houston's mayor called on the university to participate in a pilot program designed to help meet community needs. In turn, TSU sought two model cities projects, one involving the training of neighborhood commissioners and representatives, and the other providing advice for developing small businesses. Hence, the academic school year could boast of making great strides toward relevancy in urban affairs.[23]

As an active partner in the local Model Cities Program, Texas Southern moved closer to bridging the gap between academic theory and urban problem solving. Since widespread citizen participation was a fundamental part of the Model Cities Programs, TSU was in a good position to provide the skills and leadership needed to produce citizens who would work to meet

Mickey Leland walking in the Third Ward with students from Baylor College of Medecine and discussing poverty in the area, as well as the need to establish a community medical clinic. Courtesy of *TSU Yearbook*, 1969.

the needs of this urban community. Participants in this program were individuals who lived in some of the most blighted areas of Houston, who were elected by the residents to serve as representatives, and who worked closely with a competent, efficient faculty and staff from TSU. Together, this group developed methods and strategies for dealing with some of the problems in their neighborhoods and for disseminating solutions through training sessions.[24]

By the time of the 1971 planning retreat, there had emerged an obvious theme of "Excellence in Achievement—Toward an Urban University." On the eve of its twenty-fourth anniversary as a state-supported institution, Texas Southern had moved substantially toward reflecting this theme, which was clearly shown through TSU's programmatic thrust. For example, the Law School now aligned itself more closely with the university's overall urban thrust through the establishment of a Preventive Law Center, which complemented the existing Legal Aid Clinic. The School of Pharmacy undertook a clinical orientation in its program to train pharmacists to serve as therapeutic consultants to both patients and physicians. This program required that pharmacy students spend part of their learning time in the clinical environment of local hospitals and community clinics to gain experience by having direct contact with the patients. Also, in the School of Pharmacy the faculty and students engaged in community action programs such as disseminating information on drug abuse, an effort that was also considered to be one of the first substance abuse programs in the city. The School of Vocational and Industrial Education moved toward expanding its Cooperative Education Program to include students who worked in state and local governmental agencies. The School of Business had a high-quality program in 1970–71 that attracted the largest enrollment to date in its history. A special training program for prospective college business executives and a Small Business Development Center underwritten by Model Cities were begun. The College of Arts and Sciences had one of the largest enrollments in its history (2,723 students), and undergraduate course selections were made more flexible as general academic foundation requirements were reduced from sixty-four to forty-eight hours. The college also added a degree program for "allied medical health professionals" and offered minors in philosophy and African studies.[25]

The Graduate School and the School of Education also made important gains. All graduate teacher education programs received accreditation, and enrollment almost doubled, jumping from 588 to 1,029 in a single year. During that year, the School of Education came into its own. The new administrative structure gave stronger direction to the Teacher Education Program for elementary and secondary teachers, as well as to those specializing in arts, sciences, technology, and business education. Additionally, the TSU teacher-training programs were reaffirmed by the National Council for the Accreditation of Teacher Education, while the university's accreditation was renewed by SACS.[26]

By the early spring of 1972, the conceptual and programmatic commitments to an urban university had become more clearly defined. To promote the concept and to solicit support for it, the administration issued a cluster of printed and mimeographed circulations under the title "Toward an Urban University." These publications highlighted various aspects of the institution's urban concerns and were comprised of newspapers, promotional brochures, in-house memoranda, and institution-wide newsletters. Additionally, there was the circulation of an urban notebook, which was a summary factsheet designed to keep the university campus abreast of rapidly unfolding developments in the area of urban affairs. The administrators also undertook a carefully orchestrated sequence of programmatic events designed to underscore and expose the institution's minority orientation, its growing urban involvement, and the expansion of its academic and service opportunities for larger numbers of prospective students, including adults.[27]

Meanwhile, in March 1972, TSU entered into a contractual agreement (for $135,000) with the Department of Housing and Urban Affairs to establish a Model Cities Center, thereby making it the first HBCU to do so. The significance of this grant was that through its performance in the Model Cities Program via constructive and creative community action activities, TSU demonstrated itself to be a leader in urban affairs. This contract bolstered TSU's contention that it could make a definite contribution to solving problems in the area of urban affairs because the institution's personnel and expertise had been reviewed favorably by agencies of the state and federal government. Feeling comfortable with his idea of an urban institution, Sawyer began to move with alacrity to implement his plan. Speaking on TSU's silver anniversary as a state- supported institution in March 1972, Sawyer contended that the university must have a new role if it expected to survive and continue to be a viable institution—and that, moreover, that role had to be an urban one.[28]

In June 1972, the university's administration found itself in a position conceptually and programmatically to make a statement concerning urban affairs. At that time, President Sawyer went before the Texas Higher Education Coordinating Board with a prospectus for an Urban Resources Center. The purpose of this center was to bring together and to synchronize existing university programs, both regular and special ones, so that the programs already in operation would complement each other by updating and enriching more traditional disciplines at the core of the university's offering. The center was also charged with the responsibility of initiating, evaluating, and recommending to the administrators such program adoptions, innovations, and improvements as deemed necessary or desired for the university to reaffirm emphasis on urban affairs. Conceived as an agency of research and programmatic coordination, cutting across departmental and school lines, and giving more definite structure to the institution's urban thrust, the Urban Resources Center opened in September 1972 with Hortense Dixon, professor of home economics, as its first director.[29]

There were other significant developments that undergirded TSU's position as an urban institution. Not only had the university received private foundation support for its programs in law, business, and technology, but it had also begun to reap some benefits from its recruitment efforts in those areas. There were promising communications with the American

Bankers Association and with developing connections for involvement in international education. Moreover, in a period of leveling off or of general decline in college enrollment, TSU had for the past five years experienced a steady growth. It should be noted that this increase in enrollment came during a period when most historically black colleges were experiencing decreases in enrollment. It also occurred at a time when more minority students were attending college; but for the most part, they were matriculating at junior and community colleges throughout the city, state, and nation.

TSU's growth in enrollment at the same time that other universities lost students was attributable mainly to two factors: the population growth in Texas and in Houston, which affected other local and state institutions; and TSU's expansion of professional, vocational, and traditional programs via the urban thrust, which better equipped its students for the job market. This growth was positive, and TSU saw an increase both in students and in the diversity of academic and service functions, thereby likely making the university more attractive to its black and nonblack clienteles. It was at this time that Sawyer began to conceptualize TSU as a special-purpose institution of higher education for urban programming in addition to its official state-supported status.[30]

The Special-Purpose Institution

By late 1972, the Sawyer administration had begun to modify the goals and objectives of the institution to reflect the urban thrust. For those who were doubtful or opposed to change in the university's mission, Sawyer clarified his position in January 1973: "We would pose no rejection of traditional function or re-definition of the goals to which these functions are implemented."[31] When Sawyer made this statement, specific details of the philosophy and implementation of the urban thrust had already been spelled out in two resolutions that he submitted to the board of directors for approval at its meeting in March 1973. Except for a statement that called for changing the name of the board of directors to that of the board of regents, these resolutions were approved contingent on the legislature's recognition of TSU's designation as a special-purpose university. Once the board accepted these resolutions, the way was now clear for the university to make formal petition to the state legislature. After TSU made a series of presentations to several of its committees, the state legislature responded by passing Senate Bill 823, which designated

Texas Southern University as a special purpose institution of higher education for urban programing; stating limits of application of this Act as regards future designated institutions and other institutes for urban studies; amending Subchapter A, Chapter 106, Texas Education Code, by adding Section 106.02.

Sec. 106.02. Purpose of the University. In addition to its designation as a statewide general purpose institution of higher education, Texas Southern University is designated as a special purpose institution of higher education for urban programming and shall provide instruction, research, programs, and services as are appropriate to this designation.[32]

Both the state of Texas and Texas Southern University became unique with passage of the above act, which Governor Dolph Briscoe signed into law on June 17, 1973. In other states at other universities throughout the nation, the urban thrust was incorporated in their curricula and programs; but the entire university was never recognized by these states for such emphasis. More important than the recognition was the fact that this designation carved a niche for Texas Southern at a time when historically black colleges and universities were being called on to redefine their missions, and Southern states were being required to dismantle the operations of racial dualism. Not only did this new designation take into consideration TSU's historical and contemporary role, scope, and mission, but it also provided another way of securing money from the state legislature and from other state and national funding agencies.

At the time of its designation, two carefully developed prospectuses—one for a School of Public Affairs and the other for a School of Communication—were submitted to the coordinating board. Both schools were separated from the College of Arts and Sciences and were subsequently granted approval by the coordinating board. In 1975, the School of Public Affairs, under the leadership of Walter J. McCoy, and the School of Communication, with Carlton W. Molette as its first dean, became operative. These two initiatives gave rise to more generalized public awareness of the university's existence as an agency of training and service on behalf of its clientele.[33]

In the areas of federal programming, private grants, and contracts, the urban thrust (special purpose emphasis) served the university well. The American Bankers Association designated TSU as one of two subsidized training sites in the country for minority students interested in banking and finance. The university was the recipient of over fifty funded programs—many of them having "set-aside funds" from the U.S. Office of Education under the provision of the Advanced Institutional Development Program, as subsidized under certain provisions of the Higher Education Act of 1965. Also, TSU's Urban Resources Center, in addition to playing an important role in the discharge of its responsibilities in the Department of Housing and Urban Development, entered into working and operational relationships with the Department of Transportation, the National Aeronautics and Space Administration, the Texas Highway Commission, and other state and national agencies. Such efforts would eventually lead to a university transportation program and an academic major in airway sciences. Concomitant with the above, TSU had been able to enter into a number of consortium relationships with area institutions. For example, two dual degree programs were entered into with Rice University, one in geology and one in engineering. Students would take their first two years at TSU and then enroll at Rice for their junior- and senior-level courses. The degrees in geology and engineering were to be granted by TSU.[34]

What seemed to be true about the special purpose designation is that the sheer weight of TSU initiatives gave rise to a more generalized public awareness of the university's existence as an agency of training and service on behalf of its varied clienteles. During the Sawyer years, the university officially presented itself to interested patrons, to prospective and enrolled students, to community people, to business and industrial interests, to governmental agencies, and to private and corporate philanthropists as an institution of higher learning generously committed to fostering community development and to forming a better way of life in the urban community. Moreover, there had been a growing cadre of supporters for the university's urban focus in Houston's local communities, in metropolitan areas in Texas, in the Southwest region, and in the nation. Consequently, TSU became a functioning entity of the Southwest Center for Urban Research. The center at the time was a cooperative effort among the University of Houston, Rice University, and TSU.[35]

Community Outreach and Research

During the Sawyer years, the university appeared to be one of a very few historically black colleges and universities in a position to respond positively to an urban thrust. Traditionally, black institutions were not located in the city. Instead, they were isolated in the countryside or in very small towns. Texas Southern is located in Houston, which in the 1960s was the fifth largest city in the United States. Situated in the black community, TSU was mired in multiple problems peculiar to itself. Yet it was the 1967 riot more than anything else that sharpened the university's and community's awareness of each other, bringing them closer to one another. As stated earlier, the Urban Resources Center, which grew out of the Model Cities Program, engaged TSU faculty and representatives of the community in working with a drug abuse program, an urban resource center, a community legal services center, a minority manpower project, and a small business center.

The heightened awareness of community involvement at TSU was reflected in many of the schools and departments. There were community-oriented programs in pharmacy, business, education, child development, technology, and law. A very extensive Head Start program, present on campus since the mid-1960s, continued under Sawyer. Likewise, a series of public programs became illustrative of TSU's commitment to community involvement. For example, TSU became one of the grantees of the National University Year for Action (NUYA) program in 1971. Through this program, the university provided credit for student participation in service to community agencies and community activities. This program was similar to the TSU undergraduate cooperative program, but it differed in that the NUYA required courses to involve both formal study and practical work. Also, TSU received federal funding for a Teacher Corps Program and a Peace Corps Program. A product of the Great Society, the Teacher Corps was designed to train and prepare school teachers in cultural and societal traits for working in the inner cities with low-income, disadvantaged students. TSU, then, became one of the first universities to combine the Teacher Corps with the Peace Corps. The latter program prepared secondary teachers for overseas assignments in developing countries.[36] In keeping with its urban thrust, TSU established the Week-End College. Since 1970, TSU had offered graduate courses on Saturdays for teachers who wished to earn master's degrees. In the spring of 1973, the administration decided to extend both graduate and undergraduate course offerings on Fridays, Saturdays, and Sundays. The announcement of the Week-End College was met as welcome news by individuals who saw this as an opportunity to enroll as part-time students and to continue to be employed full time. The experiment began in the spring of 1973 with thirty-five students. During the academic year 1973–74, it expanded to five hundred students. The Week-End College then became the basis for the establishment of a Division of Continuing Education, a unit geared more or less to an adult clientele.

Coupled with the above outreach effort, TSU applied for and was approved by the FCC to establish a radio station on campus on June 23, 1972. One year later, it was fully operational. Various Houston stations gave time, money, and equipment to set up the KTSU studio. Starting with 10 watts; it now has 18,500 watts. The growth of this station was instrumental to the urban thrust, not only because it served as a learning laboratory for students, but also because it served as the voice of the black community in so many ways.[37]

While the above-mentioned programs were indicative of the university's involvement and commitment to the community, the Urban Resources Center was engaged in community- oriented research in mass transportation, community health, and other areas, and the results of this research were utilized by local and state agencies. It must be pointed out that individuals who worked in the Urban Resources Center did a good job of disseminating information via flyers, leaflets, and newsletters, but more often than not, they did not convert this vast body of materials that they unearthed into publications, monographs, articles, and technical papers. Perhaps because of a lack of staff, money, or expertise in the field, the research component of the Urban Resource Center was deficient.[38]

One of the requirements of faculty members working at an institution of higher learning is to do empirical or applied research. While the TSU faculty's record of such research has not been voluminous, in some areas, they have made creditable contributions. Organized research was most noticeable in the natural and physical sciences, where federal and private funds for research subsidies had been most readily attainable. In 1976, TSU produced a faculty research journal, edited by Joseph Jones, dean of the Graduate School. At about the same time two other research journals were produced—the *Ralph J. Bunche Journal* by the School of Public Affairs and the *TSU Law Review Journal*. The decision of the university administration and faculty to offer a terminal degree in education was another great commitment to research. Though not on a large scale, there was outstanding research going on in the social and behavioral sciences, as well as in the humanities, as was evident from the works of sociologist Henry A. Bullock and historian John Reuben Sheeler. Also, the creative and artistic productions by John T. Biggers and Carroll Sims placed TSU on the map.[39]

The Faculty's Response to the Urban Mission

In order for the urban thrust to be realized at an optimal level, the faculty had to buy into the idea. To be sure, the faculty had become familiar with the concept since the first mid-winter planning conference in 1968. At that time, a review of the records revealed that the faculty seemed more interested in discussing the issues of relevancy and the university's community involvement than in anything else. Yet, there were spirited disagreements and mixed reactions to the urban thrust idea, ranging from the far left to the far right, about the capacity and capabilities of the university, as well as the faculty's expertise to "handle" contemporary social problems, given the way the university was then organized.[40] Lloyd L. Woods, distinguished professor of chemistry, suggested that TSU establish a public administration department in an effort to forge a good relationship with the world in which we live. Henry A. Bullock, distinguished professor of sociology, expressed reservation to the president about his urban thrust, arguing that the university had to come to grips with three basic problems: academic conservatism, subject matter relevancy, and compensatory education. Bullock stated that "if [we were] to execute to any appreciable extent [these] propositions . . . the institution would have to undergo a complete reorganization." To say that there was uncertainty about the urban trust in 1968 is an understatement. But as H. Hadley Hartshorn put it, "If we do not determine a role and scope for TSU . . . we are going to go down the drain." [41]

After much wrangling and discussion by students, administrators, community spokesmen, and alumni, most of the faculty bought into the idea of a meaningful university participation in community affairs. The tone was now set for both university and community involvement. Consequently, a master work plan was drawn up and was facilitated by key changes in the administration. Some changes came via voluntary resignations, while others came as a consequence of an administrative reorganization. With his new team in place, Sawyer could now work toward implementing the new urban mission. As significant as these changes were for the administration's effort to push the urban mission, there was still skepticism on the part of some faculty about the university's commitment in practical and programmatic terms. These faculty members felt that "a necessary precondition to any improvement in the university's philosophy, programs and service [was an] institutional recognition of faculty organization relating to such matters as salaries, tenure and dismissal."[42]

Prior to Sawyer's arrival, the official recognized faculty organization was the university's Faculty Senate, where membership was restricted to elected faculty representatives. When the riot of 1967 occurred, another organization was formed—the Faculty Forum. In addition to discussing the causes and results of the riot, the latter met periodically to discuss faculty issues, welfare, and governance. These faculty members, who in the past had demonstrated leadership, were engaged in early dialogue with the new administration to establish a new faculty organization that would allow faculty participation in shared governance. As such, they voluntarily assumed the burden of preparing the necessary documents needed for the implementation and democratic functioning of a faculty body—that is, to establish a faculty assembly.[43]

During the 1971–72 academic year, the Faculty Assembly's constitution was drafted, and it addressed such concerns as salary inequities, insurance benefits, and academic freedom. In October 1973, the faculty held a meeting to discuss the status of the constitution and bylaws of the Faculty Assembly. When queried about such, Robert J. Terry, dean of faculty, said that "it was necessary to retype the proposed *Faculty Manual* before forwarding it to the printer." But he went on to say, "We made some minor changes, but this related mainly to changes in titles and positions." When asked again about the administration's approval of the *Manual*, Terry wrote to President Sawyer, "You will recall my having given you a copy of the Constitution and By-laws of the Faculty Assembly and Faculty Council. There is apparent disagreement among members of the Faculty Assembly as to whether or not the constitution and by-laws have been approved in the past by your office and by the Board of Directors." Sawyer did not respond.[44]

The president's stalling tactic in approving the Faculty Assembly's constitution only gave rise to more faculty cynicism, leading some to the conclusion that the Faculty Assembly was a farce. Some argued that "the administration used the Faculty Assembly to sanction its policies, to call meetings on rank, tenure, promotion, but on the other issues and on freedom of speech, it returned to its deaf, dictatorial demeanor."[45] In accordance with Article IV of the faculty constitution, the dean of faculty was charged with calling "at least two meetings [of the Faculty Assembly] . . . each semester."[46] Yet, during the academic school year 1974–75, only two meetings were held the entire year. At one of these meetings, the vice president for academic affairs was asked again when the president would sign off on the constitution. He responded with another question: "How does the President's failure to recognize the constitution harm the work of the faculty committee?"[47] In the administration's opinion, as long as faculty members (who were accepted by the administration) were part of the committee, the faculty had a voice in governance. The communication between the administration and faculty got so bad that the faculty voted in 1975 to stop holding meetings but not to stop pressuring the president to sign the new constitution.[48]

While the administration dragged its feet on approval of the constitution, several faculty members who had been denied tenure filed a class-action lawsuit. Among their many allegations was one that stated they were denied due process before they were fired. After the filing of this lawsuit, one could discern a shift in the attitude of the administration toward the Faculty Assembly. In summer 1977, a number of arduous meetings were held by the elected Faculty Ad Hoc Committee to discuss and make changes to the constitution that had remained unapproved on the president's desk for five years. When the constitution was completed, the vice president for academic affairs insisted on receiving a copy of the document for the administration's perusal before it was presented to the faculty. When the committee members voted not to concur with his request, he refused to call a meeting of the faculty. Determined to have the faculty's voice heard, the chair of the Faculty Senate, Timothy Cotton, had the entire document reproduced and distributed to the faculty.[49] To the surprise of some faculty, on October 5, 1977, President Sawyer sent a memo to the faculty approving the constitution: "I recently reviewed an updated draft of the constitution and by-laws of the faculty assembly and faculty council and I will be pleased to endorse it to the board of regents for consideration." Sawyer went on to say that the university would provide available resources as were necessary for the operation and function of the faculty organization.[50]

Despite the explicit promise made by the president, as of March 1979 the administration had not provided an office, a secretary, or budget for the faculty organization. Although Sawyer had said that his administration was centered on the philosophy of point/counterpoint, it appeared that he had a difficult time in responding to the point that the faculty made regarding the organization and its constitution. Even after the Faculty Assembly's constitution and bylaws were approved by the board of regents in 1978, it would take years before an amicable relationship would exist between the faculty organization and the administration.[51]

The Price of the Urban Thrust

The price of the urban focus can be measured both in terms of growth and management, both of which adversely affected the presidency of Granville Sawyer. During his era, the university grew physically as well as in population and programs. The student population began an upward surge that doubled the headcount in an eight-year span. The university also received more grants, contracts, and federal dollars than at any time in its history. The urban thrust brought about a proliferation of programs and projects over which the university had supervisory power. In keeping with this growth, Texas Southern had to tax its present resources—physical, personnel, and programmatic—beyond their optimal limits. Given this scenario, one can argue that it was simply not possible for statistical requirements and for fiscal procedures and financial policies geared to pre-1960 services to be transposed rapidly onto a responsive management system. In a word, the handling of fiscal affairs soon began to suffer. The handling suffered as much from obsolescence as from inefficiency and from the university's failure in updating and upgrading it.

The whole issue of university management left a lot to be desired during the Sawyer era. University management or a lack thereof included inadequate policies and procedures in fiscal affairs, a too-frequent change of personnel, conflicts of interest with people supervising cash management, and ineffective management of computer operations. Communication between various departments and computing services was not good. Internal audit reports by and large went unnoticed. Personnel management also posed a problem. A review of the records indicated that many personnel files were lacking required documents, and a personnel manual had not been updated in a timely fashion. Yet it was fiscal management more than any other area that would negatively impact Sawyer's presidency.[52]

Fiscal management plagued the Sawyer administration from the early part of his administration. From 1972 to 1978, the university operated in a climate of suspicion and mistrust in relation to the exercise of fiscal management. Coupled with this was the fact that the university was subjected to inordinately negative publicity in the news media. Much of this publicity was repetitious, but this is not to say that the university's system had been without justifiable criticism or blame. For example, there were questions surrounding Sawyer's trade mission to Africa. Some faculty members questioned the sources of funding for these trips since they were nonacademic. These trips, along with one to a TSU football game in Hawaii, gained more negative publicity. The president invited members of the board of regents, state representatives, alumni, administrators (and their spouses), and supporters of the administration to go to Hawaii at university expense and at a cost of $66,000. When the state auditor investigated this affair and found the university in violation, the state legislature threatened to place TSU in conservatorship and subsequently passed a law to place a master over any institution that would commit such a violation.[53]

Probably the biggest scandal of the Sawyer administration occurred the year he left office in 1978. This scandal involved paying out-of-state tuition for foreign students. From 1968 to 1978, TSU had a large number of foreign students, the majority coming from Nigeria and Iran. In 1979 the tuition for foreign students was raised very high; therefore, many could not afford to attend the university. In response to this situation, two churches in the city and a campus religious organization carried out a scheme for awarding bogus competitive scholarships to approximately eight hundred foreign students attending TSU. Tuition was reduced if one received a scholarship. But in this instance, no competition was involved, and the scholarship actually came from money these students paid to the religious groups. To add insult to injury, one of these churches issued a sizeable scholarship check to the university in October 1979, which was returned by the bank for insufficient funds.[54]

As the university grew, its administrative operations and management systems changed out of necessity. Such changes had not always responded to the intensified needs of a developing situation. As such, before the Sawyer era ended, there was a breakdown in virtually all management systems—in registration, in housing arrangements and accommodations, in traffic and security, and in certain student services, as well as in fiscal operations. To be sure, the university was suffering from growing pains; but it would be those growing pains that would lead to the dismissal of Sawyer and some of his staff. For example, one of the incidents that directly prompted Sawyer's departure was the 1979 fall registration. Only 8,265 of the approximately 9,300 potential students registered that semester. The situation was apparently caused by the following factors: (1) computing problems with printing fee receipts; (2) the deadlines for the submission of applications for admission and for financial aid requests were not enforced; and (3) a computer program used to calculate financial aid and dormitory fees was implemented without prior testing. The system's problems not only caused long lines but had students registering until the beginning of November. This registration issue caused a great deal of adverse publicity, resulting in student demonstrations and telephone calls to the board of regents and to the governor's office. By the time those responses reached the governor's office, a statewide

The TSU Law School was renamed in 1976 for Thurgood Marshall, the first African American associate justice of the Supreme Court. From left to right, Board Chairman George L. Allen, Justice Thurgood Marshall, President Granville Sawyer, and Dean Otis H. King. Courtesy of *TSU Yearbook,* 1976.

election had been held whereby Texas would elect its first Republican governor (William Clements) since Reconstruction. Thus, Sawyer could move in only one direction, and that was out. After receiving considerable pressure, the board of regents accepted Sawyer's letter of resignation on November 17, 1979.[55]

In sum, it can be said that the Sawyer administration appears to have verified a rationale for programmatic and service operations with respect to the black urban community and to the larger goal of cultural pluralism in the nation and in an international context. Despite its widely advertised fiscal difficulties, a breakdown in its management system, and pressure from within as well as without, the university made substantial progress under Sawyer as he carved out a niche for it as a "Special Purpose Institution for Urban Programing." Under Sawyer's watch the following were established: TSU's first doctoral program in the College of Education; the establishment of the Week-End College; the Urban Resources Center; the Banking Center; the School of Public Affairs; and the School of Communication. Also, TSU made substantial additions to its physical and service facilities, expanding from 53 acres to 125 acres. Since 1968, the physical appearance of the central campus has been altered by the construction of the School of Education

Building, the Student Life Center, and the School of Law Building (whose name changed to Thurgood Marshall School of Law in 1976). Properties in the immediate vicinity of the campus were acquired for housing both academic and support services and for certain special operations. Renovation and rehabilitation of the Fairchild Building, the dormitory complexes, and Hannah Hall were completed. In the area of extracurricular activities, the university men's basketball team captured the NAIA Championship in 1977. This accolade was coupled with outstanding performances by the track teams, a winning record by the debate team, and a university band that had come into its own and had taken the name "Ocean of Soul." From 1970 to 1976, the university also experienced unprecedented increases in enrollment of both foreign and domestic students.

During the Sawyer era, the university addressed some of the problems, issues, and situations that it had faced in 1968 and reached either partial or full resolution of others. On the other hand, the university appeared to be saddled with some of the same problems. Yet, most people will likely agree with an observer who opined that "at the end during the Sawyer's administration [the university] was no longer an infant looking for a sense of direction. [It was] a mature university undergoing certain changes."[56]

6

A New Image, a New Vision, and a New Plan

The Bell and Spearman Eras, 1979–1986

When Granville Sawyer left the office of the president in 1979, the state of Texas was entering an era of declining resources brought on by a bust in the oil industry. Likewise, a new conservatism was sweeping the state with the election of the first Republican governor since Reconstruction. A lack of fiscal accountability in the previous administration, coupled with the appointment of new members to the Texas Southern University Board of Regents, dictated change. But this change would have to wait until the installation of a new president. Meanwhile, the board sought the expertise of Everett O. Bell, a veteran administrator at the university who on another occasion had served as a member of the university's management team. A native of St. Louis, Missouri, Bell began his early education there in the public schools. After serving in the United States Army for four years, he received the BA degree in 1942 and the JD degree in 1946 from the University of Kansas. Afterward, he joined the TSU faculty and became an associate professor of law. During his subsequent career, he served the university in several capacities: assistant to the president, director of personnel, and vice president for administration services. He is also credited with establishing the university's first financial aid office.[1]

In 1979, Everett O. Bell was called on to serve as interim president. In that role, he presided over the completion of the university's self-study, which won reaffirmation of accreditation from the Southern Association of Colleges and Schools. Bell was also concerned with the image of the university and the negative press that it was receiving because of financial problems. He therefore constantly reminded TSU employees that the university's financial systems must be made current, sound, and accountable so as to maintain a good fiscal standing in the community. In similar fashion, he

Everett O. Bell, 1979–1980. Courtesy of *TSU Archives.*

held the university together for eight months until the selection of a permanent president. For his service to the university, Bell was retroactively named fifth president of the university in 1981.[2]

In June 1980, the board of regents selected Leonard Hall O'Connell Spearman, an educator and a top officer in the United States Department of Education, to head TSU. A native of Florida, he received his precollegiate education in the public schools of Tallahassee and earned his undergraduate degree in biological sciences from Florida A&M College in 1947. He subsequently earned the MA (1950) and Ph D (1960) degrees in clinical psychology at the University of Michigan. After teaching high school for a few years in Tallahassee, he became an instructor at Florida A&M University and later a professor and dean of the junior division at Southern University–Baton Rouge. In 1970, he began federal government service in the U.S. Department of Education, rising to the rank of associate deputy assistant secretary of postsecondary education. Spearman was especially instrumental in shaping and expanding the federal education opportunity programs known as the TRIO programs—originally the Talent Search, Upward Bound, and Student Support Services programs—as well as the federal student loan program.[3]

Leonard H. O. Spearman, 1980–1986.
Courtesy of *TSU Archives*.

When the TSU Board of Regents tapped Spearman to become president on June 6, 1980, he had already been selected to become head of Savannah State College in Georgia. Folklore has it that when Spearman received TSU's offer, he made a U-turn while in the air. Whatever this humor imparts, Spearman obviously considered TSU's offer to be the better one. For TSU, the 1980s could very well be referred to as both the best of times and the worst of times. TSU had potentials and opportunities rarely afforded many HBCUs: it was located in Houston's cosmopolitan community, which had grown from six to fifty-two consulates and had one of the nation's major ports in tonnage handling; it had one of the world's largest medical centers located less than a quarter of a mile from campus. TSU benefited from Houston's position as the energy capital of the world and as a major producer of oilfield equipment. To be sure, TSU had a solid base on which to grow. What was needed was a change from the proverbial status quo.

The excitement at the naming of a new president was obvious, but the challenges were sobering. When Spearman assumed the presidency on August 1, 1980, he found an institution within the shadows of the exciting Houston skyline, but one that was distant from the business and government establishments. TSU's quest for excellence was also thwarted by conditions

President Spearman and black journalists Bud Johnson, Sonny M. Giles, and George McElroy meet to discuss the changing image of TSU. Courtesy of *TSU Archives*.

all too common to public black colleges and universities—fiscal breakdown, threat of merger, neglected facilities, and relentlessly bad publicity. The situation in 1980 was that $56 million were needed just for buildings and repairs. Accreditation of four professional schools was likewise in jeopardy. Financial statements had not been produced since 1977 (nor certified since 1973). The registration process had not kept pace with the new technology; and the U.S. Department of Education's Office for Civil Rights was on the verge of announcing that the state of Texas was out of compliance with the Supreme Court's ruling in *Adams v. Richardson*, which called for ending dual racial systems in higher education. Indeed, Spearman came into office with a determination to change the image of TSU.

Reflecting on TSU's internal problems, Spearman set as his top priorities: (1) total accountability in all fiscal matters, with streamlined procedures for such functions as purchasing and prompt payment for materials and services; (2) efficiency in such routine functions as registration and in the processing of student financial aid and related services; and (3) stepped-up recruiting of traditional college-age and older students. By the time Spearman had his first audience with the faculty, this list had grown to include streamlining the administrative structure, reemphasizing scholarly excellence via rewards and incentives, improving facilities and their appearances, expanding relationships between business and government, adhering to the university's urban mission, and developing a strong alumni network.[4]

Accordingly, Spearman stressed that regaining credibility in regard to the university's financial affairs was the number one priority of his administration. Integrity in finance was at the core of his argument. In his own words, "It is essential to our legislative effort, our relations with vendors and our day-to-day business."[5] To this end, Spearman established a task force and enlisted the help of fiscal experts from other state institutions of higher learning, as well as a team of systems experts from NASA, to review the financial records of the university. But even as progress was being made in cleaning up the books, new problems were uncovered. A large deficit in auxiliary enterprise funds (ranging from bookstore and dormitory operations to athletics) had accumulated over the years. This negative cash flow in the past had been caused by transfers from unexpended funds with the intention of repayment. But given the economic state of affairs, it seemed highly unlikely that the university would be able to repay the borrowed amount. Moreover, the status of the auxiliary enterprises threatened the very survival of the athletic programs. To remedy this situation, the university asked the state for permission to use unencumbered funds from the 1979–1981 biennial budgets. The state granted that request to liquidate existing liabilities, but there was still a need for more money.[6] To complement this effort, the president called on two alumni, El Franco Lee and Craig Washington, to head up a $50,000 fund-raising drive for the athletic program, a drive that started in the summer of 1981. This effort would later be aided by the "Three of Us Dinner Dance" sponsored by Ruby Mosley, Polly Turner, and Ruby Jefferson.

At the same time that Spearman was seeking to get TSU's fiscal house in order, he also named his own team to carry out his goals and objectives. Within three months after he assumed office, Spearman asked for the resignations of all top-level administrators (deans and vice presidents). After two weeks, he announced that he had accepted the resignations of the deans of education, law, pharmacy, public affairs, and of the director of the Week-End College, as well as the director of athletics. These officials were replaced by individuals who would serve in interim posts and in some cases be promoted to permanent positions. Beginning with the 1981–1982 school year, his top-level executives included: Llayron L. Clarkson, academic affairs; Plummer Austin, fiscal affairs; Wayne Carle, institutional advancement; and James Race, student affairs.

Almost as soon as Spearman arrived on campus, he had to deal with budget issues. Prior to his coming, TSU had presented a budget of $62,613,491 to the Legislative Budget Board (LBB); but in the summer of 1980, the LBB cut that amount to $49,424,410, a reduction of $13,189,081. If the reduced budget were allowed to stand, it would wipe out much of the proposed renovation for substandard facilities and the other special items that dealt with both old and new programs, research, student services, institutional support, and accreditation of professional schools. Responding to this situation, Spearman went before the Senate Finance Committee and the House Appropriations Committee in March 1981 to lobby for the restoration of the funds. In part, he was successful because the state of Texas was at that time in negotiations with the U.S. Office of Civil Rights to comply with *Adams v. Bell*. Consequently, the LBB recommended a special fund of $12 million above the formula funding for TSU.[7]

The Texas Plan and the Future of TSU

Much of Spearman's presidency was consumed with the Texas Plan, a plan that greatly impacted the university's present as well as its future. A history of the Texas Plan is therefore instructive. In 1964, Congress passed the Civil Rights Act, which outlawed segregation in public facilities. Later, Title VI was added to the Civil Rights Act, thereby prohibiting racial and ethnic discrimination in educational programs financed with federal funds. It was not until 1969 that the Department of Health, Education and Welfare (HEW) took steps to enforce the nondiscrimination clause embedded in Title VI at institutions of higher learning. At that time, the department sent letters of noncompliance to twelve southern states. The letters indicated that they were operating a segregated system of higher education; and it requested each state to submit a desegregation plan within 120 days. Some states ignored the letter, while others submitted plans that were unacceptable. In 1972, the NAACP filed a lawsuit, *Adams v. Richardson* (later changed to *Adams v. Bell*), to remedy this situation. The plaintiff in the case asked the court to remove the dual system of education in institutions of higher learning in the noncompliant states. After the filing of the lawsuit, several southern states entered into an out-of-court settlement with the Office for Civil Rights and the Department of Education. In a consent decree, these states agreed to several offers to bring HCBUs up to parity with their white counterparts via new programs, faculty salaries, new buildings, equipment, and scholarships for students of all races. Because the state of Texas had failed to be proactive during the 1970s in rectifying inequities at TSU and Prairie View, it was cited for noncompliance. In response to the court's citation in 1980, the state submitted what became known as the Texas Plan to eliminate the vestiges of its dual system of education. The Department of Education provisionally accepted the plan, contingent upon additional commitments that were to be incorporated by June 15, 1981.[8]

For TSU, the additional commitment would come in the form of a mission and enhancement study, as well as funding from two special sessions of the state legislature held to address inequity issues at the university. The mission and enhancement study would provide an opportunity for the university to define its long-range mission, goals, and programs that should either be developed, strengthened, or changed. This study, which did not begin until September 1981, would analyze the university's historical and emerging mission as well as its present findings and recommendations for implementation within the next five years and beyond.

In order to fulfill the commitment of the provisional plan, Governor William Clements called a special session of the legislature in August 1981. The Texas Legislature approved $1.4 million to address accreditation of the professional schools and $15.8 million for construction, renovation, and repairs contingent upon the passage of the ad valorem tax referendum in the November election.[9] Consequently, by early March of 1982, one could begin to see the impact of the legislative measures. By that time, campus beautification became evident as sidewalks and other accouterments were installed in a three-year face-lifting project. Moreover, twenty building projects got underway with the support of state appropriations for construction. These included a laboratory and classroom addition for the School of Pharmacy, a new central plant for heating and cooling, a new Technology Building, a new General Services Building, a new health and Physical Education Building, underground utilities repair, a major addition to the Nabrit Science Center, an additional floor for the School of Education and the construction of Graystone Apartments for students. Also, $2 million in instructional equipment were used for the Law Library, and $1 million went to the School of Business for computer materials.[10]

Meanwhile, the mission and enhancement study, completed at the end of the summer of 1982, called for specific improvements in the physical plants and equipment, in quality and range of program offerings, in numbers and qualifications of faculty, and in student services and financial assistance over a period of three biennials. Some of the new programs included the pharmacy's doctoral program and the masters of science program in petroleum engineering technology. Included also were a new School of Human Ecology and a request for an increase in faculty salaries. The enhancement of myriad student services included counseling, health services tutoring, financial aid, expanded recruitment, and scholarships for nonblacks. Additionally, this study called for campus expansion via construction of eighteen buildings and for major repairs and renovations to existing structures. In physical terms, this study proposed that the campus be expanded to include the physical area bounded by the following streets:

Ennis on the west, Scott on the east, Blodgett on the south, and Alabama on the north. Also included in the plan were catch-up appropriations for financial management, data processing, institutional marketing, dormitory management, and the Week-End College.[11]

It is interesting to note that before the TSU mission and enhancement study was completed and before the state of Texas could present an acceptable plan to the Office for Civil Rights, the University of Houston asked the Texas Higher Education Coordinating Board (THECB) to approve new courses and programs for the University of Houston Downtown (UHD) that would impinge on TSU's course offerings. Writing on this matter to Charles E. Bishop, president of the University of Houston, President Spearman did not mince words when he said, "Expansion would have a negative impact on TSU in the availability of these programs and would bring about reduction in enrollments, present and potential, and almost inevitably would constitute an unnecessary duplication of curriculum offerings."[12] And as if this argument were not enough, Spearman made a strong case to Kenneth Ashworth, executive director of THECB, stating that "TSU cannot support the establishment of the new degree programs as proposed by UHD. These programs are represented [in our] college of arts and sciences. They differ little, if any, in course identification and content."[13] Further, he went on to make the point that these programs were already operational at TSU and had been there since its inception; therefore, he begged for a dialogue between the two presidents. Instead of answering Spearman, Bishop responded to Kenneth Ashworth, saying that "the role and scope of each university are considerably different, and that the mission of each institution is such that each serves different populations and offers similar educational opportunity."[14]

When Spearman's plea fell on deaf ears, he turned to state representative Wilhelmina Delco for assistance. He told her that in 1980 the Office for Civil Rights (OCR) had cited the negative impact that duplication of courses at UHD would have on the academic community served by TSU and that it was important for the state to address this needless and costly duplication.[15] Delco responded by preparing a bill that would create a Texas Southern University System, a system that would give it a satellite campus downtown. Spearman was pleased with this proposal because such "would return TSU its clientele that was siphoned off by UHD." As will be discussed later, Delco's bill became convoluted and blown out of proportion in 1987, when attempts were made to send the entire TSU campus to the UH Downtown Campus.[16]

After the completion of the mission and enhancement study, the Texas

Plan was revised and submitted to HEW in October 1982, but the plan was returned by OCR for further negotiations.[17] While negotiations between the state and OCR were going on, a gubernatorial campaign and election was held between incumbent governor William Clements and Attorney General Mark White. During the campaign, Governor Clements was invited to address the fall convocation at TSU. In response to a query from one of Clements's staff persons about the content of his speech, Spearman wrote, "He should speak on his commitment to TSU, but [should] feel free to give commentary on whatever emphasis [he] ascertains to be timely at this point."[18] True to form, Clements spoke of his commitment to the university but afterwards proceeded to make a political speech. His commitment to TSU notwithstanding, Clement and the Republican Party did not have strong supporters at TSU nor in the black community in Houston. This notion became evident in the November election when Democrat Mark White won both the governor's race and the black vote.

Upon assuming the office of governor, Mark White encountered many challenges, not the least of which was a downturn in the state's economy and the Texas Plan. To remedy the former, Bob Bullock, state controller, warned President Spearman, as he did with other state agencies, that the Texas state government faced a financial crisis. "The legislature has options, but they are limited—cut the budget, raise taxes or risk deficit spending. You are affected by this crisis. You have a right to know the situation and to try to help solve it."[19] Following Bullock's edict to cut the budget, TSU's president then announced his plan to reduce the number of instructional personnel and support staff and also to realign various units at the university. Realignment would streamline and strengthen academic support programs and at the same time realize a projected savings of nearly a quarter million dollars per year in operating costs. The results were that nine schools and colleges were reduced to seven, forty-six academic departments became twenty-three, and the office of the president went from six to five staff workers. Some schools, colleges, and departments were combined with others, whereas others were phased out. Under the new alignment, an authorized new School of Allied Health Professions, which was slated to begin in 1986, was instead combined with the existing School of Pharmacy to form the School of Pharmacy and Health Sciences. The College of Arts and Sciences was separated into two units—a College of Humanities and Communications, and a College of Sciences and Technology. A new School of Management incorporated the Schools of Business and Public Affairs. A new School of Education and Behavioral Sciences absorbed the existing School of Education and the Departments of Psychology, Sociology, Social Work, and Home Economics from the College of Arts and Sciences. The former School of Communication was merged with the new College of Humanities. The Thurgood Marshall School of Law and the Graduate School remained as they had been structured in previous years. The School of Technology became a unit in the School of Science and Technology.[20]

Meanwhile, the Texas Plan was still front and center for both the governor and the president. Having served as attorney general, Governor White was thoroughly familiar with the Texas Plan, so he immediately set up a Governor's Special Committee to negotiate the plan with the federal government. President Spearman served as a member of this committee. When the final draft was completed and submitted in the spring of 1983, it included commitments for the funding of new facilities and programs, for removing deficiencies in salaries, for strengthening existing program, and for recruiting, scholarships, and counseling. More specifically, provisions of the plan indicated that the state should (1) provide resources comparable to white institutions with similar missions; (2) rectify inequities in salaries with special appropriations by achieving a higher faculty-to-student ratio; and (3) enroll 25 percent of the student body in high demand areas or in unduplicated degree programs, attractive to all races within five years. These new programs, subject to revision at TSU's option, included bachelor of science programs in sports health, in environmental health, and in petroleum engineering technology; masters programs in professional accounting and in transportation; and a doctoral program in pharmacy. The plan also called for the enhancement and strengthening of programs and physical facilities. Bilingual education, fashion merchandising, foods and nutrition, consumer education, early childhood education, and business education were listed as the programs to be enhanced, while the School of Law was to be strengthened. The plan also called for new construction, major repairs, and renovations.[21]

The Texas Plan further stipulated that there should be cooperative agreement between TSU and the University of Houston because these institutions had distinctive and complementary programs. While it called for both universities to promote high demand courses, it did stipulate that priority consideration should be taken not to duplicate programs at TSU. It also asked for reinforcement of coordinating board policy against intercession by other institutions in the Houston area. The cooperative agreement further called for cross-registration of students for up to nine semester hours of elective courses without additional fees for joint degrees and other academic ventures. Integration and an increase in the student body at the undergraduate, graduate, and professional levels were critical parts of the plan. Also, there was a special appropriation for scholarships for minorities and for the recruitment of nonblack students. Likewise, the plan called for a 5 to 10 percent increase of black and Hispanic enrollment and graduation rates.[22]

When Spearman went before the legislature in March 1983 to seek a budget for the next biennium (1984–1985), both he and Governor Mark White were aware that Judge John H. Pratt had given the state forty-five days to complete its plan for desegregation. So, Spearman asked for a budget of 60 percent above the formula funding, and the legislature approved it. This money was used for construction, repairs, renovations, and special items. The legislative appropriation also helped strengthen student service through scholarships, recruitment, counseling, and academic advisement. Likewise, it supported the accreditation of the professional schools, the implementation of new degree programs, the purchase of new instructional equipment, and increases in faculty salaries. The legislature also pledged to continue to bring TSU's physical facilities up to standard. In addition, five major projects were added to twenty-two construction and renovations projects already underway or completed on campus since 1980. The priorities for this work were older buildings, a run-down central plant, and underground utilities. At the end of the session, Spearman told the faculty that the governor had interceded in both the regular and special sessions of the legislature on behalf of TSU, and that as a result TSU received $33 million above the state formula.[23]

It is instructive and informative that before the Texas Plan was accepted by the federal government, the University of Houston's Board of Regents moved toward obtaining the pharmacy doctorate, a degree program specifically denied under the state's plan for desegregation of higher education. This degree program was one of the new programs reserved for Texas Southern because one of the goals of the Texas Plan was to have more white students attend Historically Black Colleges and Universities with new high demand programs such as TSU's pharmacy doctorate. Robert Maxson, the UH system vice president for academic affairs, argued that both UH and TSU could have pharmacy doctorate programs because TSU's program stressed clinical work, whereas UH's focused on research, and Houston was big enough to justify both. In the end UH's argument prevailed.[24]

Meanwhile, the revised Texas Plan was accepted by OCR in May 1983. Both the governor and the legislature were committed to providing funds to TSU for the purpose of improving deficiencies in facilities and salaries, for implementing new programs, and for strengthening existing program areas, scholarships, recruiting and counseling. Among other things the plan called for were (1) the implementation of at least six new degree programs—the doctor of pharmacy, masters of accounting, masters of transportation, bachelor of environmental health, bachelor of sport health, and bachelor of petroleum engineering technology; (2) the organization of a School of Health Sciences by the year 1987; (3) the continued strengthening of the Schools of Law and Education, as well as programs in insurance, consumer education, foods and nutrition, fashion merchandising, business and bilingual education. Upon hearing that the plan had been accepted, Spearman wrote the governor to tell him "congratulations to you and other state officials who are handling this matter . . . the State of Texas will be the chief beneficiary of an effective implementation of a Plan which is bold and far reaching."[25]

Rumors of Spearman's Departure

Although the completion and implementation of the Texas Plan was a milestone for the state of Texas, Texas Southern University, the governor, and the president, rumors about Spearman's ouster, which had begun with the election of Mark White, were now rife. In an attempt to allay these rumors, and to show his commitment to the Texas Plan, Governor Mark White came to Texas Southern University on June 28, 1983, and signed into law a bill giving $15 million to the university for new construction.[26] There, he also swore into office two regents—Arthur M. Gaines and Larry Greenfield—stated his support for Spearman, and presented the president with $20,000 from the Lockwell Foundation to establish a bar review course for TSU graduates of the School of Law. During his presentation, White indicated that he "was concerned about rumors of disruptive interference in the educational process here, distracting the administration, faculty and students from pursuing their primary purpose."[27] But White's coming to TSU did not happen fortuitously. According to the *Houston Informer*, one of the two regents recently appointed by White had called Board Chairman Howard D. Kirven and asked him to call a special meeting in June to fire Spearman. When the story leaked out to the public, a rally was held by his supporters urging the board to keep Spearman and carrying signs that read "We want Spearman."[28]

Suspicions about Spearman's departure were fueled even more when it was discovered that his contract was not going to be renewed in the summer of 1983. Responding to this situation, the *Houston Defender* published an editorial titled "Leave Spearman Alone" in which it argued that "we don't want our community's university to be so subjected to political whims that every time the administration changes in Austin, we have to adjust to a new president."[29] TSU student James H. Lang wrote to the governor the same month, stating that "I read an article in the *Houston Post* that you were opposed to the Board of Regents' renewing Dr. Leonard Spearman's contract. I cannot understand why. . . . It is extremely important to the continued success of TSU that your office not allow TSU to become a political football."[30] After reviewing many similar letters, including one from Mike Petrizzo, executive vice president of KCOH radio station, the governor responded. Writing Petrizzo, White said, "Like most executives in private industry, most presidents of the state colleges and universities in Texas serve without a written contract. Instead, they continue employment at the discretion of the Board of Regents." He went on to say that his interest on the issue of Spearman's contract involved only the policy questions.[31]

The issue of Spearman's contract would not be resolved until several months later. While Spearman continued to perform his duties as president, rumors of his ouster continued to haunt him. On December 20, 1983, a newspaper reporter requested documents from the university about contributions that Spearman had made to the Democratic Party and members thereof, including Mark White. Spearman argued that contributions to the campaign for Anthony Hall and Glen Scott were made before the election. The others, including White's campaign, were made after the election to retire debts. Spearman contended that he gave to White's campaign to "mend fences."[32] What caused so much consternation was that Spearman asked the university to reimburse him. The money was taken from a regents fund—a special discretionary fund that was to be used for enhancing TSU, not for political contributions. If any of this money were used for political purposes, the university could lose its tax-exempt status. Spearman readily acknowledged that he was wrong and paid the money back.

The above incident certainly did not help Spearman in his battle for a new contract. It only added more fuel to the fire. Subsequently, a rally was called by TSU alumni on February 14, 1984, in support of Spearman. To many, the end was imminent; to others, there was a need to keep the embattled president and to keep the university from becoming a political football. Congressman Mickey Leland said, "In the absence of any charge of malfeasance in office, I am hard pressed for an explanation to move Spearman." Frank Burns of the NAACP stated that the university should be insulated from the political whims of state officials who may use "strong-arm" tactics to render the university helpless. City councilman Anthony Hall argued that under Spearman "the university has made significant progress and the city has benefitted directly from [those] programs."[33] Spearman did not take this matter lightly as he thanked his supporters and indicated to them that he was not dismissing this matter as a "tempest in a teapot." He began to look for another job. He applied for and became a finalist for the presidency of Morgan State University in Baltimore, Maryland. Before a commitment could be made in August 1984, Spearman wrote the chairman of Morgan's board: "The roller-coaster ride I have been on here in Houston over the past year seems finally to be slowing to a stop, with the Board of Regents acting to renew my contract for the coming two years."[34]

The Last Two Years

With a two-year contract in hand, Spearman was ready to embark on pursuing the opportunities and challenges that lay ahead. Texas Southern University continued its enhancements of infrastructure, of its management system, of its degree programs, and of its faculty development. One of the most visible accomplishments was the completion of the university mall in the center of the campus—a place that was formerly used as a parking garage. Major new computer acquisitions and new fiscal accounting software strengthened the management systems. Fiscal affairs installed a new system and won another clear audit from the state. In terms of faculty development, personal computers were awarded to the faculty, along with accompanying training and laboratories, and the state increased scholarships for nonblack students. Progress was made by implementing four of six new degree plans: the doctoral degree in pharmacy, the master's degrees in transportation and in professional accounting, and the bachelor's degree in environmental health.[35] During these two years, the board of regents approved a plan for the establishment of the Frederick Douglass Institute of Liberal Studies. The institute had a twofold purpose: to improve the general literacy of undergraduate students, especially those who were taking remedial courses; and to revise the Honors Program. As conceived by Patricia Williams, the first academic, female dean of the university, the Honors Program was designed to recruit talented students, to establish honors courses, and to provide the students with scholarships.[36]

The last two years of the Spearman era brought about visible changes in fund raising and extracurricular activities. Building on the successes and innovations of previous years, fundraisers' efforts broadened and intensified. In 1984, the Marvin Zindler Roast, coordinated by development vice president James Cunningham, netted $165,000. The 1985–86 People-to-People Capital Campaign had as its goal $50 million, as opposed to the $1 million goal of its previous campaign. In 1985, TSU also became the beneficiary of 2,500 vintage 78-rpm recordings. Edward (Ed) Brunson, a resident of Conroe, Texas, donated these recordings, which were appraised at $17,500. Houston's tenor sax great Arnett Cobb headed the lists of jazz artists represented in a collection that reads like a virtual Who's Who in jazz. Other notable musicians represented included Duke Ellington, Erskine Hawkins, Benny Goodman, Louis Armstrong, Tommy Lanceford, Count Basie, Chick Webb, and Ethel Waters. The ultimate goal in acquiring this collection was to start a jazz archive.[37]

In the area of extracurricular activities, the athletic programs were strengthened, while the national conference on educational excellence placed TSU on the map. A new track field was installed with artificial turf, which contributed to TSU's track team winning the 1984 SWAC Championship and making a remarkable showing at the NCAA Championship competitions. One of the most outstanding events of 1984 was a TSU-sponsored National Conference on Educational Excellence and Economic Growth, with keynote presentations given by three governors—Mark White of Texas, William "Bill" Jefferson Clinton of Arkansas, and Charles Robb of Virginia. In the words of Spearman, "[These] governors' [appearance] cannot be underestimated in the history of Texas Southern University."[38]

Despite the above accomplishments, Spearman also faced a number of challenges, a major one being that of mergers. This age-old issue resurfaced as soon as Mark White appointed a Select Committee on Higher Education to do a study on Texas colleges and universities. The talk of merger had arisen several times during the Spearman administration, but with the formation of Governor Mark White's Select Committee on Higher Education in November 1985, a group charged with taking a hard look at the possibility of closing or merging some of the state-supported institutions, merger talks carried more weight.[39] Shortly thereafter, uneasiness began to creep into TSU board meetings and prompted lengthy discussions of issues that might hurt the predominantly black university if the legislature seriously considered a merger. The board members almost immediately became upset at the November meeting, when the president announced that the School of Business had lost its accreditation, which it had gained three years earlier. Regent Larry Greenfield quipped, "We can ill afford this loss. That just gives them [i.e., the proponents of merger] what they need." Among the many things the business accrediting agency cited were the need for more faculty with terminal degrees, insufficient research, and excessive faculty turnover.

While Spearman assured the trustees that the administration had done everything possible to maintain accreditation, many faculty contended that the university had gone up for accreditation prematurely. Regardless of the reason, many board members felt that the Schools of Pharmacy and Law might suffer the same fates because of low passage rates on professional exams.[40]

Following a period of student growth, the 1985–86 school year reflected significant losses of student enrollments in the wake of tripled state tuition rates and the inability of students to pay overdue tuition and old bills. Consequently, the university experienced a loss of the following students: 9.3 percent from Texas, 24.5 percent from out of state, and 34 percent from other nations. The spring 1986 enrollment dropped by 10 percent, due largely to the loss of 911 students who failed to pay $424,261 in overdue tuition. Even with those numbers, Spearman assured Commissioner Ashworth, "There is no reason to believe that overall enrollment cannot continue to grow through redoubling our efforts to identify and recruit urban Texans who are part of our special mission." Spearman also sent Ashworth the university's plan designed to overcome this deficit in recruitment and enrollment. This plan called for articulation agreements with community colleges; placing the offices of recruitment, admissions, and student financial aid under an Enrollment Management Center; and establishing an Academic Advisement and Counseling Center to improve retention.[41]

With a decline in enrollment, a loss of the School of Business's accreditation, low passage rates on other professional schools' examinations, new members being added to the board of regents, and an upcoming gubernatorial election between the incumbent Mark White and William Clements, it was not surprising when rumors began to fly early in April 1986 that Spearman's tenure in office would soon come to an end. On the eve of the June 5th board meeting, the *Houston Chronicle* reported that Spearman's resignation was imminent. Spearman was told on the next day by the board chairman Milton Carroll that he no longer had the confidence of the board. Subsequently, Spearman tendered his resignation on June 6, 1986, and returned to the Psychology Department as a distinguished professor.[42]

In sum, Spearman can be credited with improving the infrastructure of the university and with establishing a number of new programs during his tenure as president. Wheeler Avenue was officially closed to traffic after many years of protest to that effect; and a university mall was constructed out of a parking lot to enhance the learning environment of the campus. The physical conditions of some buildings were changed almost completely, while new construction gave rise to the new General Services Building, the

Health and Physical Education Building, a new Technology Building, and the renovation of the Nabrit Science Building. A new track field and four tennis courts also graced the campus. Additionally, the acquisition of new land expanded the boundaries of the campus. Spearman had forged a new image for the university, but numerous challenges yet remained with the Texas Plan and the issue of merger.

7

The Fight against Merger

The Interim Years of Robert J. Terry, 1986–1987

Robert J. Terry, a distinguished professor of biology at Texas Southern, succeeded Leonard H. O. Spearman and became interim president on June 18, 1986. He ascended to power at a time of falling enrollments, tightened budgets, and the controversy over merging TSU with the University of Houston. A native of Crockett, Texas, Terry had held several positions at the university before assuming the post of interim president. He had been vice president for academic affairs, 1973–1978; dean of faculty, 1971–1973; and dean of the College of Arts and Sciences, 1969–1971. After attending the public schools of Crockett, Terry matriculated and graduated from Houston College for Negroes in 1946 with a bachelor of science degree. He was later awarded the master of science degree from Atlanta University in 1949 and the PhD in biology from Iowa State University. He further distinguished himself by serving as a consultant to the government of India in 1965 and was an associate director at the National Science Foundation from 1966–77.[1]

Upon his acceptance of the interim post, Terry convinced the board that he was up to the task of moving the university forward. Pledging to work for the best interests of TSU, he indicated that "he recognized the challenges in higher education which TSU faced" and predicted that "the University" would meet those challenges—low performances on exams, falling enrollments, and the issue of merger. With regard to students' performances on standardized tests, Terry first pointed out that the university would not waste time criticizing the content of the exams but would instead teach the students in such a manner that they would overcome their difficulties and would pass all required examinations. In his view, preparing students for the future went beyond test taking. It required having a solid foundation, which entailed strengthening and

Robert J. Terry, 1986–1987. Courtesy of
TSU Archives.

improving all academic units and programs at the university.[2] But while
he worked toward that end, he had to deal with the falling enrollment. The
university's enrollment had fallen by 1,089 students in 1986, a 13 percent drop
that officials blamed on a second round of tuition increases (from $12 to $16
per semester credit hour) and hard economic times. The result was that low
and moderate income black families, part-timers, full-timers, foreign, and
out-of-state students were hardest hit by the increments. Although Terry
proposed using installment payment plans to allow students to remain
enrolled, the slide in enrollment did not stop.[3]

While Terry worked on the above issue, his major headache appeared
to have been the issue of the merger. In one of his first speeches given to
an outside group after becoming interim president, Terry told the Houston
Business and Professional Men's Club on October 8, 1986, "I think we are
going to win the confrontation about merger, if it is about to occur." He went
on record as opposing any efforts that would result in "TSU's not remaining
an autonomous university with its own administration and own governing board."[4] Almost from its inception, TSU had been threatened (verbally
or practically) with merger. Arguably, TSU's *raison d'être* and its location
dictated that merger would be in its future. Integration of the University of
Texas as a result of *Sweatt v. Painter* (1950) and the TSU Board of Regents'

resolution to admit all applicants who applied to TSU regardless of race in 1956 indirectly suggested this future.

Every president has had to deal with the issue of merger, but seemingly this issue reached a crescendo under interim President Robert J. Terry. A history of the issue of merger is therefore instructive. The first attempt at merger came in 1962 when the coordinating board called for a feasibility study on TSU's law and pharmacy schools. The study revealed that the cost was greater to educate fewer students at TSU than it was at UT and UH. Motivated by the student-teacher ratio, as well as by the cost to maintain these programs, the commission's study revealed that the University of Houston had about 350 law students and was integrated, whereas TSU's law school had about 30 students. Yet, the cost of educating TSU law students was five times as high as the cost at UT and nearly four times as that at UH. During the 1963–1964 school years, it cost TSU $2,236 per law student, whereas it cost $444 per student at UT and $1,622 at UH. President Nabrit's reply was that 93 percent of all black lawyers in the state were TSU graduates, and that TSU had more African American law graduates than all other southern law schools combined.[5] Despite the arguments and pleas of President Nabrit, on October 9, 1964, by vote of 11–2, the commissioners agreed to phase out the law school beginning in the fall of 1965, with a total phase out in September 1967.[6] THECB made its decision in the same year that it acknowledged that enrollment at law schools would have to double in the next decade if Texas were to maintain an adequate supply of attorneys.

As stated previously, in 1962, a similar study was done on the School of Pharmacy and yielded results similar to those concerning the Law School— TSU and UH were duplicating each other. TSU's School of Pharmacy got a reprieve, however, when the director of the THECB, Lester Harrell, disputed the above findings. Harrell said that the facts surrounding the Schools of Law and Pharmacy were different. TSU's was one of three pharmacy schools in the state; it awarded thirteen pharmacy degrees in 1963–64, which indicated that the school had a good enrollment.[7] For those who would criticize the School of Pharmacy, Nabrit pointed out that "TSU had as many [pharmacy] students as our facilities will permit us to accommodate and . . . as many students as there are Negroes in the entire University of Texas, and it has been desegregated since 1955."[8] The THECB, then, decided to delay a decision on the School of Pharmacy until it could do further study on methods of combining the physical facilities and programs of TSU with the University of Houston's. As previously stated in chapter 3, after a meeting between TSU president Samuel Nabrit and Governor John B. Connally in January 1965, there was a halt to the issue of merger for a brief period of time. Afterward, the Texas Commission on Higher Education hinted that TSU would keep its pharmacy school, but the Texas State Legislature would have to decide if the law school would be closed in 1967.[9] The TSU Board of Regents rejected the THECB's recommendation to phase out the law school; and when President Nabrit went before the House Appropriations Committee in Spring 1965, he asked for more funds for the law school, arguing that "it is premature for Texas to abolish programs in a predominantly Negro institution on the theory that they are not needed because they are not legally required."[10] After Nabrit's presentation, some members of the Harris County delegation moved quickly to halt a rider to the House and Senate versions of the proposed TSU state appropriations, which read "None of the funds appropriated to Texas Southern University for the year ending August 31, 1964, may be expended for the instruction for first- or second-year law students."[11] TSU appealed this decision on April 4, 1966. Notwithstanding this appeal, after a site visit to TSU School of Law, the coordinating board still voted for closure but changed the date to 1973.[12]

TSU's law school got a new lease on life in 1969 when the Ford Foundation awarded the school a $550,000 grant. According to newspaper accounts, the grant was contingent upon the coordinating board rescinding or modifying its decision to phase out the school in 1973. Consequently, the THECB reversed itself. In keeping with the decision, Representative Jamie Bray of Pasadena asked the House appropriations chairman, William S. Heatly, to remove a rider from his committee's general state appropriation bills that would force the shutdown of the law school starting in 1971.[13] Not only was the rider removed in conference committee, but the law school was spared.[14]

The issue of merger came up again during the Granville Sawyer era. According to state representative George Thomas "Mickey" Leland, a TSU alumnus, in February 1975, an official of the University of Texas approached him and asked if he would request a suspension of the rules to submit a bill for merger between Texas Southern University and the University of Texas. Leland said that he "did not know who wrote the bill, but Michael Hudson, director of public affairs for the U.T. System asked [him] to consider introducing it."[15] Although Hudson reportedly told Leland that the bill would be introduced with the understanding that it would not be pushed if the board and administrators of TSU did not approve, it is hard to believe anyone would make such a proposal without the direction or authority from the chancellor or the board of regents of the UT system.[16] As soon as Leland released this information, rumors and suspicions became rife that a merger between TSU and UT was in the offing. Leland acknowledged that "a merger would be a way to get more money for TSU, but indicated that

[he] would not introduce a bill [late] unless the Board of Regents and President Granville Sawyer call an emergency board meeting and decide that
such was necessary for TSU's survival."[17] A meeting was never called, and
the issue of merging would not resurface at the state level again until 1981.

Fears about the future of Texas Southern as an independent entity were
further compounded or aggravated by the Office for Civil Rights' campaign
to dismantle segregated institutions of higher education in the South during
the early seventies. As a result of *Adams v. Bell* (1972), which called for integration of institutions of higher education, a study of Texas institutions was
conducted and completed in the spring of 1978. An investigator for the U.S.
Office for Civil Rights found a degree of segregation in Texas public institutions of higher education. As was discussed in the previous chapter, the state
of Texas initiated a plan to comply with the federal government's ordinance
to bring the two black universities, Texas Southern and Prairie View, up to
parity with their white counterparts—a plan that many thought would be
very expensive and could be resolved via merger. While the Texas Plan was
being negotiated, Governor William Clements set up a thirty-member committee to study higher education in the state and to make plans for improving it. Not long after the committee was formed, it approved a controversial
proposal to group most state colleges and universities under five boards:
(1) the Texas A&M System would include Prairie View, Tarleton State,
Texas A&M, and Texas Tech; (2) the University of Houston System would
include the central and downtown campuses, as well as Texas Southern;
(3) Texas State University would include Sam Houston State, Angelo State,
Sul Ross, Stephen F. Austin, West Texas State, and East Texas State; (4) the
North South University System would include North Texas State College
of Osteopathic Medicine, Midwestern University, Texas Woman's, Texas
A&I, Laredo State, and Pan American University; and (5) the University of
Texas System would remain intact with its branches and satellite campuses
because most of these colleges and universities were already governed by the
board of UT.[18] Oppositions to these recommendations were swift. TSU was
one of the first to respond. Its board chairman argued that "TSU is serving the minority community . . . and should stay as it is." In part because
of the negative response to the above proposal, it was placed on the back
burner until the Texas Plan was negotiated and accepted by the Office for
Civil Rights.[19]

Governor Mark White, who assumed the office in 1983, not only played
a leading role in negotiating the Texas Plan but also established a Select
Committee on Higher Education. That committee was charged with taking a hard look at the possibility of merging some of Texas's state-supported

institutions. Talks of merger had been heard for many years, but now the proposal earned new weight. As soon as the Select Committee was established, uneasiness began to creep into TSU board meetings, prompting lengthy discussions on issues that might hurt the predominantly black university if the legislature ever seriously considered a merger. A merger with UH was uppermost in the committee's mind. The rationale for combining UH and TSU was vague but included such arguments as that the two institutions were too close together, that it was unnecessary to have a separate law and pharmacy school for minority students, and that TSU and UH offered many of the same programs.[20]

When the Select Committee met on October 18, 1986, Robert J. Terry had become interim president; and one of its members, George Mitchell, suggested that Prairie View, Texas Southern, and the University of Houston–Downtown should be phased out because they served to perpetuate segregation. George Mitchell went on to say that "if not closed, they should be redefined as academic institutions and placed under a different governing structure."[21] In keeping with his plan, Mitchell proposed that state-supported institutions be grouped under regional governing boards in order to eliminate turf battles among the thirty-seven separate boards. In other words, one board of regents could serve the University of Houston, TSU, Lamar University, and Sam Houston State University. Mitchell's comments came as the Select Committee neared the final phase of its year-long task to conduct an in-depth study of Texas colleges and universities.[22]

Although Mitchell argued that his comments were presented only as items for discussion, TSU faculty, students, alumni, and friends, as well as Houston's higher education leaders, were disgruntled over the potential dangers inherent in his proposal. Some saw it as an assault on the city; others saw it as diminishing the research role of the University of Houston. Still others viewed it as diminishing the independence of a black institution. TSU students, faculty, alumni, and friends were more vocal and aggressive in their protests over the merger. Mickey Leland, a TSU alumnus and a state representative, accused George Mitchell of pushing for a merger to pave the way for a University of Houston empire in the Woodlands. He also denounced Houston's business leaders and the chamber of commerce members for failing to speak out against the merger. Rodney Ellis, another TSU alumnus and city councilman said, "It is important that the city go on record saying we think our institutions are important and ought to remain the way they are." Harold Dutton Jr., a state representative and TSU alumnus, wrote an Op-Ed piece against merger in the *Houston Post*. Representative Larry Evans said that merger was a deliberate attempt to undermine the

... Ain't Nobody Gonna Close This University

TSU board members, alumni, city councilmen, state legislators, and friends rally to prevent TSU's merger with another university. Courtesy of *TSU Yearbook*, 1987.

Students rally to prevent the merger of TSU with another university. Courtesy of *TSU Yearbook*, 1987.

desegregation plan, and he volunteered to be the first plaintiff to oppose the state in court if a merger occurred.[23]

In 1986, after listening to, studying, and discussing various concerns and issues relating to a merger between TSU and UH, the commission came up with another proposal. This one would allow TSU to remain autonomous but called for the relocation of Texas Southern University to the campus now used by the University of Houston–Downtown. In return, Texas Southern would sell its Third Ward facilities to the University of Houston, and UH–Downtown would be phased out. To effectuate this plan, the commissioners resurrected Wilhelmenia Delco's bill, which called for a Texas Southern University system with a downtown satellite campus. Whatever assumption or intention the commissioners had in mind, Delco's bill never called for doing away with the TSU Third Ward campus.[24]

Without a doubt, the planned move of TSU to the UH downtown campus galvanized the black community like no other issue dealing with merger had before. TSU Board of Regents quickly requested a hearing before the Select Committee. When it was granted on November 21, 1986, ten buses and a caravan of cars with over one thousand supporters of the administrators, faculty, students, allies, and friends converged on the state capitol in Austin. Most prominent among the speakers were Congressman Mickey

Leland and interim President Robert Terry.[25] Mickey Leland reminded the commissioners that TSU was established "to educate African Americans and now it's being taken away. It's being taken away although blacks have never been given their forty acres and a mule."[26] Terry had the most direct and piercing assault on the proposal. As he stood before the committee to a thunderous ovation from supporters, Terry made it clear that TSU viewed the current proposal "not as defining our role, scope and mission, but as affirming to disestablish TSU as a viable institution."[27] He minced no words in saying that the proposal made no sense educationally, economically, legally, or morally. "To be asked to surrender our traditional identity, our history, our integrity, one hundred and twelve acres, and forty buildings in exchange for a renovated fifty-year-old office building, a downtown motel and parking garage is hardly a fair or equitable exchange or trade," said Terry. While admitting that the university understood the state's need for money in hard economic times, as well as its responsibility for better management and accountability, Terry urged the committee to be cautious about the explication and assumptions inherent in the proposal. He further pointed out that (1) TSU had been a victim of discrimination, but did not perpetuate segregation; (2) TSU had been a part of the Texas State System of Higher Education for many years, longer than UH; (3) TSU was not a duplication of UH; and (4) TSU did not seek to take any part of UH.[28] Part of his speech is therefore instructive:

> Officials of the state of Texas needed simply to recognize that it had erred in offering this specific and far-reaching merger proposal. Forty years ago in 1946, my state erred when it denied Heman Marion Sweatt admission to the University of Texas solely because he was black. The state of Texas, which has been the state of my family for more than a hundred years, increased that error in 1947 when it bought the Houston College for Negroes for the sole purpose of perpetuating segregation through the establishment of Texas State University for Negroes. The state of Texas magnified that error in 1963 when it ignored Texas Southern University's existence and brought the University of Houston into the Texas State System of Higher Education, thereby perpetuating segregation by creating a second state-supported university in a city where one already existed.
>
> The state of Texas further confused the matter when it gave permission for the creation of the downtown campus of the University of Houston, which duplicated Texas Southern's open admissions policy and thus brought it into direct competition with TSU for its

traditional clientele. It is the same catch-22 that has always thwarted the legitimate aspirations of blacks. We are most often excluded from the game, and then when we are finally granted admission, the rules have all been changed. There obviously was no perpetuation of the segregation rule in 1947 when Texas Southern was established or created. Evidently, there was no "one state university per city" rule in 1963 when the University of Houston was brought into the system. And undoubtedly there was no duplication of effort prohibition in existence when the downtown campus was created. Now that all these things over which we had absolutely no control are in place, the rules are once again to be changed—to our detriment. That is not fairness, and to us that is not justice.[29]

After TSU's presentation before the Select Committee, Chairman Larry Temple admitted privately that he did not have the votes to effectuate the merger, but he did not make such an announcement until Governor Mark White came out against the proposal. White argued that "merging Texas Southern University with the University of Houston–Downtown would hurt alumni participation at these institutions and damage the University of Houston's chances of becoming a major research center." Texas Southern's backers celebrated on December 12, 1986, when the Select Committee formally dropped any further consideration of moving and merging TSU with the University of Houston–Downtown.[30]

With the issue of merger behind him, Terry then turned his attention to the upcoming budget (1987–88). As the university prepared to go to Austin to request funds, an undetermined number of students owed tuition fees for the 1986 fall semester; and the governor-elect William Clements proposed to eliminate at least $49 million in special line items in universities across the state. These special line items included funds for Thurgood Marshall School of Law and over $3 million for scholarships. Terry asked the legislature for an $18 million increase in the next biennium. Included in the addendum appropriation was $3 million for students who could not afford the escalating college costs. Terry was successful in getting the budget increased from $35.7 million to $37.5 million. The extra money was to be used to strengthen the law and pharmacy programs and student scholarships.[31]

Six months after TSU's budget was approved, Terry met an untimely death on September 12, 1987, when his car was hit by a train not far from campus. Again, the university was left without a permanent president. The search for a president, which had begun prior to Terry's death, was now expedited. Meanwhile, from October 1987 to July 1988, the Office of the

President was run by Otis King, assistant to the president, Melvin Bergeron, vice president for financial affairs, and William Moore, vice president for academic affairs. After months of this leadership, the board decided that the university would fare better with an interim president; therefore, it called on E. O. Bell to assume the helm until the search committee and the board decided on the next president. By December 1987, the board had decided on William H. Harris, but he did not assume office until July 1988.[32]

8

Toward a Bold New Vision

The Harris Era, 1988–1993

Texas Southern's seventh president, William Hamilton Harris, came to the office with a bold new vision to make "academic excellence" the cornerstone of a new era. At age forty-three, Harris became the youngest president of the nation's third-largest historically black institution of higher learning. Prior to his sojourn to TSU, Harris had served as president of Paine College in Augusta, Georgia, for six years. He earned a bachelor's degree from Paine in 1966 and was awarded the master of arts and the doctor of philosophy degrees in history from Indiana University (Bloomington) in 1969 and 1973, respectively. After serving as a Fulbright Scholar in Hamburg, Germany, for one year, he returned to Indiana University, where he served as associate professor of history and associate dean of the Graduate School. Harris was also the founder of the Committee on Institutional Cooperative Minorities Fellowship Program (a successful project designed to encourage and help finance minority attendance in Graduate School). During his stay at Indiana, Harris wrote and published two books—*Keeping the Faith: A. Philip Randolph, Milton P. Webster, and the Brotherhood of Sleeping Car Porters, 1925–1937,* and *The Harder We Run: Black Workers since the Civil War.* He also served as president of the Association for the Study of African American Life and History, the oldest black learned organization in the country.[1]

When Harris assumed the presidency in July 1988, the university faced many challenges. Shortcomings in its accounting system, low graduation rates, and problems relating to accreditations of professional schools all plagued the university. Not only had TSU's enrollment plummeted from 9,500 to 7,000 in two years, but it did so at a time when the Texas Higher Education Coordinating Board was predicting that by the year 2000 the

William H. Harris, 1988–1993. Courtesy of *TSU Archives*.

fastest growing colleges and universities would be minority institutions—UT–Pan American, UT–El Paso, Texas Southern University, and Prairie View University.[2] Also, at this time, the School of Business was trying to regain its accreditation, and the School of Law was in need of money to maintain its own. The university itself was going through a routine review by the Southern Association of Colleges and Schools for reaffirmation. Moreover, the new president would have to stave off regular attempts to close or merge the university and adroitly juggle the inadequate funding that had plagued the university for years. Without a doubt, TSU needed a strong leader with a vision and determination to bring the university to a point of excellence. Harris believed that he had this vision. As he boldly proclaimed, "Any institution that would have a future must have a vision and that vision must be sufficiently bold to point the direction for decades to come."[3] Only time would tell if he would be that leader with a vision to implement plans with boldness, courage, persuasion, and integrity.

In Harris's first appearance before the board of regents on July 15, 1988, he described what he considered the objectives of his job as president. They were to secure the academic integrity of the university; to secure the financial integrity of the university; and to maintain the university as a pleasant, dynamic, and diverse community in which to live, work, and study.[4] Harris enlarged on these points at a specially called meeting of the Academic

Council four days later. In expanding on his first priority of academic integrity, Harris argued that it was the administration's and faculty's duties to establish a strong academic foundation, but this foundation could come only with good teaching and by maintaining standards. "We must know what a baccalaureate degree means," said Harris, "and [must] make sure that everyone who graduates has the knowledge and qualities we have determined to be essential."[5] While his emphasis was placed on the undergraduate program, Harris was quick to add that "we must not build undergraduate strength at the expense of reducing the quality of graduate and professional training. . . . We will work with the weaker ones and encourage and support the stronger ones."[6]

At the meeting, the president spoke of the need for fiscal integrity and for making the university a more humane community. "In order to maintain fiscal integrity, the university must pay its bills on time,"[7] said Harris. "We must stop our auxiliaries from failing us. We must organize our resources along functional levels."[8] This statement was undergirded by the state auditor, who said that TSU's bookkeeping should be improved. While acknowledging that planning had occurred in various units of the university, Harris pointed to the need to develop a long-range strategic plan for what the university should be and how to get there. Thus, Harris's first two years can be dubbed as a time of challenge and discovery.

Challenge and Discovery

A month after speaking to the Academic Council, Harris addressed the TSU family—the administration, faculty, and staff. There, he spoke of the dawning of a new era of academic excellence and reiterated the three objectives of his job. Before a packed house in the university auditorium and responding to the rumor about a possible merger of TSU with another Texas university, Harris told the crowd, "I came to TSU because of my belief in the mission of TSU, not to oversee its demise."[9] His words were well-received as applause and cheers erupted from those in attendance. He then proceeded to speak of TSU's future and of how he expected to bring the university into the vanguard among colleges and universities. "Our future," he emphasized, "is not in the past, but in the students who are here now and in the years ahead."[10] At this meeting, he also spoke of some of his personal goals for TSU. He wanted to set up three centers—for educational outreach, for the dissemination of cancer research information, and for black males. The audience was attentive as Harris concluded his speech by invoking the words of Benjamin Mays: "Failure [comes] not in failing to reach one's goals, but in having no goals at all." He went on to say that "even if we fail to reach the goals we set, no one can say that we had no goals at all." In launching this new era, Harris was quick to add that "a new era does not suggest that the past is less worthy." To him, it meant that "now was the time to take stock of where the past had brought us and to reach for a new era of greatness."[11]

Two of the major problems that confronted Harris during his first two years were a negative financial report from the state auditors and the state-mandated Texas Academic Skills Program (TASP). To tackle these and other issues, Harris set up an interim leadership team that included Llayron L. Clarkson, interim vice president for academic affairs; Deanna Lott Burrell, interim vice president for student services; Donald Mullet, vice president for financial and fiscal affairs; Joshua Hill, vice president for facilities planning and operations; Melvin Bergeron, special assistant to the president; and Nell S. Cline, executive assistant to the president. Putting a good administrative team together was of course extremely important to Harris. This would be the team that would place him on the road to realizing his vision.[12]

Meanwhile, Harris moved quickly to resolve fiscal issues amid mounting criticism. Early in 1988, it appeared that TSU had started to iron out some of its longstanding financial problems; but when the audit report came out in October 1989, it revealed that "TSU continued to have major weaknesses in its finance and accounting systems—resulting from spending and investing irregularities."[13] This report was followed by two negative articles in the *Houston Post*, which indicated that TSU had a multimillion dollar deficit in one year, when in reality the figure was a cumulative deficit covering a period of several years. Harris immediately accepted full responsibility and took corrective action. He sent a written response and had a face-to-face meeting with the audit committee, as well as a face-to-face meeting with Governor William Clements. These efforts, however, were not enough to convince the governor that TSU was moving in the right direction or to deflect the cries for merger or conservatorship.[14]

To overcome this financial hurdle, the administration took steps to put policies and procedures in place that resulted in the employment of a major consulting firm, Deloitte and Touche. This firm advised the university on ways to reorganize and restructure the entire fiscal and management information service area. Subsequent implementations of the recommendations were costly to the university in terms of software and personnel, but they led to the purchase of the Banner Information System Software, which placed the university in a much-improved position with regard to management information retrieval and dissemination, on the one hand, and creditable financial reporting, on the other. As a result of action taken, the university received a clean audit in 1991. Jubilant over the outcome, Harris wrote Governor Ann Richards about the state auditor's report for the period during which he was fully in charge: "I am delighted to let you be among the first to know that it shows our central weaknesses are resolved."[15]

While working to correct the fiscal problem, the Harris administration had to deal simultaneously with the Texas Academic Skills Program (TASP). In 1988, state law mandated that all students entering Texas's public institutions for the first time in the fall of 1989 would be required to take a state test to demonstrate certain proficiencies in English, mathematics, and reading. TASP was destined to have a great impact on TSU, which was an open-admissions university wherein a large percentage of the students were required to take remedial courses.

To respond to the challenges inherent in the Texas Academic Skills Programs, Llayron Clarkson, interim vice president of academic affairs and a former vice president under Leonard Spearman, organized the General University Academic Center (GUAC) as the academic home for all entering students and as the main office to house the developmental courses required by the Texas Academic Skills Program (TASP), namely, reading, English, and mathematics. As a self-contained unit, GUAC had oversight for the following: (1) all advisement services for freshmen; (2) all adjunct teachers in remedial courses; (3) the reading unit, which was removed from the Department of English; and (4) all schedules for remedial classes and the enforcement of class attendance policy. From time to time, Harris reminded the faculty that nothing was more important for the long-range future of the university than improving students' performances, especially on TASP. Harris lamented the fact that students' performances on examinations had become the centerpiece for what is done in higher education, but he maintained that TASP was a matter of both law and fact. It was, therefore, incumbent on the faculty members to do everything they could to assist students in demonstrating adequate performance. Among the many reasons TSU should have been concerned about TASP was the fact that it was an open-admissions university with a large number of students who did not meet TASP requirements, a fact that could impact the university's funding and graduation rates at a time when the state was contemplating performance-based funding.

Concomitant with the previously mentioned challenges, Harris had to prepare a budget and go before the Legislative Budget Board (LBB) for its approval in 1989. In keeping with his theme of academic excellence, Harris went before the LBB with five priorities. First, realizing that the single most essential element of any university is the faculty, he asked for funding for faculty salaries so as to enable the university to recruit and maintain a faculty of high quality, as well as to make TSU faculty salaries competitive. Second, he requested funds for departmental operating expenses to make available to university personnel the resources necessary to carry out their responsibilities. Priority three dealt with special items to support academic programs. Because the legislature recognized the impossibility of providing adequately for the support of all institutions through a single formula, it complemented university budgets with special items. But in the 1989–90 academic year, TSU's special items were under assault. The TSU administration was concerned with the devastating impact that a lack of special items would have on its professional schools' accreditations, as well as on students' performances on TASP. If these funds were cut, TSU would likely lose $2.7 million, which Harris argued was absolutely necessary if TSU were to protect the integrity of the academic programs.[16]

Harris's fourth priority was closely related with that inherent in the above. Whether as a special item or otherwise, funds were requested for TASP. Given the history of test results both in Texas and the nation as a whole, black students (the vast majority of the overall population at TSU) required remediation in larger numbers than did the general college population. While not squabbling with this disparity, Harris pointed out that once the tests show the weakness, "TSU can provide the remediation that has been proven in the past. But the fact that if the state required the university to perform their responsibility, it is incumbent on the state to provide the financial support that this task will require." Priority five asked for the continuation of the Texas Plan and support for maintenance and safety. While acknowledging that funds from the Texas Plan had transformed TSU in terms of quality programs and physical facilities, Harris argued that much work remained undone.[17]

Harris reminded the LBB that a lot of the commitments made under the Texas Plan had not been realized. For example, the proposed College of Education Center for Excellence never got off the ground. Funding for maintenance did not keep pace with the expansion of buildings and other facilities, nor did the statewide formula for police protection provide equitably for maintenance of safety and prevention of crime for TSU. Just as TSU benefited from its location in Houston via its association with businesses, the medical center, and other educational institutions, it suffered from that location regarding matters of safety. Located in a depressed economic area of the Third Ward, the very dynamics of the nation's fourth largest city carried with them high crime rates; therefore, a request for additional funds was not unreasonable nor extravagant.[18]

Harris and his team left the budget hearing hopeful but with mixed feelings since there was talk that the proposed budget would be cut. So, after returning to TSU, Harris wrote Representative Larry Evans, in whose district the university resided, and asked for his support and influence in getting the LBB to restore $57,000 in special items for the law school, which had been cut to 25 percent of its total budget. Were the legislature to sustain this and other cuts, it would have been devastating to TSU. The law clinic would disappear and the university would lose $253,000 in faculty salaries. This essentially would have meant an end to TSU's law school. Likewise, Harris wrote State Representative Wilhelmina Delco and asked her to use her influence as chairperson of the Higher Education Committee to restore TSU's special items. Harris minced no words in telling her that "if the goal of TASP is to be achieved, there is need for more money. [TASP] placed additional requirements upon the academic community without reducing one bit of responsibility we already have." Harris also wrote Lt. Governor William P. Hobby and asked for his intervention in having riders removed from TSU's appropriations bill. His letter writing continued as he thanked Representative Evans for writing to Governor William Clements and asking him to place TSU's fee increase for the Student Life Center on the calendar during the special session.[19]

As Harris strove to achieve academic excellence, his mantra was "good teaching," teaching that would build a strong foundation, teaching that would develop the strong, the average, and the weaker students. Harris was wholly mindful of the number of students who came to the university with academic deficiencies, but at the same time he did not overlook those who came with above-average abilities. Not only were the administration's recruitment efforts focused on getting the "best and the brightest," but the Honors Program under the leadership of Professor Patricia Williams was greatly enhanced. More importantly, the president emphasized the fact that the great majority of TSU students were neither highly gifted nor in grave need of remediation. So, part of the university's challenge was to make sure that it met the needs of those who were gifted as well as those who needed remediation, on the one hand, and those mainstream students who were progressing at a regular rate, on the other hand. A necessary ingredient in meeting this challenge was good teachers. So, Provost Bobby Wilson, along with a faculty committee, developed an evaluation instrument that would reward good teachers. At the same time, U.S. Congressman Craig

Washington, an alumnus of TSU's School of Law, assisted the president in procuring more funds for the professional schools via Title III.[20]

Concerned about extending the university's activities beyond the normal classroom relationships, the university created and funded a number of outreach centers. The first was the Cancer Awareness and Prevention Center. It had as its major goal the dissemination of information concerning ways to prevent cancer and to inform poor and minority people about how to get the help they deserved regarding this disease. Another center, commonly referred to as the Center on the Family, housed the Black Male Initiative (BMI). In the 1980s, TSU, like many HBCUs, faced a problem of retaining the black male population. The BMI's main objective, then, focused on improving the social and educational conditions of the black male by developing plans that included mentoring, counseling, and tutoring. The expectation was that TSU would take the leadership role in increasing the number of black males graduating from college. Complementing this center was the proposed Center for Teaching Excellence, which focused on improvement in the levels and quality of the faculty's and students' relationship, but the center never came to fruition.[21]

The center that stirred the most excitement and offered the widest possibilities for innovative leadership was the Mickey Leland Center on Hunger, Poverty, and World Peace. Mickey Leland, a Texas Southern University alumnus and a U.S. congressman from the Eighteenth Congressional District of Texas, dedicated a great portion of his life to providing for the less fortunate, especially through efforts to provide food for the hungry. It was on such a mission that Congressman Leland lost his life in August 1989 in an airplane crash in the mountains of Ethiopia. As a part of carrying forward the work of Congressman Leland, Texas Southern University established the Mickey Leland Center on Hunger, Poverty, and World Peace to serve as the centerpiece for disseminating information and for developing policy statements on a wide range of matters having to do with hunger, distribution of food, and the problems of peace throughout the world. The center was funded from private sources in the amount of $1.6 million. TSU purposely defined hunger and world peace broadly so as to enable a wide range of scholars to bring their best thoughts and ideas to matters having to do with peace, hunger, and conflict resolutions. This center added a unique and exciting new element to the life and development of Texas Southern University.[22]

Though not a center in the same vein as those described earlier, a major effort was made to reestablish Texas Southern University as a center of culture in Houston. The university reestablished the Cultural and Lyceum

Committee, both to focus attention on the importance of art, music, and literature as a part of the students' larger education and at the same time to expose the students to outstanding artists and scholars. TSU's emphasis on the arts enabled it to reactivate the jazz archives and make available to both students and the public this rich and rare repository of African American music, a unique collection at Texas Southern University.[23]

In addition to meeting the usual challenge of carrying on the regular activities required of the university in establishing community outreach centers, the Harris administration made a concerted effort to improve the overall quality of life and work at the university. With the availability of Higher Education Assistance Funds, major renovations were done to buildings and grounds. Major steps were undertaken to intensify campus beautification, lighting, and cleanliness. Funding sources were also provided for student services, which expanded student operations year-round.[24]

Within two years of Harris's administration, one could easily see changes at the university. Two years prior, a number of prominent Texans had been questioning the relative benefits and costs of maintaining TSU as an independent university and thus called for its closure or merger. Since then, TSU's burgeoning enrollment seemed to demonstrate that such a course would have been ill-advised. Though the university had received bad press in the past, by the beginning of the 1990–91 school year, the university appeared to have received more positive press, perhaps in part because of a good relationship established between the university and the media, and because TSU was given an opportunity to participate in the 1990 Economic Summit of Industrialized Nations, held in Houston and hosted by President George H. W. Bush. TSU was involved in the local planning for this worldwide event, and it also provided a collegiate exhibit allowing the public to view TSU.

The Last Two and One-Half Years

The first two and a half years of Harris's tenure were marked by strenuous institutional self-examination, collegial deliberations, and creative thinking, which led to a strategic plan. The next two and a half years would be ones of change and implementation for the future. For example, the 1990–91 school year was exciting not only because it was the first full year of operation in a new decade prior to the advent of the twenty-first century, but it also was the year that TSU held a very important conference. It was a year during which President Harris would unveil his bold new vision and began talks of ending the open-admissions policy and of capping enrollment.

Faced with the challenges of a changing society, demographic realities, an evolving global economy, emerging new technologies, and environmental and health issues, the university's leaders decided to organize a conference titled "Developing Partnerships and Building Futures: TSU 2010–2020."

This conference was based on a premise and a belief that are worth noting. The premise was that TSU had a proud heritage, a dynamic presence, and a challenging future. The belief was that TSU must pursue the highest levels of educational development through a partnership between citizens and government if it was to educate, train, and prepare a competent workforce for the future. The objectives of the conference were (1) to develop ideas, goals and objectives central to the continued growth and survival of Texas Southern University; (2) to provide a forum for communication and cooperation between and among Texas Southern and its various publics; (3) to promote a better understanding of the university through dialogues about various programs; (4) to provide accurate and complete information on the university's accomplishments and projected needs; and (5) to develop priorities for action that would facilitate the development of educational activities responsive to the current and future needs of society. In a word, this conference was designed to elicit input from community, business and industry leaders, educators, alumni, public officials (elected and appointed), students, and citizens about issues, problems, policies, and programs that TSU should address in order to effectively meet the needs of society now and through the year 2020.[25]

The conference opened on November 9, 1990, with President William H. Harris laying out his visions: "Any institution that would have a future must have a vision, and that vision must be sufficiently bold to point to the direction for decades to come." Six goals projected within the "bold new vision context" were contingent upon TSU (1) becoming a national repository of black culture and art; (2) creating special programming for the education of black males; (3) becoming a national force in the preparation of a new generation of urban public school teachers; (4) designing and implementing programs specifically for the purpose of increasing the number of minorities who hold doctorate degrees; (5) enhancing health care programs, especially those designed to reach minority group members; and (6) increasing alliances with public school officials, community groups, and parent groups to ensure educational access for all students. Harris also targeted the establishment of new degree programs in the sciences and emphasized the continued development of nationally recognized outreach centers as a part of the new "vision." Harris was optimistic about the possibilities that these innovative and intellectually exciting initiatives could be achieved at TSU by 2020. Yet not unmindful that modern university presidents seldom have a thirty-year tenure, Harris still insisted on planning for the future, positing that "TSU will be here in 2020 and we must plan for its future."[26]

After this historic conference, the administration received a number of recommendations on how to effect the above goals, but at the same time the university had to deal with three major problems: a burgeoning enrollment; the call by the Texas Higher Education Coordinating Board to cap enrollments at public colleges and universities; and the issue of open admissions. In the spring of 1991, Harris reported to the board that there was an increase in enrollment. In fall of 1991, he wrote the board again, pointing out that "the university now has 10,080 students which put us over the 10,000 mark for the first time." But this growth was not achieved without producing some problems. Harris argued that this unprecedented enrollment was taxing on the university with regard to adequate space for teaching and adequate faculty members to provide instruction for this large number of students. He asked the board and the administration to take a serious look at what needed to be done about the future of the university in light of the increased numbers of students. At the November 1991 board meeting, Harris informed board members that the question of capping enrollments at state colleges and universities was being discussed by the state coordinating board. Because TSU was included among those institutions that were discussed, Harris told the board that "we must begin a serious study of what effect this would have on the university."[27]

When the discussion on capping enrollment began, Harris made it clear that he did not consider a cap as a potential denial of access to those who desired a college education. In his opinion, rather than placing a cap on enrollment, TSU should establish admissions standards. Currently, students were required only to have a high school diploma or to make a passing score on the GED to be admitted to the university. It should be pointed out that this was not always the case. From the inception of the university to the late 1960s, entering students had to have followed a college-preparatory curriculum that included coursework in English, mathematics, reading, social studies, history, and science. TSU, like many other colleges and universities, relaxed its standards in the late 1960s as more students entered college and more financial aid (Pell Grants) became available. But Harris did not want to impose admissions standards based on grades or on entrance examination scores. Rather, he wanted to return to the standards that predated the Sawyer administration. Once these standards were in place, TSU would inform its feeder schools (especially those in the Houston area), prospective students, and their parents about the academic requirements a student must meet before he or she could be admitted to the university.[28]

Discussion of capping enrollment at TSU was intermingled with the open-admissions policy, although formal discussion of the latter would not occur until March 1992. The issues of providing for an education of high quality and of ensuring access to educational opportunities to underserved populations have bedeviled the higher education community for decades. Because Harris was convinced that the two were not mutually exclusive, and because he believed that TSU was uniquely positioned to demonstrate the fact that both goals could be accomplished, he asked William Harrell, chairman of the Faculty Assembly, to establish an ad hoc committee to study ways to assure the students of both access and quality, and to issue a preliminary report accordingly. When the faculty committee completed its work, it issued a preliminary report, a portion of which was in the form of questions for the president. Many of these questions— regarding a cap on enrollment, the minimum requirements for admissions, and a college-preparatory curriculum in high school—had already been answered by Harris in prior meetings with the faculty, the local press, and the board; but he reiterated them again. When the committee's report was finally completed, it supported the position of the president. So, on June 5, 1992, Harris went to the board meeting with a proposal for imposing admissions standards at the university.[29]

No sooner than the June 5, 1992, board meeting was over, the media, some alumni, and students were screaming that the open admissions policy was under assault. Harris responded with an article in the *Houston Post* entitled "If our children are going to learn more, we must demand more." In it, he admitted that he had recommended to the board of regents that "TSU should consider setting a wide range of expectations for high school graduates who would apply to the university." More specifically, he recommended that prospective students follow a college-bound curriculum before being admitted to the university. Harris further argued that the admission criteria should not work a hardship on students who came from schools that simply did not have the resources to offer a broad range of proposed courses. Instead, he envisioned that a university admissions committee would make appropriate evaluations of the records of such applicants. These statements were not enough to quell the concerns of many. One regent, Walter Criner, did not agree with the recommendation, stating that he stood alone against the idea when it was first mentioned and that he still stood against it. Regent Odysseus Lanier stressed that the admission policy had potential, but that he was weighing the pros and cons. Rufus Cormier emphasized that the

admissions policy requirement was only a proposal that had to be scrutinized and developed in great detail.[30]

Because a large percentage of TSU students were enrolled in developmental courses, Harris felt that it was incumbent upon the university to
be bold and courageous in pushing for a change in the admissions policy.
So, he went before the board with a completed proposal in December 1992.
There, he informed the board that the TSU faculty had voiced its approval
of the coordinating board's recommendation that by 1996 all public colleges
and universities should have a college-preparatory curriculum requirement
for admission. Though he believed that admissions standards were essential
to the future of the university, he argued that the faculty, students, and general public ought to be clear on the steps the university should take to effect
the change. He asked the board to consider establishing certain admissions
standards. Following a positive board recommendation, the administration
would make its decision within several months so that all constituencies of
the university would have ample opportunities to have appropriate input
into the decision. Harris admitted that when discussion began on this topic,
it deserved the widest possible debate. Later, he remarked rather facetiously,
"I am not sure that I envisioned that the debate would be quite as wide as it
has been."[31]

To convince the board, and at the same time to allay some fears about
admissions standards, Harris repeated some of his previous assertions.
"Students with potential will not be denied access as the faculty committee was considering a two-step admissions procedure whereby applicants
without the requirements might be conditionally accepted and monitored
closely for a period and then be given an opportunity to earn unconditional
admission by diligent work." Harris argued that TSU was on the right track
with its admissions standards and that the debate about this issue was help-
ful if it did nothing more than make a few potential students and their parents choose a course of study wisely while students were still in high school.
Again, he implored the board to study this proposal and to make a decision
that would benefit all of the people of Texas.[32]

Time is seldom kind to people who dream and have bold visions, and
Harris was no exception. One week after Harris submitted his proposal
for admissions standards to the board, some members of TSU's marching
band, the Ocean of Soul, who had been selected to play for a football game
in Tokyo, Japan, at the Coca-Cola Bowl, were accused of shoplifting $22,000
worth of merchandise from a Tokyo store. This event made worldwide news.
After an investigation, not only was this charge confirmed, but the investigation further revealed the fact that twenty-two persons who accompanied

the band were not students at TSU. Moreover, $30,000 in band funds could not be accounted for. Harris subsequently closed down the Ocean of Soul, fired its director, and suspended several students. Harris's action led to an outburst of indignation not just over the band's many problems, but over his decision to dissolve the band since not every member was involved in the illicit activities.[33]

In the wake of very little support and of mounting opposition, including rallies, petitions, and a television editorial by investigative reporter Marvin Zindler, Harris gave ground, saying that the band would be reorganized but under a different name. That still was not good enough for State Representative Ronald D. Wilson of Houston, who filed a bill in the Texas Legislature requiring that the school retain the name "Ocean of Soul" once a new band had been formed. Perhaps yielding to all of this, Harris allowed twelve of the suspended students back in school provided they would take an ethics course; another seventeen were put on probation. Shortly thereafter, for whatever reason, Harris submitted a letter of resignation on February 17, 1993, and stated his intention to give up the presidency at the end of August 1993.[34] "There comes a time in our career, when we look back on our accomplishments and measure the distance that remains to fulfill our personal sense of purpose," wrote Harris.[35]

When Harris's tenure as TSU's president ended, he could point to several significant achievements. Enrollment rose from 7,500 to more than 10,000 students. Sponsored-research grants increased from $6 million to $18 million annually. The university's first PhD program was created in environmental toxicology. Harris also increased and enhanced the academic programs and started a Black Male Initiative Program under former Houston mayor Lee P. Brown. Likewise, the Mickey Leland Center and the Center on the Family had their beginnings under Harris's leadership. In dealing with low graduation rates, Harris sought to raise the admissions standards and to expand the appeal of TSU beyond open admissions. Under Harris's tutelage, the museum and culture committee brought to campus such notables as Nelson Mandela. After the university's many years of inaccurate bookkeeping, Harris and his staff won a clean bill of fiscal health from the state auditor in 1991. It can also be argued that he established the best presidential relationship with the Faculty Assembly since its establishment in 1978. He likewise created the Office of Provost and Vice President for Academic Affairs, and the Office of Senior Vice President for Business and Finance. Together with the Office of the President, these two constituted the senior leadership at the university.

President Harris and TSU Basketball SWAC Champion, 1990.
Courtesy of *TSU Yearbook*, 1990.

Without having received a statement from either Harris or the board, one can only speculate about the reasons for his departure. It was well known that he was trying to upgrade the university by setting admissions standards that were higher than those of the open-admission era. Ironically, for attempting to do this, he obviously had made some enemies. He also made some people angry when he dissolved the TSU band. A number of TSU officials said Harris resigned because he wanted to initiate the six goals in his "Bold New Vision" and to make TSU a comprehensive university with a full range of academic programs, whereas regents wanted to direct resources toward a few specialized areas where TSU could excel. In a word, the regents wanted to cut out or do away with programs that were not attracting enough students. Some even opined that the disagreement between Harris and the board over the direction of the university intensified when he was given a five-year contract extension with the possibility of his taking a sabbatical leave if the two parties could not reach an agreement. If one accepts the speculation about the disagreement, the relationship was likely to have gotten worse, given the imminent appointment of four new regents who were pushing for TSU to reduce its scope. The regents' secrecy regarding their differences with Harris did nothing to strengthen the institution entrusted to their care. One observer of institutions of higher education seemed somewhat prophetic when he opined that the board's action regarding Harris's departure could only make TSU's future a tumultuous one.

9

In Search of a New Direction

The Horton Era, 1993–1995

Joann Horton, the first female and eighth president of Texas Southern, assumed office in September 1993, at a time when the university was in search of a new direction. Six months prior to her arrival, the university was in a state of flux. While the TSU family, as well as the larger Houston community, was transfixed by the scandal surrounding the Ocean of Soul Marching Band, the leaders of the university were wrestling with issues more important than extracurricular activities. They were dealing with preexisting management problems and had to find a new president. Rather than conduct a long and arduous search for Harris's successor, the board decided that it was possible to name a new president in six months. A nineteen-person search committee was subsequently formed and chaired by regent Walter Criner. The committee consisted of five board members and one faculty member, along with alumni and community and business leaders of diverse ethnicities. The faculty component constituted the smallest group of the committee, yet it was the faculty whom the president would come in contact with most frequently.[1]

By May 1993, the committee had reviewed sixty-five applicants. In June, the board narrowed the finalists to five and later to three: Otis King, former dean of the law school; Leonard Hayes, former Department of Education assistant secretary for post-secondary education; and Joann Horton, a community college administrator. After a five-month search, the board of regents selected Joann Horton; and on Friday August 6, 1993, the TSU board chairman introduced Joann Horton as the university's eighth president. At forty-six, Horton became the first female to head the forty-four-year old state institution. She earned two degrees in French from Appalachian State University before receiving her PhD in higher education and public

Joann Horton, 1993–1995. Courtesy of *TSU Archives.*

administration from The Ohio State University. Prior to assuming the presidency of TSU, Horton was an administrator in the Iowa Community College System, which consisted of fifteen institutions. In that role, she was responsible for providing leadership and implementation for system-related policies, planning, and budgeting. Before 1989, when Horton took a job with the Iowa Junior College system, she had spent ten years as an administrator in the Chicago Community College System. A cursory review of her vitae revealed that her skills were more managerial than scholarly. That the regents would turn to Horton seemed to suggest something about what they felt TSU needed at the time.[2]

Horton came to the university at a time when it was beset by many problems. Although Texas Southern University had received one clear audit from the state in 1991 and had ironed out a number of fiscal issues, there were still many problems that remained when Harris left office. For one thing, financial aid and the athletic department had deficits that bordered on scandals.[3] The faculty was in somewhat of a quandary as to the direction of the university. An unprecedented growth in students was taxing the university in terms of both space and instruction. In addition, the university lagged far behind in technology, and there was a need for a new strategic plan that incorporated both long- and short-range goals. The chair of the Faculty Senate, William Harrell, questioned whether Horton was up to the task.[4]

Many individuals had questions as to whether Horton's background and experience adequately prepared her to take on a "troubled" histori-cally black institution. Others argued that a male would be more suited for the position. Horton's reply was that "when the TSU Board of Regents employed me as president, they charged me with improving the administra-tion and operation of the university." More importantly, the board pointed out to Horton particular areas of concern that called for immediate atten-tion. Some of these included TSU's lengthy response time to requests, the university's seeming inability to make decisions in a timely fashion, and its alleged failure to follow policies and procedures. Coupled with these alle-gations, the university was also riddled with lawsuits.[5] How Horton would meet these challenges would, in time, determine her presidency. Would she listen to all sides of the story, or would she simply follow the dictates of the board? What would she do about problems that were not clearly delineated by the board? For example, what would she do about open admissions, an issue that was left unresolved by the last president?

When Horton arrived on campus in September 1993, she, like other past administrators, enjoyed a honeymoon. The faculty seemed willing to give her administration a chance; and many of the females on campus were pleased about her presidency and viewed the board's selection as a step in the right direction for the women's movement. While a few men thought that the job should have gone to a man, Horton felt that she had broken a glass ceiling. For those who asked about the gender issue, Horton said that before she arrived at TSU, she was informed that a male-chauvinist environ-ment existed at TSU, but that she was up for the task.[6] On the other hand, members of the board, all men, were protective of Horton. At the opening fall convocation, the board set a new precedent by formally introducing the president to the faculty, students, and staff, thus undergirding their support for her.[7]

During the first semester of her administration, Horton spent most of her time meeting formally and informally with faculty, staff, and students to ascertain their feelings and concerns about the university. As she met with these groups, they were interested in finding out her views about an open-door admissions policy for students, about how to attract more gifted stu-dents to the university, and how her past experiences could help improve

TSU. In her responses, Horton stated that she was opposed to eliminating open admissions but that she would work to establish quality programs that would attract gifted students. It was her feeling that the university could establish a better relationship with business by providing quality programs. Horton further believed that her "hands-on" management style allowed her to better understand what was happening on campus and at the same time allowed students to approach her more easily. But as she met with various audiences, she informed them that she was working on a "change agenda" given to her by the board.[8] This board agenda included some concerns about policies and procedures, about improving the quality of education, about customer service, about improving management organization, and about planning at the institution. Horton made it clear that she would rely on her experience as a manager in the implementation of this agenda.[9]

By December 1993, Horton had formulated and presented to the board her goals and objectives for the coming academic year, 1994–95. These goals included (1) establishing a strategic plan for the university (including refinement of its mission by 1995); (2) reviewing the organizational structure and making realignments to improve effectiveness; (3) establishing a coordinated plan for fundraising and development; (4) improving the registration process by 1995; (5) establishing and implementing a communication plan within the internal and external communities in 1994; and (6) improving the organization and operation of board-related activities. After making this presentation, Horton informed the board that she "was now ready to make recommendations for change, both in organization and personnel." Faced with the many challenges that TSU presented and with the implementation of these goals, only time would tell if and when she could fulfill these objectives.[10]

At the same time that Horton was defining her goals and objectives, she was preparing for her investiture. As the event approached, excitement about the first female president made it appear that everyone on campus was preparing for the inauguration. The inaugural activities included a student visual and performing arts tribute, an inaugural symposium, an inaugural community program, the investiture ceremony, an inaugural reception, the inaugural ball, the alumni inaugural brunch, and an inaugural ecumenical service. At the investiture ceremony, held December 15, 1993, the following dignitaries attended: Texas governor Ann Richards; Houston mayor Bob Lanier; members of the Texas House and Senate; members of the Texas Black Caucus; and representatives from institutions of higher learning. Horton's theme for this ceremony was "Change, Renewal and Redirection." At this ceremony, she also laid out her vision for the university: "My

21st century vision for Texas Southern University," said Horton, "is one of an open, dynamic, learning center environment dedicated to excellence and empowerment of students and its broader community in order to be competitive in the international marketplace."[11] Her vision also included a viable plan that "would position the university to establish a clearly focused strategic direction." Horton, therefore, called on each of TSU's supporters to play an active role in shaping the university.[12]

In keeping with her "change agenda" and her goal to restructure the administration, Horton made a bold move by removing seventeen administrators in six months. One week before her inauguration, Horton asked for the resignations of the provost and academic vice president and the director of institutional research. Later, in December, the football coach was relieved of his duties. He did not leave quietly. He refused to serve in any other capacity and demanded the university honor his contract for the rest of the year. This was a sign of things to come. With the opening of the spring semester, the president was well on her way to a complete administrative shake-up. Beginning with the reorganization of the Office of Academic Affairs in May 1994, Horton asked the board for approval to abolish four positions: associate vice president for academic affairs and director of the Frederick Douglass Institute; director of the Weekend College; associate vice president for academic affairs and dean of the Graduate School and Research Studies; and assistant vice president for academic affairs and director of the GUAC program. Afterward, she asked the board to establish the following positions: assistant vice president for institutional enhancement; dean of the College of Continuing Education; dean of the Graduate School and Research Studies; and associate dean of the College of Arts and Sciences. Likewise, she requested to reassign the GUAC program to the College of Arts and Sciences and to redesignate the Weekend College as the College of Continuing Education.

Subsequent to the May board meeting, Horton told her acting provost, Franklin Jones, to notify six administrators that they could either sign a letter of resignation or be terminated from their administrative duties by 5 p.m. on the same date. These administrators included the director of Title III; the associate vice president for academic affairs and director of the GUAC program; the director of the Leland Center; the director of academic computing; and the vice president for the Graduate School and Research Studies. Two other resignations would come by the end of the summer—the dean of the College of Arts and Sciences and the vice president for student affairs. The associate vice president for academic affairs and the director of Frederick Douglass Institute resigned prior to May 27, 1994. So, in her first year, seventeen TSU administrators were removed from office via firings or resignations. Responding to critics of her action, Horton informed the board that while the changes in leadership were unsettling to some, they were designed to accomplish her goals and objectives. The changes, she said, were made to move the university forward.[13]

There were mixed reactions to Horton's action. Some praised it and said that it was long overdue. Others contended that it caused controversy that would haunt Horton throughout her administration because some of the firings were considered to be handled insensitively and because the firings left the school without much experience at the top. There were some who said the firings were justified, that TSU had hired too many of its own graduates and kept them in place too long. Others argued that whether or not the firings were deserved, some people who had devoted twenty to forty years of their lives to TSU should not be told one day that they must submit letters of resignation and be out of their offices by 5 p.m. on the same day. The editor of the *Houston Sun* said, "[Horton] always had the power to fire, but I think I would look at people first and make assessments, and if I made changes, I would have made competent replacements." State Representative Ronald Wilson took the opposite view. He said, "Of all the presidents in the last 20 years at TSU, Horton has taken the boldest steps to clean it up."[14]

Horton's firing of so many administrators at one time not only drew media attention and gave her critics something to "chew on" but also cost the university money. Rather than waiting for the administrators to complete their twelve-month contracts, Horton dismissed them with time remaining on their contracts, filling their vacancies with interim appointees. The contracts had to be honored and the new appointees had to be paid, requiring two salaries for a single job. It is estimated that these redundancies may have cost the university up to $300,000. In July 1994, a few months after the firings, the university posted a $2.8 million shortfall that required laying off many staff and part-time instructors and implementing a hiring freeze. Not only did faculty morale sink, but student enrollment decreased. Coupled with all of this, the local media had a field day reporting negative stories about the university. Things got so bad that Reverend William A. Lawson wrote Rufus Cormier, chair of the board, about the president, saying "I love supporting the university . . . but the university is in pain. . . . The media is not friendly to us right now and we cannot allow an unfriendly media to define us. Will you convene a meeting so that we can discuss this matter?" A lack of evidence prevents one from knowing if this meeting ever took place.[15]

After one year in office, Horton had completed only one goal (restructuring the administration) and had worked on others—students' empowerment, customer service, and strategic planning. On the issue of customer service, some student groups praised Horton for being less aloof than the previous administration and for meeting with them at regular intervals.[16] Although Horton spoke of strategic planning, the bulk of the work on this goal did not come until her second year. During her first year, Horton contended that she was simply trying to deal with problems she had inherited; but her critics charged that many of her problems were of her own doing. Some claimed that she was too disruptive and was only taking advice from a small group of faculty, commonly referred to as her "kitchen cabinet." [17] Important items such as faculty promotions and tenure were postponed during her first year because of what the administration described as a lack of funds to comply with these achievements. Some critics said that as a leader, Horton failed to engender the respect and loyalty of her faculty, the very individuals who were responsible for the most crucial work of the university. Instead, they charged that she played the game of symbol and rhetoric: "Fire people, send press releases to the media, present new faces in new places and that will equal change." When asked about any of her actions, Horton simply said that she was pursuing a change agenda mandated by the board.[18]

In all fairness to Horton, not all of the problems she faced in 1993–94 were of her own creation. The $2.8 million shortfall that the university experienced can be attributed to many factors: a $250,000 (buyout) liability to comply with the contract of former president William Harris; overestimating an increase in spring enrollment; and housing costs for Horton at the Warwick Tower because she had refused to live in the Presidential House.[19] Additionally, the July and August 1993 state audit reports criticized TSU's board for not effectively dealing with a $495,000 deficit in the athletic program.[20]

Horton did not do a great deal to explain her actions during her first term. Instead of discussing the state of the university with the faculty, Horton decided to give an assessment of her first year in office in an article in TSU's 1994 *Fall Quarterly*. Responding to changes she had made in the administrative structure, Horton made it clear that in keeping with her mantra of "change, renewal and redirection," the need to change the administrative structure had become paramount. She further pointed out that the cornerstone of her administrative plan was to create a structure that would do the following: link the university and the community together in the attainment of achievement and institutional effectiveness;

enhance the university's accountability; eliminate slowness in decision-making processes; strengthen internal as well as external communications; and allow the university to establish standards against which to measure performance.[21] To many, Horton seemed to have been long on "talk" but short on details. Despite Horton's "cornerstone" statements, as well as the hiring of a new provost and a special assistant to the president, the faculty still questioned the direction of the university.

In an attempt to respond to faculty concerns, Horton called a meeting of faculty and staff on the evening of September 21, 1994. At that time, no one knew for sure what the president was going to say. Horton chose the student cafeteria for the meeting place instead of the auditorium because she did not want to "sit above her audience." She wanted to be on the same level with the faculty, to touch and be touched. Among many things, she talked about preparing students for the twenty-first-century marketplace, about building her team, and about empowering students. She said nothing about the budget or programs but made it clear that the university would enforce policies and procedures, and that those external reports would be delivered on time. During the course of her presentation, and in what may be perceived as a swipe at her critics who questioned her academic credentials, Horton noted, "I, too, have a Ph.D. degree." Following her presentation, when asked "why no one had heard of the promotion and tenure decisions," Horton evaded the question by saying, "The letters are forthcoming." When one of her critics from the *TSU Voice* asked if she was satisfied with the manner in which the former administrators were fired, she said, "Yes, next question."[22] Once again, most faculty felt that the president had not made the case with regard to the direction in which the university was moving.

Horton went into a second year amid a great deal of criticism from within as well as from outside the institution. By this time, she had appointed Vernon Clark as provost, and apparently she felt that she could devote her attention to developing a strategic plan and to carrying out her priorities for the 1994–95 year. These included initiating curriculum reform, improving graduation rates, restructuring the financial aid delivery system, securing adequate resources to compensate faculty, improving the student learning environment, and enhancing computer assisted support. But these items were not accomplished. Instead, Horton soon found herself responding to the state audits in August 1993. Three separate audits about the operations at TSU had identified three similar problems. Specifically, these audits determined (1) a material weakness in the Office of Financial Aid; (2) a material weakness in the central environment of the athletic operations; and (3) significant control weaknesses in the registrar's office, in human resources, in athletic operations, in student services, and in the university-wide monetary system.[23] Horton and the board were informed of these findings in March 1994, but she did nothing about them. In fact, Horton, the board chairman Rufus Cormier, and other regents held extensive discussions regarding preparation of an appropriate response when the audit would be released. Later, when the audit was made public via the *Houston Chronicle*, Cormier had to write Horton about her response to the press.[24]

In July 1994, the *Houston Chronicle* released excerpts from the audit indicating that the auditor had informed the university that he had found $300,000 in questionable costs in the university's financial aid awards. This included payments to ineligible recipients, excessive payments, and payments that were not properly documented.[25] Financial aid was important to TSU since 80 percent of its students depended on it. When Horton responded, she conceded some problems, saying that the school had a short-term plan to stabilize this situation, including several thousands of dollars in student loans. Horton also indicated she had fired the financial aid director and the registrar and replaced them with interim appointments. But in the case of financial aid, her replacements had limited or no background relative to the complexities of the job. By making such appointments, Horton compounded the problem of financial aid. Consequently, registration became more chaotic, and enrollment began to drop. In the end, the TSU internal audit office pledged corrective action was being taken on each of the items mentioned above.[26]

While working to achieve compliance with the audits, Horton continued to discuss her agenda items with the board for the next year. Her plans included developing criteria for curriculum reform, improving student graduation rates, restructuring the financial aid delivery system, securing adequate resources to compensate faculty and staff on a more equitable basis, improving the quality of the students' learning environment, and enhancing the computer system support services.[27] Before Horton could address these and other issues of her job, she found herself having to respond to two more audit problems—in the athletic program and in the School of Pharmacy. Deficits and discrepancies in the athletic program had shown up in the August 1993 audit report but had not been dealt with by the president. These came up again in the June 1994 audit, and in 1995 they were being disclosed by the *Houston Chronicle*. This time, Horton cooperated with the auditor and acknowledged TSU's wrongdoing and also the firing of the track coach. Coupled with the problems in athletics was an ongoing investigation of at least one pharmacy student who allegedly had received the state pharmaceutical licensing test prior to sitting for the exam. While this charge was eventually dropped, it was nevertheless a distraction for the president.[28]

Amid all of the aforementioned negative publicity came a silver lining. In April 1995, an exhibition of the works of John T. Biggers, a nationally renowned artist and retired TSU art professor, was featured by the Houston Museum of Fine Arts. "The Art of John T. Biggers: A View from the Upper Room" traced Biggers development as an artist over five decades. Biggers, who had retired in 1986, had lived in Houston since 1949 when he established the Art Department for Texas Southern University. This exhibit generated great publicity for the university; but it was not enough to ease criticism surrounding the embattled president.[29]

Arguably, the beginning of the end for Horton came on March 10, 1995, when the TSU chapter of the Texas Association of Colleges and Universities held a press conference and demanded the resignation of the president. A flyer was passed out which read, "Faculty, Staff and Students: Take a Stand and Vote No Confidence in Joann Horton to our Regents." When Otis King, the chair of the Faculty Senate Assembly, participated in the press conference, many felt that this was a result of "sour grapes'" because King had not been selected as the eighth president of TSU. The board of regents had simply ignored the outcry for the removal of Horton, but one month later, when King was elected chair of the TSU Faculty Senate, King called his election a repudiation of the Horton administration. "If you vote for a person as outspoken as I have been, I think you are in general agreement with my positions."[30] To a certain extent, this statement was true. King's publication, *The Voice*, relentlessly attacked Horton throughout her administration; and King, who had lost a previous Faculty Senate election, now ran on the slogan, "You know where I stand." In this 1995 election, King emerged victorious.[31]

By May 1995, the campus was rife with rumors that Horton's days were numbered. State Representative Al Edwards, president of the Texas Legislative Black Caucus, took those rumors seriously and a made a plea to the board to keep and extend Horton's contract after its date of maturity. One member of the board of regents responded to this request by outlining the board's plan and its expectations of Horton. "I think it would be in the best interest of TSU for the Black Caucus to support the Board and acknowledge the fact that the Board made an error in its decision to choose her and move on down the road to make Texas Southern the outstanding school which it can become."[32] Whether Horton had been informed of this regent's criticism during her annual performance review is not certain. What is known is that rumors intensified and expanded throughout campus the last week

President Joann Horton congratulates John T. Biggers on the naming of the John T. Biggers Art Center. Biggers, a distinguished faculty member, is a world-renowned artist. Courtesy of *TSU Yearbook, 1996.*

in May, suggesting that something would surely happen at the next board meeting.

At the board meeting on June 2, 1995, the earlier rumors were confirmed. The board voted not to extend President Horton's contract beyond its current maturity date in August 1995. It was further agreed by members of the board that a search would begin immediately for a new president and that this person would assume office on September 1, 1995.[33] The board gave no reason for its action beyond the fact that Horton had lost the confidence of the board. This decision put the university in a state of confusion. Notwithstanding the action by the board, Horton would be allowed to remain on the campus as a lame duck for four months. During that time, Provost Vernon Clark and pharmacy dean Henry Lewis would resign from the university. On August 2, 1995, Horton named James M. Douglas, dean of the law school, as interim provost.[34] Inasmuch as Horton had worked to put financial aid policies in place and was responsible for the newly installed Banner Information System, she wanted to (and did) monitor the fall registration, but much to her chagrin, the fall registration was not a success.

By the end of the registration process, Horton and the TSU Board of Regents entered into an agreement for her to resign from the university. The agreement was intended to be maintained in a privileged and confidential file in the custody of TSU's General Counsel Office. Neither Horton nor the board was to discuss in writing or orally the terms of that agreement. But according to a copy of this agreement, obtained under the state's Public Information Act and published by the *Houston Chronicle*, TSU regents paid Horton $216,000 to buy out the last eleven months of her contract. So, she exited the university campus on October 1, 1995.[35]

It can perhaps be said that Horton's administration was uneventful in the life of the university, with nothing accomplished, nothing gained. No doubt she followed the dictates from the board in an administrative shakeup of the university, but other problems ensued and therefore she left the university in a very unstable condition for years to come. To be sure, two years are a short period of time to accomplish much, especially with regard to the typical length of a university presidency. But if the board decided to end Horton's tenure with good reason before her contract ended, one has to wonder whether Horton had been very impressive in the presidential search interview or had become totally overwhelmed by the university's problems after she arrived. Did politics play a role in the selection process, or did having only one member of the faculty on the search committee prove vital enough to inform members of the search committee of the pressing problems of the university's past, present, and future and so influence them in a different direction? Neither Horton's coming, her two-year stint, nor her departure from Texas Southern advanced the institution in any positive way.

10

Toward an Urban Academic Village

The Douglas Era, 1995–1999

When Joann Horton left the TSU presidency on October 1, 1995, the university was in a state of confusion and uncertainty, and it was beset with management and fiscal problems. The expansion of the student body by 3,000 students since 1992 strained the Office of Financial Aid and created a new series of problems that the university thought it could resolve under Horton, but the problems were still haunting the institution when she left, the state auditor's findings notwithstanding. To give immediate attention to this matter, the board turned to its newly elected chair Enos Cabell, a former Astros baseball player and businessman, and to James M. Douglas, who was named as interim president. These two individuals had a monumental task before them. For Douglas, the university administration was still reeling from massive turnovers from the past two years. Many faculty and students had complained publicly about low morale. As for Cabell, he was elected as chair to a divided board by a 3–2 vote over his opponent, a board which gave the appearance of being more concerned with politics than with the best interest of the university. By Cabell's own admission, the board of regents was divided. "We're not really a board right now . . . we've got to get to know each other so that we can become one." Cabell went on to say that the board's first objective was "to get everyone to pull together and heal the university and the board." Despite what appeared to be a chaotic and divisive situation, both Douglas and Cabell said they were determined to resolve TSU's problems. Douglas expressed confidence that he could perform at a level that would make the university remove "interim" from his title. Cabell echoed Douglas's statement by adding that he also hoped Douglas's performance would be such that the regents would not have to launch a national search for the president. Whatever inferences that can be drawn

James M. Douglas, 1995–2000. Courtesy of *TSU Archives*.

from the above statement, on December 8, 1995, Douglas was selected by the board as the ninth president of the university.[1]

A native of Onalaska, Texas, Douglas graduated from Texas Southern University in 1966, receiving a bachelor of science degree in mathematics. He earned his JD degree in May 1970 from the Thurgood Marshall School of Law at Texas Southern University, where he graduated first in his class. One year later, he continued his legal studies at Stanford University's School of Law, where he received a master's degree in computer law. Douglas began his teaching career as an assistant professor of law at TSU in September 1971. He then continued his teaching career at Cleveland State University's Marshall College of Law in September 1972. In September of 1975, he joined the faculty and administration at Syracuse University's College of Law. In July of 1980, he joined Northeastern University School of Law and remained there as a faculty member until returning to his alma mater in 1981, when he became the seventh dean in the history of TSU's Thurgood Marshall School of Law.[2]

There was a swift reaction to the announcement of Douglas as president. Despite being a veteran administrator, a former dean, and provost, he had many detractors. One of his main nemeses was Otis King, chair of the Faculty Senate. Furious that the faculty had not been involved in the selection process of the new president, the Faculty Senate voted 18–1 to censure the board of regents for ignoring the by-laws of the Faculty Senate, which called for such participation. Since the faculty is the group with whom the president interacts closely and directly, and since the university's accreditation agency (SACS) called for shared governance, the faculty felt that the board was making a grave mistake by not asking for the faculty's input. Some faculty members argued that the Douglas appointment could serve only to divide the faculty. Still others contended that the university now should put the students first and end these rumors over the president. Given the state of affairs at the university, many faculty members felt that this was not the time for the board, the faculty, or the president to be at odds with one another. These concerns notwithstanding, the board's decision stood.[3]

Before Douglas could lay out the plans and goals of his administration, and before he could prepare for his inauguration on March 4, 1997, he had to give his undivided attention to the financial aid crisis. Financial aid problems did not start with Douglas, but they were now under his purview. In December 1993, President William H. Harris had been informed by the internal auditor that the university's financial aid records were in disarray. The state auditors confirmed the same. In that same year, Congress toughened the accountability rules for institutions receiving students' grants.[4] TSU subsequently purchased the Banner Information System Software to assist in this regard. Six months thereafter, Harris resigned and was succeeded by Joann Horton. During Horton's tenure, the auditors continued their investigation and in March 1994 reported to Horton that they had found more than $300,000 in questionable costs in the university's 1993 grant awards.[5] When nothing was done about the situation, the Department of Education kept the pressure on the state auditors to review TSU's 1993 grant awards in more detail. The auditors then inspected a cross section of files, noting further discrepancies and questionable costs. Based on these findings, a projection was made for all of them. By the time Douglas assumed the office of president in October 1995, the questionable cost had grown to $13.6 million. Shortly after he was named permanent president, the state auditors issued a financial aid compliance report for the university. The auditors' report cited inadequacies in the administration of Federal Family Education Loans and Federal Pell Grants that had combined expenditures of over $41.5 million.

It should be noted that managing financial aid at any institution is a complex task. For the process to work smoothly, there must be coordination among the admissions, registrar, and bursar (business) offices. Also, students are required to document their financial needs and to provide academic transcripts from universities or colleges attended. Copies of all documents are supposed to be maintained in confidential files in the financial aid office, and the contents of these files are to be placed in the university's computer. Maintaining such records at TSU had not been easy. To do so was often complicated by the following: a large number of transfer and part time students; TSU's open-admissions policy, which allowed students a second chance if they failed at another college; students' decisions to apply for financial aid and admission to the university at the last minute; and an increase in the student population, which caused the financial aid office to make awards and then hope to catch up on the record keeping later.[6]

Douglas had been on the job only two months when he received a letter from the state auditor stating that TSU was now at risk of losing its financial aid. If the university were to lose financial aid, this would have had a devastating impact on enrollment since over 80 percent of the student body depended on this aid. Upon receipt of this letter, Douglas called a press conference and sent an open letter to the faculty and staff informing them of the situation. He informed the media that he accepted responsibility "to get [TSU's] house in order," but that it would take time because both he and over half of the regents had been in office only a few months. In his letter to the faculty, Douglas laid out his strategies for improving the financial aid services. They included an audit of all financial awards made during fiscal year 1995–96, random audits by internal auditors to ensure integrity, continued evaluation and training of staff, and periodic audits of the financial aid unit to ensure that these guidelines and strategies were monitored. The financial aid director was subsequently removed.[7]

Despite these efforts, in March 1996 the federal government placed TSU on reimbursement. Under reimbursement, the university puts up the money for student grants from its own state resources. The federal government repays the university when the university provides documented proof that monies have been properly awarded. The auditors predicted that TSU might have to advance its students as much as $8 million for 1996–97; and if TSU did not get the money back in time, the May 1997 checks could start to bounce. In April 1996, President Douglas and the board of regents chairman Cabell went before the Legislative Budget Board (Higher Education Committee) and intimated that they were working on the financial crisis. They said that they would resign if the university's financial affairs were not in order by January 1997. The task before them proved easier said than done.[8]

In November 1996, the state auditors warned black state lawmakers that TSU's financial situation had been reviewed and had reached such a crisis stage that the school's very existence was in peril. The *Forward Times* reported that the state auditors had been put on notice by the Department of Education (DOE) that reimbursements for federal loans and grants were being withheld until TSU made outstanding federal payments. In a word, the auditors recommended that TSU be placed under a conservatorship and be run by a special team answerable to Governor George W. Bush, Lt. Governor William P. Hobby, and Speaker of the House Pete Laney. While most faculty members opposed the conservatorship, Otis King, chair of the Faculty Senate, embraced it as "the only way to save the university."[9]

Shortly after the audit report was issued, Douglas released his "management principles"—to make the train run on time (toughen control and responsibility); to improve services to the most important customers, namely, the students; to increase student academic performances; to maintain compliance with all audits; to initiate teamwork and team spirit throughout the university's workforce; and to render fair compensation. These principles were to serve as the blueprint for the day-to-day operations of his administration. To ensure consistent follow-through on these important principles, Douglas created an oversight system that consisted of an executive committee, a special-purpose task force, and the president's cabinet. Together, these groups were to determine the university priorities and strategies in order to make sure that the university's mission and goals were communicated to faculty, staff, and students and to target special areas of the university for improvement.[10]

Coupled with his management principles was Douglas's vision for the university. But before he released his vision, Douglas solicited from the university faculty and staff answers to four questions. What kind of campus do you envision—comprehensive, commuter, residential? What should the role and status of the General University Academic Center (GUAC) be? What is our commitment as an open-admission institution to develop education? And what is the role of athletics? [11] Douglas considered answers to these questions in formulating his vision for the university. His vision was to broaden TSU's scope as a special-purpose institution for urban programming by transforming the campus into an urban academic village. The latter focus included developing a residential academic environment designed to nurture academic excellence in personal growth and in civic responsibility. With this vision, Douglas went before the Seventy-Fifth Legislature in January and requested approval of $8.5 million in special items for the purpose of maintaining and improving the academic infrastructure of the university. Some of these funds were to be used for building an Urban Academic Village.[12]

The Academic Village was the focal point of Douglas' inaugural address, given on the same date as the fiftieth anniversary of TSU's Charter Day, March 4, 1997. In Douglas's view, TSU could and would become an academic and cultural oasis in Houston's Third Ward. It would be a place where students would live, study, work, and play in a highly charged educational environment. Douglas explained his concept of the Urban Academic Village thus: "We will return to the basics. We will require a more structured . . . and intellectual environment. We will require more production in the classroom. We will work the minds of our students on campus." He further contended that bringing the students to campus and into an academic village was imperative if TSU were to accomplish its mission; that moving them from an old environment to an academic village would transform the students from passive learners to active learners. Ideally, the village would be a community wherein students, faculty, and staff would live in a twenty-four-hour intellectual environment, replete with housing, recreational facilities, and retail zones—all dedicated to the purpose of preparing students for the future. The optimistic Douglas was proposing an idealistic vision at a time when the university was beset with financial problems, when 80 percent of the students depended on financial aid, when the university's dormitories had deteriorated, and when the trend for most college students was to live off campus. Only time would time reveal whether his dreams would be realized.[13]

Meanwhile, Douglas's inauguration was a unique occasion. Sharing the stage with him at this august event were four of the five living university presidents—Samuel Nabrit (1955–66); Granville Sawyer (1968–79); Leonard Spearman (1980–86); and William H. Harris (1988–93). These former leaders shared experiences during their administrations and discussed current issues facing higher education.[14]

After the inaugural day festivities filled with pomp and circumstance, Douglas had to return to an issue that would determine the fate of the university—financial aid. Prior to the inauguration, black lawmakers had entertained the idea of drafting a bill to assist TSU with its financial troubles. On March 10, 1997, the president was greeted with good news when he was informed that state lawmakers had approved a $10.4 million loan to the institution to be used during the 1997–99 fiscal biennium to pay off debts and loans.[15] The bill called for the board of regents to appoint a team of outside experts to assist in establishing a comprehensive internal oversight system of control in finance and accounting, human resources, management information systems of planning and communications, and student financial aid. The bill also called for the administration to produce quarterly reports of fiscal and administrative practices. And if state auditors determined that substantial and demonstrable progress had not been made by June 1, 1998, a recommendation would be made to the Seventy-Sixth Legislature in 1998 to place TSU under another system.[16] Because this bill concerned the autonomy of TSU, Douglas was reluctant to accept the money. Still hopeful, the Douglas administration argued that the university was up to the task of improving financial aid. The administration had put rules and regulations in place to make certain that students would provide proper documentation before receiving an award.[17] But did TSU have the manpower, computer system, and a sufficiently trained staff to effect this change, and how soon would students accustomed to submitting paperwork at the last minute change their habits? Time would be the judge of these concerns.

Although elated over the bailout money that was promised TSU by the legislature, the Regents at the board meeting on August 29, 1997, unanimously approved a $60.6 million budget without having to dip into the $10.4 million bailout fund.[18] The university officials estimated that the university would finish the fiscal year with a surplus of $5 million.[19] This announcement prompted an Op-Ed in the *Houston Chronicle* titled "Getting It Right: TSU . . . Making a Good Faith Effort to Get Its House in Order." It argued, "The TSU boat is floating on serene financial waters . . . a bit of good news that everyone needs to hear."[20] But was TSU floating on serene waters or thin ice? Did the board's action lead to unity or to division? Preoccupation with the university's financial difficulties seemed to have overshadowed all other concerns, namely, recruitment, falling enrollments, and graduation rates.

In the midst of the financial aid crisis, an election of board officers resulted in the ouster of Enos Cabell, board chairman and strong supporter of Douglas. At the October 10, 1997, meeting, Willard Jackson, a Houston businessman, was elected by a 6–3 vote over Cabell. Sentiments expressed at the meeting made it clear that the next two years were going to be strained. Partisan politics had become more apparent than ever. Cabell, a Republican, had not been successful in unifying the board. Douglas, a visible and outspoken Democrat prior to becoming president, was not totally embraced by some Grand Old Party regents, although he said he was willing to work with the board regardless of regents' political affiliations.

Despite the president's olive branch, the fight with some of the regents became evident early into his administration. For example, Willard Jackson and Douglas got into a squabble regarding who had the authority to hire personnel at the university. According to Jackson, Douglas told him that he was not going to let the board tell him whom to hire. Jackson, in turn, questioned Douglas's hiring of two staff persons and so cautioned him that he should inform the board of his action in this regard. Short of this, Jackson quipped, "We may take necessary steps to select your replacement." Douglas's response was that the board delegated authority to the president to hire personnel for the administration, including employment and termination. Under the university policy, it seemed clear that the president of the university had the authority to hire members of his own staff, and that the lines of authority and responsibility of the president and the board chair were clearly drawn. Yet the scope and limitation of their individual and collective responsibilities remained blurred.[21]

The next board meeting did not occur until November 21, 1997; and with only two weeks left before the president's contract expired, the meeting ended without a statement about it. Inferences drawn from the above action indicated that silence did not mean approval. At the same meeting, the board denied the Douglas's recommendations for a law school dean by a 5–2 vote. Four days after the meeting, the student body president and about one hundred students staged a rally in support of Douglas.[22]

Whether in response to the student demonstration or not, on that same day Willard Jackson issued a ten-page statement arguing that the flow of inaccurate information made it necessary for him to address the severity of the situation at the university. In bold print the statement read: "The overall financial situation at the university did not improve over the past year, but rather deteriorated." Willard Jackson further said the only reason the university was not out of money was that more financial aid reimbursements had been collected than the state auditors had projected, and that more grants and contract monies had been collected than expected. In the all-important category of cash balances, state treasury account number 247, which previously totaled $2.8 million in 1995, had now dropped to $1.4 million in 1996, and it dropped even further in 1997, according to Jackson. Jackson argued that there was not a $5 million surplus as reported by the president at the August meeting. Moreover, no student files had been submitted to the U.S. Department of Education since the past August.[23] To rectify the situation, the board began to make plans to use the $10.4 million to meet some of the university's obligations and to put together a team of experts to bring Texas Southern into compliance with the state audit to help strengthen the financial affairs at the institution. At this point, Douglas appeared to be at odds with the board on this issue, but he obviously believed that his administration could overcome the indebtedness without using the bailout money.[24] This schism between the board and the president would widen even more at the next board meeting.

Student rally to keep James Douglas as president. Courtesy of *TSU Yearbook,* 1998.

When the board allowed Douglas's contract to expire and commented only at its December meeting that the chairman was appointing a committee to review the president's performance, everyone, including the *Houston Chronicle,* agreed that TSU faced a leadership crisis.[25] The issue most agreed upon was that long-term, stable leadership was crucial to TSU's survival as a freestanding institution. The question was, who would be the best to lead? Uncertainty sparked demands from students, alumni, and community leaders to retain Douglas. Students occasionally staged rallies, and black lawmakers lobbied the regents to keep Douglas in order to maintain stability. Their pleas came amid plans to place TSU under another university system if both fiscal and management progress was not shown by June 1, 1998.[26] State Representative Garnet Coleman asked the board to keep Douglas since he was the administrator the legislature had been dealing with and a lack of sustained leadership would hurt the university.[27] During the prior legislative session, Douglas had assured the lawmakers that he would be at the helm of the institution a long time and would make every possible effort to fix financial aid.

In fairness to him, Douglas had made a concerted effort to overhaul the financial aid areas. Students were now required to provide proof that they qualified for federal aid before Pell Grants, loans, and work-study monies were awarded. The president put new policies in place and replaced the financial aid director with one who was more knowledgeable about college financial aid. Douglas and his staff also worked on the university's master plan—a plan that included a study by a team of planning professionals, TSU faculty and staff, the Metropolitan Transit Authority of Harris County, the University of Houston, the Houston Independent School District, and the Third Ward Development Corporation. Together these professionals were to come up with ideas that would transform the Third Ward area where TSU resides. The plan also called for renovated and new campus facilities and housing to encourage students to spend more time on campus and on their studies.[28] As a result of this plan, the Fairchild Building was renovated, and plans were made for a university museum. But even these efforts were not enough. Without having its financial house in order, the university was still at a crossroads.

The longer the regents took to make a decision regarding Douglas's contract, the more Douglas's supporters coalesced and vowed to keep him in office. This coalition consisted of community leaders, students, ministers, elected officials, business owners, and TSU alumni. By February 1998, Douglas's contract and the autonomy of TSU had become one and the same. Prior to the April board meeting, the student body president issued a statement indicating that the students were taking over the negotiations for the president's contract. Expressing similar sentiments for Douglas was the Inner City Network of community supporters, which issued an even harsher statement that urged "saints, soldiers, scholars, and dealers to mobilize and go to Austin to express their sentiments [about the leadership at TSU] to Governor George W. Bush."[29] With tension building, when the board meeting was held on April 21, 1998, it lasted only ten minutes because students and community residents occupied the boardroom floor and demanded that Douglas's contract be renewed immediately.[30] Unwilling to forcibly remove the students, Chairman Willard Jackson adjourned the meeting. This action only exacerbated the friction behind closed doors among members of the board. According to excerpts of a confrontation published in the *Houston Chronicle*, Anthony Lyons asked Willard Jackson to resign as chairman after the April meeting, citing "an inability to exhibit essential leadership skills." Jackson replied, asking Lyons to "do TSU a favor and quit." Many individuals left the meeting feeling that if the situation went unresolved, it would result in violence against some of the university regents.[31]

While the regents prepared for their May meeting and awaited the committee's performance review of Douglas, the "Coalition to Save Douglas" held a news conference at the NAACP's local office on May 18 and called for a march on the same day. Nearly three hundred people rallied at TSU and made clear their demands that TSU should remain an independent institution, that President James Douglas ought to be awarded a contract, that no chief operating officer should be hired, and that Regent Thomas Friedberg should be asked to resign.[32] Protestors accused Friedberg of favoring placing TSU under another system. Claiming "We have documented proof," Justice of the Peace Al Green went on to say, "You can't sit on the Coca Cola Board and push Pepsi."[33] Others saw the action of the board as purely political, with a Republican majority controlling the board of an HBCU. As the discord between Douglas and the board grew wider, more and more faculty aired their grievances with the regents rather the administration. Instead of referring disgruntled employees to department heads, immediate supervisors, or top-level administrators, some regents entertained the issues all by themselves. Such action by the regents was not unique to this administration. Many exhibited such behavior since the inception of the university, but during the Douglas era, this behavior seemed to have happened much more frequently than at any other time. Coleman called the situation surrounding Douglas's contract a "pressure cooker in the community."[34]

Bowing to pressure in a hastily called meeting on May 22, 1998, five out of nine board members voted to give Douglas a two-year contract extension, thereby ending speculations about his tenure.[35] There were unconfirmed rumors that those who voted for Douglas did so because of pressure from community leaders and elected officials. Yet, the two-year contract was a compromise because Douglas had been negotiating for a three-year deal, and some regents supported him, while others were considering giving a one-year contract or even just dismissing him.[36] According to Otis King, Douglas was supposed to have been fired at the May board meeting but wasn't because troopers from the Department of Public Safety and at least one Texas Ranger were present on campus in anticipation of violence in the absence of the approval of a contract.[37] Moreover, these troopers, along with TSU's security force, cleared the TSU library, where the board meeting room was located. There were also rumors that Houston's riot policemen were stationed a few blocks away from campus in case they were needed. On the contrary, the announcement of Douglas's contract was met with cheers and applauses in a jam-packed board room that included such individuals as State Representatives Garnet Coleman and Harold Dutton Jr., NAACP president Howard Jefferson, Reverend James Dixon, and the Nation of Islam minister Robert Muhammad.[38]

Although many had hoped that the extension of the contract would at least give the appearance of stability at the troubled institution, it did not. Needless to say, the discord between Douglas and the board grew even stronger after the May board meeting. The regularly scheduled board meeting for June was cancelled, prompting Douglas to write members of the board: "I want to make it perfectly clear that the administration is in no way at fault for the cancellation. Much has been said lately about the necessity of my administration to get things done and I totally agree [but] we must work collectively to get things done."[39] In what appeared to have been retaliation against the regents who opposed Douglas's contract renewal, when the board met in July, the regents who were present voted 3–2 to replace the current chair Willard Jackson with Gene Moore.[40] Jackson was not present at the meeting; and Moore, who at first was opposed to Douglas, was now willing to side with his supporters to become chair of the board. Voting along with Moore were Anthony Lyons and Enos Cabell. Martin Wickliff and Albert Black Jr. opposed the motion.[41] When Jackson heard of the board's action, he took his case to court. In a court settlement, the judge ordered Jackson to hold another election at the next board meeting, and whoever received the majority of the votes would be declared the winner. At the October meeting, Jackson received the majority of the vote and was therefore reinstated as chair.[42]

Now with his having a two-year contract in hand, more pressure was placed on Douglas to straighten out financial aid. The university had entered into an agreement with the Department of Education (DOE) to settle the debt by August 26, 1997. This debt was based on a total liability that had risen to $40 million from fall 1993 to spring 1997. The DOE was ready to settle for $20 million. If the university would accept the offer, the DOE would lift the reimbursement restriction and again advance financial aid payments to students. Douglas's much smaller counteroffer was rejected almost immediately. David L. Morgan of DOE wrote the university in April 1998, telling the president that $20 million was a very conservative estimate that TSU would be required to pay. He went on to say that if TSU would pay that amount, the DOE would forego the review it had made of TSU in May 1994. On the other hand, if TSU did not pay, the DOE would proceed with a review, which the university could not appeal.[43] As the fall semester approached, the admissions office was projecting a decline in enrollment, and Douglas began to consider using the bailout money. His decision to use this money was reinforced, in part, by the state auditor Lawrence Alwin's report on October 3, 1998, that stated "TSU has made some progress toward improving accountability . . . ; however, the actions taken have not yet achieved the result or outcome needed."[44]

Needless to say, board members were concerned about what could happen when the legislature reconvened in January. In short, the university's future was once more at risk. So, when the board met in November 1998, it voted to establish the position of chief operating officer, and it stepped up pressure on Douglas to fill other vacant jobs quickly. During the board meeting, even some of Douglas's staunchest supporters criticized the number of jobs that were still occupied on an interim-state basis. For example, Regent Anthony Lyons stated that there were interim deans in five out of six academic colleges. "Things continue to haunt us. Please fill these jobs by January. People don't see stability."[45] Other regents took turns showing their impatience with Douglas's inaction. "We cannot go into the next session without stability," said Willard Jackson. Douglas's response was that he expected two deans to be appointed by early January, and he downplayed the regents' concerns by stating that "I can't think of any major company that doesn't have vacancies."[46]

A week after the November board meeting, TSU students staged a rally and asked administrators to take steps to get the much-delayed financial aid from the federal government. Checks for nearly half of the student body had not been issued because DOE still was reviewing files to ensure that students qualified.[47] In response to this rally, Board Chairman Jackson issued a statement saying that he would be convening a special meeting of the board to address all student concerns, including those related to student services. "Clearly we are at a critical crossroads and we intend to solve the problems,"[48] said Jackson. Four days after Jackson's statement and before he could convene the board, the *Houston Chronicle* issued an Op-Ed titled "Warning, Texas Southern A Harrowing Place to Seek College Education." The Op-Ed argued that TSU has made a historic contribution "(that) runs mainly toward the past." It went on to suggest that "enrolling in TSU at this point would be like buying a ticket on the Titanic after it had hit the iceberg."[49] Despite the best efforts of the regents and administrators to dispel this view, it seemed that the students, faculty, and alumni were the ones most affected by this article. Many faculty did not take kindly to this Op-Ed, stating that it was unfair to link academics of the university with the financial and administrative problems. Others criticized it for suggesting

that the students should check out other local schools, such as UH–Downtown and community colleges.

Within two weeks, the outlook at the university began to change.
Whether in response to student demonstrations, the memo from the board
chairman, or the November 24th editorial in the *Houston Chronicle*, the
administration issued a statement stating that 80 percent of TSU students
who lacked financial aid two weeks prior could now receive their monies.
In other welcome news, the TSU board and administrators received a letter
from Representative Robert Junelle and Senator Bill Ratliff of the Appropriations Committee giving TSU permission to use $3.5 million in bailout
funds. But the monies had stipulations: "access to this emergency fund
[was] contingent upon successful resolution of the [TSU] problems and if
not resolved satisfactorily in the next 90–120 days [the state would pursue]
having a university system take over TSU." This was not the first time that
TSU had dipped into the bailout money. It had been used before, but this
time, the usage did not include restrictions.[50]

As the time approached for the legislature to reconvene and to make
a determination on the fate of TSU's autonomy, the board at its January
meeting discussed the hiring of a chief operating officer.[51] If hired, this person would oversee finance, administration, student affairs, external affairs,
budgets, and personnel. The vice president of those departments, many of
them interim, would report to that person. But the board did not vote on
that position because the president did not want to move forward since the
number-one candidate, Don McAdams, was being considered for another
position. Subsequently, McAdams withdrew his name as a candidate for the
other position, and at a specially called meeting, the board hired McAdams
as the chief operating officer.[52] Two weeks prior, Governor George W. Bush
named two new regents to the board and issued a statement expressing his
support for an autonomous Texas Southern, but he cautioned that a plan
was needed to address serious issues raised by auditors.

A few weeks later, after meeting privately behind closed doors on talks
about Douglas's performance since he had been given a new contract, the
board fired Douglas at its February 1999 meeting.[53] The regents referred to
this action as a "bold move" to stabilize the political and financial troubles
at Texas Southern. They also contended that the financial and administrative health had not significantly improved since June 1998. While newspaper accounts said that Douglas was stunned by the announcement of his
firing, he should not have been given several red flags—the board's refusal
to renew his contract, the hiring of a chief operating officer, and a divided
board.

Douglas's vision was to transform the TSU campus into an urban academic village and also to restore TSU to its former place of pride in the black community during the 1960s. Part of this vision was achieved, whereas another part was lacking. For example, under his watch, TSU established strong ties between itself and the constituent community, and it also established a transfer system to allow Houston Community College students to easily transfer their credits to TSU. The university during this time also formed a master plan calling for the renovation of the Fairchild Building and initiated the idea of the Urban Academic Village. Other parts of Douglas's vision were not realized, such as the need to fix the financial aid and other fiscal problems, to restore accountability, and, to use his own words, "to make the trains run on time" as far as the fiscal health of the university was concerned. To accomplish the latter, both he and the board needed to be in basic agreement. Instead, their disharmony left the university at the same crossroads in 1999 that it had faced in 1995. Douglas's departure meant that the university had seen three presidents come and go within ten years. Board members too often bickered among themselves or placed their own interest over the common good of the university. If such trends were allowed to continue, they would have a devastating impact on the future of the university.

11

Challenges, Opportunities, and Accountability

The Slade Era, 1999–2006

Texas Southern University was at a very critical point in its existence when James Douglas left the presidency in February 1999. The university was facing an April 1, 1999, deadline set by the state legislature for it to show cause as to why it should maintain its independence. Black lawmakers were calling for a reconstitution of the board of regents, a board that would fight to keep TSU from being placed under another university's system. As was the case in 1995, TSU now again faced many challenges. Chief among them were financial aid reimbursement, declining enrollments and declining cash flow, demographic shifts, leadership instability, and a negative press that impacted enrollment. Most of the rapidly changing technologies that would require innovative approaches to improve delivery of higher education services were lacking on the campus. While public and private resources were diminishing, demands for accountability at the state and local levels were increasing. Yet despite these challenges, there was a glimmer of hope for the university and for the opportunities that lay ahead in the Texas Plan that the state was negotiating with the Office for Civil Rights to bring TSU up to parity with its white counterparts in the state.

Given the above scenario, the board moved rapidly in naming Priscilla Dean Slade as acting president on the same day as Douglas's departure. Prior to being named to this position, Slade had served as dean of the Jesse H. Jones School of Business from 1992–97. She joined the TSU faculty in 1991. Shortly thereafter, she became chair of the Department of Accounting and then dean. Slade received her bachelor of science degree in business administration from Mississippi State University, the master's degree in professional accounting from Jackson State University, and a PhD in accounting from the University of Texas at Austin. Since the fiscal problems

Priscilla D. Slade, 2000–2006.
Courtesy of *TSU Archives.*

were the most pressing at the university, the board felt that a person with a background in accounting would be a good fit for the university at the time.[1]

Challenges and Opportunities

When Slade became the acting president, she said, "I feel as if I have a tremendous responsibility," and she did. She was assuming a job known for its political strife, financial migraines, and an ebb and flow in enrollment. One of her first tasks was to assemble an interim team to assist her in meeting the state's deadline for fiscal and administrative performance compliance in order to prevent a conservatorship of the university. In an unprecedented move, when the board fired Douglas, it also called for the resignations of the provost and the vice president for finance. This action made it easier for Slade to fill these and other positions. As such, Slade named the following interim team: Paulette Frederickson, vice president for finance; James Race Jr., provost; Gayla Thomas, director of institutional research; and Charlene Evans, executive vice president (a former assistant to Douglas). Less than six weeks on the job, Don McAdams, a Houston Independent School Board trustee, who had been hired in February 1999 as executive vice president and chief operating officer, submitted his resignation, citing overlapping responsibilities with the acting president. When questioned about the resignation, the chairman of the board stated that "the initial assignment given McAdams changed because of the strong financial and accounting background of Priscilla Slade."[2]

At the time that Slade assumed the presidency, Lawrence F. Alwin, state auditor, informed the board that "despite extensive assistance from [his office] and other agencies, the University has not made substantial, demonstrable progress."[3] Two weeks later, Terry Holderman, project manager from the State Auditor's Office, told the board of regents that the acting president and her staff had worked feverishly to meet short-term goals to improve the overall operation of the university. Thus, he was guardedly optimistic that TSU would meet the April 1 deadline of showing progress in stabilizing its finances.[4] When juxtaposing Alwin's statement against Terry Holderman's, several questions come to mind. How bad was the financial situation? What was the measuring stick for progress? And how much political influence was involved—Democratic vis-à-vis Republican?

Bolstered by the auditors' comments, Slade made her first appearance as acting president before the TSU family at the Charter Day celebration on March 4, 1999. In an attempt to pump up the audience, and perhaps to lift morale, Slade constantly reminded the group that the university was on its way back, that TSU's problems would be solved, and that the university would return to greatness. "Our eyes are not on the past but on the future,"[5] said Slade. A few days after Slade's remarks, Lieutenant Governor Rick Perry toured TSU's campus at the invitation of Senator Rodney Ellis, whose district included the historically black university. At the time, Perry indicated that an independent TSU was in the best interest of the community. "I think," he said, "if this board of regents empowers the President to address the issue of concerns at the university, it will go forward."[6]

Meanwhile, at the end of March, the state auditors reported that TSU officials had made substantial progress in stabilizing the university's finances and in implementing some different administration policies. They cautioned, however, that long-term stability would depend on how generous the state would be in providing TSU funds for the hiring of more staff and for the training of current employees.[7] This audit report bolstered Slade's efforts to seek more funding when she went before the Legislative Budget Board to try to convince lawmakers that TSU was moving in the right directions of meeting the performance measures as set forth in the audit report.[8] In June 1999, the state auditors reported that TSU still needed to improve its oversight of financial data entry, but that it had made substantial improvement in other areas. More specifically, the university had begun to pay bills within thirty days and had secured help in fixing software problems to produce and balance financial statements. Additionally, TSU was leading an effort, via consultants, to satisfy the state auditors' longstanding demands that university officials follow university bookkeeping policies.[9] The auditors' report was good enough to persuade state lawmakers not to move TSU under another university system. Instead, the legislative session ended with TSU remaining autonomous and with more than $9 million in additional state funds over the two-year budget cycle. This legislative action also prompted state representative Garnett Coleman to withdraw House Bill 3525 from the legislative calendar—a bill that would have removed TSU's board of regents and replaced it with a temporary one.[10] Moreover, the chairman of the board informed Slade that Lieutenant Governor Perry wanted to be informed about "all fiscal activities, university publications, press releases and meetings with an agenda." In his own words, Perry said, "I would like to be advised in a timely fashion of the issues likely to garner the attention of the media."[11]

After nine months, and in part as a result of the above accomplishments, Slade was named the tenth president of TSU on October 27, 1999.[12] Immediately after commencing her tenure, President Slade established and articulated a vision for the university. "I envision Texas Southern in the 21st century as an independent institution of higher learning of the first class."[13] This vision would be more clearly delineated in her inaugural address in the spring of 2000. Her theme for this occasion was "Honoring the Past, Inventing the Future." This theme was undergirded by Slade's "Five Points of Vision": (1) fiscal responsibility—commitment to working diligently to attain fiscal responsibility for all operations, programs, and facilities; (2) service and accountability in administration—commitment to maintaining accurate record keeping and adhering to policies and procedures; (3) a hospitable learning and living environment; (4) commitment to community outreach; and (5) academic and faculty excellence via shared governance, training, and professional development. In order to accomplish all of this, Slade had to have a turnaround strategy. This strategy included repositioning the university and restoring stakeholder confidence, restructuring the university to facilitate growth and accountability, and reengineering business processes to accomplish mission-centered goals and objectives.[14]

More important than a turnaround strategy was a strategic plan. Strategic planning and consultant expertise provided core ingredients for the development and implementation of Slade's long-term comprehensive plan for sustainable growth and improvement. This plan included putting a senior-level team in place, having an aggressive enrollment and management plan for recruitment and retention, and adopting an image campaign, a capital campaign, and a finance management plan for state and federal funds accrued from the settlement the state of Texas made with the Office for Civil Rights. As soon as she was appointed president, Slade moved quickly in naming her team. The team included Bobby Wilson as provost, Gayla Thomas as vice president for enrollment management, Nina Wilson Jones as vice president for institutional development, and Quentin Wiggins as vice president for finance.[15]

After TSU rebounded from its serious audit concerns and precipitous enrollment declines, Slade wanted the university to be known for more than its problems. So, she began what some called the first image campaign in TSU's seventy-year history. This estimated $1 million campaign featured pictures of successful TSU graduates and community leaders on billboards and in thirty-second commercials on television, as well as in print media— all thanking the university for providing educational opportunities and for contributing to the local economy. The Office of Public Relations and the Office of Marketing and Communication established a new logo to go along with the campaign—TSYou. This marketing slogan meant that whatever your association was with TSU, it was about TSYou.[16]

While the image campaign was being launched, the state of Texas and the Office for Civil Rights were in negotiations over the final phase of the Texas Plan. The Texas Plan was implemented in 1983 in response to an investigation of higher education in Texas conducted by the U.S. Department of Education's Office for Civil Rights (OCR) from 1978 to 1980. The OCR's review of Texas higher education institutions came as a result of the *Adams v. Richardson* case filed in 1970 against states that maintained dual systems of higher education. Having found vestiges of segregation that were in violation of Title VI of the Civil Rights Act of 1964, the Supreme Court ordered them to take corrective action. Thus came the various phases of the Texas Plan. The first phase was federally monitored and was effective from 1983–88. A second five-year phase was effective from 1989 through August 1994 and continued the effort of the first phase. It was from these two phases that TSU would improve its infrastructure and the qualities of many of its programs, though much remained to be done. A third phase, designed to take Texas into the next century, became effective in September 1994 and lasted until 1997.[17]

Arguably, the fourth phase of the Texas Plan began in February 1997, when the state was notified by OCR that it was going to conduct a review of the Texas system of higher education to determine if Texas had eliminated vestiges of the formerly *de jure* system. When OCR completed its review in 1998, it found that Texas still had vestiges of prior segregation in the follow-ings areas: missions of the two historically black universities; the land grant status of Prairie View A&M University; program duplications; inadequate facilities and other resources; inadequate funding; and racial identifiability of public universities.[18]

Faced with the possibility of a loss of federal dollars for noncompliance with Title VI, and at the same time eyeing the presidency in the November 1999 national election, Governor Bush responded to the OCR's concerns via the Texas Coordinating Board, a state agency charged with oversight and developing new plans for public higher education in Texas. To address the urgency of these concerns, a committee was established by the Texas Coor-dinating Board to make recommendations to strengthen education at TSU and Prairie View. This committee consisted of representatives from Texas Southern and Prairie View, from other Texas public universities, and from business and state employees. Divided into subcommittees, this commit-tee met monthly from November 1999 to April 2000 and examined the following items: the mission of each university; their land grant status; the presence of program duplications; university facilities; and recruitment, retention, and graduation rates. A coordinating board staff member met with each subcommittee. The public was invited to present testimonies at any of the subcommittee meetings as well as throughout the process. The result was that the committee adopted a set of recommendations known as the Priority Plan for both universities at its final meeting on April 28, 2000.[19] In May 2000, Governor Bush and the Office for Civil Rights approved the Texas Plan as an agreement intended to provide a framework for developing and implementing recommendations for removing vestiges of segregation.

The recommendations for TSU called for an ambitious set of actions to strengthen its operational systems related to finance, academics, human resources, facilities planning, information technology, and an effective institutional development office. The Texas Plan required the state to take action to improve recruitment, retention, and graduation rates of stu-dents; to develop an attractive and well-maintained campus; to strengthen the academic programs (especially those in law, pharmacy, business, and teacher education); to construct a new science building; to add ten new high-demand programs in several fields; to reestablish the School of Public Affairs; to create twelve endowed chairs for new and existing programs; to develop a program of merit scholarships; to make a change in the statutory mission statement as it relates to race; and to remove the apparent limit on Texas Southern University's mission focus on "urban programming."[20] All of these recommendations were made in conjunction with those of the university administration.

In refining some of the recommendations, the university administrators proposed the following programs: doctoral programs in administration of justice, urban planning, environmental policy, and pharmaceutical sciences; masters of science programs in management information systems, health care administration, computer science, and biomedical science; and masters of arts programs in urban planning, administration of justice, computer science, and social work. Coupled with these programs was a proposal for the reestablishment of the School of Public Affairs. Funding under the OCR Priority Plan began with the 2001–2003 biennium budget. At that time, the Seventy-Seventh Texas Legislature appropriated $25 million each to TSU and Prairie View above the regular budget formula for the next biennium.[21]

Although well-intentioned and designed to make up for prior years of discrimination, some of TSU's proposals were neither well thought out nor carefully planned. Some were offered by OCR, and others were made by politicians who did not take into consideration whether TSU would have enough money to sustain some programs in the future. Other proposals were made without taking into account assessments of student needs, of faculty expertise, and of costs. For example, someone outside the university proposed a master's degree in social work at a time when the undergraduate program needed strengthening to maintain its accreditation. The undergraduate program was suffering from inadequate faculty, staff, support services, and an inadequate operating budget. In some cases, the administration took the attitude of "the more the better," without looking seriously at the immediate and long-range cost of these programs. For instance, the university proposed to have twelve endowed chairs, with half of the money coming from OCR and the other half being matched by the university.[22] Given the financial condition of the university, it would have been better to propose three or four chairs that the university could realistically match by securing matching funds in the future. The "more-the-better" attitude would come back to haunt the administration in the future. But in all fairness to the administration, a four-month window was a very short time to respond to or to erase seventy years of discrimination.

At about the same time that these recommendations were being confirmed, an inauguration was held for President Slade. On this auspicious occasion, Slade vowed to make TSU an institution of the first class by continuing to improve the university's bookkeeping and by implementing her

Five Points of Vision plan—fiscal responsibility, service and accountability in administration, hospitable learning and living environments, commitment to community outreach, and academic and faculty excellence. Acknowledging that TSU was on its way to recovery, Slade announced the launching of a $50 million fundraising effort that would be spearheaded by former president George H. W. Bush, who was one of the dignitaries at her inaugural ceremonies. Other good news relayed in her inaugural speech included an 8 percent increase in enrollment and a 3 percent raise for faculty. And although she did not mention it, the university museum had been opened in the Fairchild Building two weeks prior to the inauguration. Perhaps in the views of Slade and others, TSU was on the move.[23]

Within three years, one could see the handiworks of Slade's Five Points of Vision. With regard to fiscal responsibility, one year after she assumed office, the U.S. Department of Education removed TSU from reimbursement and resumed giving financial aid directly to the university after TSU devised a plan for lowering its student loan default rate. The university also received high marks from the State Auditor's Office on the Rider 5 Performance Measure and the subsequent removal of the rider from the current appropriations bill.[24] Likewise, the university successfully implemented the 126 recommendations made by the State Comptroller's Office. In September 2001, to fund the university's future, Slade took a leading role in building public, political, and corporate awareness for the open-door campaign—a $50 million comprehensive fundraising plan designed to fund the university's future.[25] It was perhaps because of her relationship with former president George H. W. Bush that she and members of her staff were invited to meet with major potential corporate donors at two retreats in Kennebunkport, Maine. In 2003 the university received a favorable audit opinion from the Texas state auditor, who said, "The university's financial statements were materially accurate and the legislature and other oversight bodies could rely on them for accuracy."[26]

Under the leadership of Provost Bobby Wilson, the university made progress in the creation of new programs, in the enhancement of existing programs and the strengthening of others via program reviews of instructional assessments, and in the addition of new faculty. Per the OCR agreement, new high-demand degree programs were created in computer sciences, biomedical and pharmaceutical sciences, and urban planning and policy. The College of Arts and Sciences was split into two areas—the College of Liberal Arts and Behavioral Sciences and the College of Science and Technology. The reestablishment of the Schools of Public Affairs and

Communication occurred in 2004 and 2005, respectively. Permanent deans were hired in education, business, pharmacy, law, science and technology, and liberal arts and behavioral sciences. Of special note a Distance Education Program was developed through the Jesse H. Jones School of Business. Also research capabilities and funding increased. Additionally, the MCRI Biomedical Research Center and the Tobacco Center for the dissemination of information on the health hazards of smoking were established. Finally, salaries, which lagged far below the national average, were raised to 80 percent of the national average per professional rank. The university experienced a 6 percent enrollment increase in fall 2000, 18 percent in 2001, 20 percent in 2002, and 11 percent in the fall of 2003.[27] Despite all of the above accomplishments, the graduation and retention rates remained low. In an attempt to help change this number, the university developed a summer academy to bridge and to help provide undergraduate readiness for underprepared high school students who needed remediation to pass an entrance test before moving into their major areas. It should be noted that although TSU was an open-admissions university, and despite the impact that this aspect had on graduation and retention rates, Slade was opposed to changing the admissions policy.[28]

Historically, students and faculty had long voiced concerns about the condition of the university's buildings and grounds. To address these issues, the administration launched several major and minor initiatives. The result was that at least 90 percent of the current buildings were earmarked for construction or renovation. Major renovations and new construction included the Roderick R. Paige Education Building; the Hannah Hall Auditorium, whose name was changed to the Granville Sawyer Auditorium after renovation; the Technology Building, whose name was changed to the Leonard H. O. Spearman Technology Building; the Sterling Student Life Center; the Bell Building; the Thurgood Marshall Law School Building; the Pharmacy School Building; the Science Building; the Allee Mitchell Building; and the Radio Station Building. The Recreation and Wellness Center and a new Public Affairs Building were also on the drawing board. In large part because of OCR, a construction renaissance took place on campus from 1999–2005. But this renaissance was both good and bad—good in the sense that it was sorely needed, bad in the sense that there were too many projects occurring at the same time with limited oversight over the construction. The result was that the great majority of the new buildings were completed with many defects. Moreover, renovations to the Student Life Center and the Law School Building exceeded budget by $5 million, and the same fate befell the new science building.[29] In a word, there were too many contractors doing a

Ground-breaking ceremony for one of many buildings slated for construction during Slade's tenure. Courtesy of *TSU Yearbook*, 2005.

less-than-stellar job without any accountability, and the university was left "holding the bag." Management of construction left a lot to be desired.

As the Slade administration tried to implement the provisions of OCR, it also made concerted efforts to infuse the campus with new and upgraded technology. Computer access labs were expanded and upgraded for students throughout the campus. Not only were personal computers upgraded, but for the most part, one was placed on every faculty member's desk. Most important, registration was improved via the Banner web system. Also, a $5 million building was constructed to house the radio station, while a new electronic data base was implemented in the library.[30]

From all indications, Slade seemed to have been putting the problems of the past behind. From 1999 to December 2004, the enrollment doubled to 12,000; and as enrollment increased, so did the university's revenue from tuition and fees, which reached $48 million in 2004. When OCR settled a longstanding case regarding unequal funding of HBCUs in 1999, TSU received $12.5 million a year above normal funding for at least six years; and at about the same time, TSU also received $2.7 million from the tobacco settlement. In part because Slade had also established good relations with the corporate community, the capital campaign she initiated in 2002 also reached approximately $30 million. When speaking of the distance that TSU had come under her administration, one regent was quoted as saying,

Slade and former secretary of education Roderick Paige at the naming
of the School of Education building in Paige's honor. Courtesy of *TSU
Yearbook*, 2003.

"I don't know if that would have happened with just anyone. It could have,
but I doubt it." One could argue that Slade had achieved all of her Five Points
of Vision save one—accountability.[31]

Accountability

Just as everyone thought that things were going well at the university, the
murder of a TSU student near campus on the night of December 4, 2004,
demonstrated (to many) that Slade's administration was marred by deeply
serious problems. On that night, Ashley Sloan, a student from Dallas, Texas,
was struck in the temple by a bullet as she left a party at the University Oaks

housing complex. A fight inside the apartment continued outside when a young man pulled a gun and fired the shot that struck the twenty-year-old sophomore, who died in the parking lot. Soon after this incident, accusations of poor campus security arose. Many thought that when Slade had improved the infrastructure on campus, security had also improved. As it turned out, this tragic event set into motion a set of events that would reveal a campus administration riddled with scandals, some of which would eventually bring Slade down.[32]

A few weeks after Sloan's death, three students, Justin Jordan, Oliver Brown, and William Hudson, organized a student safety committee. They began by documenting areas in need of additional repair, such as street lights and red-box emergency call stations. During a walk around the campus, they came across an abandoned dump truck behind TSU's General Services Building that contained copies of the university's payroll, complete with employees' names, salaries, and social security numbers. The three students used the documents to ask for an audience with the administration to discuss what they believed to be corruption at the university.[33] When these students confronted Quentin Wiggins, vice president for finance, and inquired about the security on campus, Wiggins blamed "the white boys and Republicans" for inadequate funding.[34] Not satisfied with this answer, the students insisted on an audience with the president. One meeting occurred at a later date, but it was of no consequence.

Getting no response from the administration, these students became active on campus in order to make their voices heard. Not only did they draft a petition calling for the president's resignation, but on January 11, 2005, they wrote an open letter to the public disclosing alleged corruption at the university. On February 2, 2005, "TSU Day" at the Texas capitol, Jordan, Brown, and Hudson met with legislators and discussed what they perceived as allegations of wrongdoing at the university. They also listed their findings in a twenty-page booklet titled "Special Crisis Report" and submitted it to TSU's board and to the governor, who ignored it. As a consequence of their continued protest, these students became, in the words of their lawyer, "victims of unwarranted retaliatory discipline."[35] For example, on March 22, 2005, when Jordan and Hudson disrupted Wiggins's meeting, the police were called and they were charged with insubordination, disrupting a meeting, and threatening to do intentional physical harm. While these charges were sent to the Student-Faculty Hearing Committee, the TSU police filed charges against Hudson and Jordan for allegedly printing an article and publishing an employee's social security number without his permission. On March 24, 2005, Judge Don Strickland dismissed the charges.[36]

Later in the spring of 2005, the administration brought these students before the Student Faculty Disciplinary Committee on charges that
included insubordination, using vulgar language, and disturbing a meeting.
When the verdict came down, Hudson would be suspended for a year and
asked to take anger management classes in order to return to the university.
He was also fired from his campus job in the Office of Enrollment Management. Jordan was placed on probation, but he appealed his sentence and
won.[37] Consequently, these students were forced out of their roles in student
government. On September 21, 2005, the TSU Three (as the students were
known on campus) filed a lawsuit against TSU's board of regents, President
Slade, five administrators, and a campus police officer, alleging retaliation
for publicly criticizing the administration.[38] Having had to wait a long time
for a court date, the TSU Three took supporting documents of their investigation to the Harris County District Attorney (DA). What role this evidence
played in the DA's office taking an interest in what was happening at TSU is
unknown. What is known is that in November 2005, a TSU regent gave the
DA's office cause for further concern.

Regent Belinda Griffin's visit to President Slade's newly constructed
home near Memorial Park to pick up a gift Slade had purchased for her during a university-related trip to China set things in motion. As Griffin walked
into Slade's house, she was awed by Slade's expensive taste and asked Slade
how she could afford such expensive artwork and furnishings. Slade's reply
was "the university is paying for it."[39] Griffin was stunned further by what
she had seen because the purchases appeared to be more than the $25,000
for which Slade did not need authorization from the board. Griffin was on
the Finance Committee and did not recall the board giving the president
authorization to buy such items. She therefore reported Slade's purchases to
the chairman of the board, Paul Johnson, and asked him to place this item
on the agenda for the January board meeting.[40]

At the committee meeting and again at the regular board meeting in
January 2006, Slade was quizzed about her spending. During the query,
board members soon discovered that Slade had spent $138,000 of the uni-
versity's money on landscaping for her private home. Slade's reply was that
the landscaping bill was accidentally sent to TSU's address rather than
to her home.[41] After the board meeting on January 30, 2006, Slade wrote
a personal check for $138,000 to reimburse the university for landscaping
at her new home. When asked about Slade's spending, the chairman of the
board replied, "We trusted her and I think she misinterpreted the rules and
regulations governing housing purchases."[42] But while Johnson thought
the board could handle the matter internally, such was not to be. The day

after the board meeting, the district attorney's office subpoenaed the minutes of the executive board meeting and began to call board members in for questioning. As soon as the district attorney became involved, everyone and everything were fair game. Facing the district attorney's scrutiny, the board members, who still had questions about $8,700 spent on furniture, took action to check Slade's spending and to place Quentin Wiggins, senior vice president for finance, on administrative paid leave. The regents met again on February 3, 2006, stripped Slade of her spending authority, and announced the hiring of the law firm of Bracewell and Giuliani to conduct an external audit of the university's spending.[43]

At its March 17, 2006, meeting the board of regents placed Slade on paid leave after a nine-hour meeting and asked Bracewell and Giuliani to expand its investigation to other purchases Slade may have made with university money. The regents then placed Provost Wilson in charge of university matters.[44] According to reliable sources at the meeting, Slade was offered a severance pay if she would resign. Accompanied by four attorneys, Slade refused the offer on the grounds that she had not done anything wrong.[45] A rally to support Slade was held by students the next day, but a week later, the newspapers revealed more detailed spending by Slade.

Prior to April 12, 2006, Slade had not spoken publicly about her spending allegation. On that day, she decided to explain her spending in an open letter in the *Houston Chronicle*. After speaking about her accomplishments at the university, Slade got straight to the point. "When Regent Belinda Griffin complimented my choice of furniture, I thanked her and cordially pointed out the furniture was owned by TSU as was the university's practice." The next day Slade went to the public again on KCOH AM Radio, the city's oldest black radio station. Again, Slade defended her spending and highlighted the achievements of her seven-year presidency. She made her case on the radio talk show as she interacted with callers without assistance of the show's host.[46]

Meanwhile, Slade's audit did not look good. The board's inquiry, conducted by the Bracewell and Giuliani law firm and completed by mid-April, found that Slade and her chief financial officer, Quentin Wiggins, had failed to follow university policies and state laws, including long-accepted principles of prohibiting the use of public monies for private gain. The details of Slade's lavish lifestyle indicated approximately $260,000 in unauthorized spending for landscaping and furniture for her home (which included $9,000 for a bed). Documents also showed that Slade furnished and bought a security system for her multi-million-dollar home, employed a full-time maid, bought drinks, and learned to play golf—all at university expense.[47]

Bobby Wilson, acting president, June–November 2006, May–September 2007.
Courtesy of *TSU Yearbook*, 2007.

The *Houston Chronicle*'s analysis of 2003 financial records from twenty-six public institutions showed that Slade's expenditures generally exceeded those of her cohorts. After receiving, reviewing, and discussing the audit, the TSU regents by an 8–1 vote on April 17, 2006, dismissed Slade on grounds that she had brought shame to the university. After the meeting, Slade's supporters held a rally equating her firing with that of the independence of TSU. For her part, Slade vowed that she would stand up for her rights. The next day, the district attorney indicated that he would bring charges against Slade, thereby raising the specter of a criminal investigation.[48]

After the April 17 meeting, Slade sued TSU regents, claiming that they had failed to provide her with a mandatory hearing before summarily firing her. Slade's attorney, Ron Franklin, requested a hearing as stipulated in her contract before the firing became final. The hearing was granted and scheduled for May 10, 2006, but Slade failed to show up. At the June 2006 board meeting, Slade's firing was made official by a vote of 8–1 for the reasons stated above. Bobby Wilson, the provost of the university, was then appointed acting president.[49]

The news of Slade's firing drew mixed reactions. The *Houston Chronicle* complimented TSU regents' decision as a "move in the right direction, fair, decisive and best for the university."[50] Some individuals said she was not fit to be custodian of finances of a public institution such as TSU. For others, her firing revived anxieties and memories of the revolving door of the TSU presidency and of the fear of merger. "I think the merger issue is coming up absolutely," warned Robert Muhammad of the Nation of Islam's Southwest Region.[51] Many students, alumni, and friends of the university felt that various instances of mismanagement during the Slade era would have to be attributed to the board's lack of due diligence. Sylvia Brooks, a TSU alumnus and CEO of the Houston Area Urban League, said of the board that "they come for personal reasons or political reasons and don't really have the interest of TSU at heart."[52] In his column in the *Houston Chronicle* titled "Governor Has to Find Right People for the Board," columnist Rick Casey said, "Few would suggest that governors have made it a practice of recruiting regents for TSU with the same level of interest as for the University of Texas at Austin."[53] Representative Harold Dutton Jr., speaking at TSU's summer commencement exercises in 2006, told the regents, "You are directly responsible for the unsuccessful management and governance at TSU." He went on to tell the audience, "We cannot allow the same Board to choose the next President."[54]

After losing her first case against the board of regents for a breach of contract, Slade and her attorney made a concerted effort to keep the embattled president at the university. Her attorney, Ron Franklin, appealed to the First District Court of Texas, but in July 2006, the court handed down a decision that said that the board could indeed fire Slade because her contract was valid and enforceable.[55] Adding insult to injury, on August 1, 2006, a grand jury indicted Slade and two university administrators, Bruce Wilson, director of purchasing and senior vice president for administration, and Frederick L. Holt, senior safety systems engineer. By this time, Quentin Wiggins, vice president for finance, had already been indicted, tried, and sentenced to prison for his role in the scandal.[56] Two weeks after Slade was indicted, she made a move to return to the classroom via her attendance at the university's opening faculty meeting. After much outcry from within, as well as outside the university, Bobby Wilson, acting president, relieved Slade of her duties as a tenured faculty member, saying her presence in the classroom posed an ongoing threat to disrupting the academic process.[57] Under the university rules as stipulated in the faculty manual, Slade had thirty days to file a grievance with the provost, who would then appoint a committee of seven tenured faculty members to consider her case. Perhaps acting on second thought, Slade decided not to pursue the issue.[58] Instead, she worked with her attorney in preparing for her trial.

Slade's trial began on September 1, 2007, and lasted nearly six weeks. She was charged with a felony count of misapplication of fiduciary property of $200,000. Testimonies during this trial came from current and former board members and from TSU employees and officers who were in a position to detail Slade's spending habits and financial management during her seven years as leader of TSU. Although Slade was charged with misapplication of $200,000, the prosecutor accused her of misspending more than a half million dollars of the university's monies for extravagant purchases for her home, including a dinner plate set worth nearly $40,000, a $17,000 sectional sofa, a $9,000 bed, and silk chairs that cost approximately $10,000.[59] Mike DeGuerin, Slade's defense attorney and a very a prominent criminal lawyer in Houston, argued that Slade's spending was legitimate and was done to woo donors for the university and not for self-enrichment.[60] The eight-week proceeding ended in a mistrial when jurors became deadlocked after deliberating for five days about whether Slade's spending amounted to criminal behavior. Both faculty and students were somewhat disappointed with the outcome of this trial because a second trial would keep the university in a negative spotlight. Sanders Anderson, chair of the Faculty Assembly, expressed it best when he said, "What we all wanted was for this ordeal to be over." Yet the prosecutor vowed to retry the case in the future.[61]

Slade's questionable spending was not unique among university presidents. For example, a president of American University lost his job over $500,000 in unauthorized spending, which included European vacations and private parties. A Vanderbilt University chancellor spent $6 million to renovate his university-owned mansion. A Texas A&M chancellor used the university's airplane to transport his friends to certain destinations at university expense. A Stanford University administrator used grant money awarded to the university to purchase a yacht. But each of these cases occurred at a different time, in a different location, under different circumstances. In the Slade case, the prosecutor decided to take her to court. Although each case was different, none of the above individuals were taken to court for the reason Slade was taken, namely, to determine criminal behavior.[62]

The Slade Fallout

Slade's spending scandal, fiscal mismanagement, and lack of accountability left the university in a state of chaos and financial ruin, and almost placed it in conservatorship. For the first five years of Slade's presidency, the university received very good press, and most people were under the impression that everything was going well, especially the finances. But when Slade's spending scandal came to light, the picture was quite different. When she was fired in June of 2006, the university was facing an anticipated $4.5 million shortfall at the end of the 2006 fiscal year, as well as a projected $13.7 million shortfall in 2007. Such numbers forced acting president Bobby Wilson to impose a hiring freeze and to cut approximately 178 jobs, including some faculty and the entire Office of Development in 2006. For the same reason, the board approved a 22 percent tuition and fees increase, and faculty salaries remained unchanged. Because of management woes and bad publicity, the university's bond status was lowered to a negative rating. Also, there were questions about how much money had been raised via the capital campaign after an audit revealed poor record keeping. In addition, the athletic department was operating at a $12 million deficit.[63]

Responding to Wilson's instructions, Bobby Smith, TSU's interim chief financial officer, performed an internal review of the financial practices and oversight of the university's financial management prior to fall 2006. Smith found that the institution did not have adequate financial resources to complete the 2007 fiscal year without a reduction in its operations. The anticipated shortfall for 2007 was due in part to the following: (1) deferred maintenance had not kept pace with new construction; (2) TSU had outstanding payables from the previous year that were being paid from the 2006–2007 budget; and (3) a proposed transportation system that had $4 million of debt. Two garages were built to ease student parking with money coming from student fees. But the students, via a referendum, rejected the proposed plan; therefore, the university was left without revenue to pay an annual fee of $1 million for thirty years.[64]

Without a doubt, the university was in need of financial assistance. But just as Bobby Wilson and Bobby Smith were wading through this financial malady trying to find solutions to it, Governor Rick Perry sent Carin Barth, a CPA, to take over the finance department at TSU. Barth's coming caused immediate resentment on the part of many who felt that her presence was the first step toward conservatorship. There were disagreements among Wilson, Smith, and Barth over how to fix the financial problems. In the absence of prima facie evidence, one does not know if these disagreements played a role in the removal of Bobby Wilson as acting president. What is known, however, is that on November 27, 2006, the TSU regents hired seventy-six-year-old retired NASA manager and Air Force brigadier general Timothy Boddie as interim president.[65] General Boddie had a BS degree in chemistry from Howard University and a master's degree in public administration

Timothy Boddie, interim president November 2006–May 2007,
September 2007–March 2008. Courtesy of *TSU Yearbook*, 2007.

from Auburn University, but he had no experience in academia, much less in an HBCU.[66] Again, this appointment caused concern about the revolving door for presidents at the university. The faculty, students, alumni, and seemingly the entire black community were concerned about the status of the university, most especially about its autonomy.

The eyes of Texas were indeed upon TSU in January 2007 at the opening of the legislative session. Governor Perry moved quickly to create the TSU Blue Ribbon Advisory Committee to deal with this situation. Established by an executive order of the governor, the committee was asked to examine the financial oversights, the governance, and the mission of the university with the objective of providing recommendations to the governor, lieutenant governor, speaker of the house, and TSU's board of regents within forty-five days. In order to arrive at its recommendations, the committee examined administrative governance, financial management, financial aid, technology, instruction, and strategic planning. The committee held five meetings in Houston and by teleconferencing in order to get input from as many constituencies of TSU as possible. Likewise, it convened town hall meetings on the campus to determine the interests and opinions of the local communities regarding the future of the university. The committee invited a number of individuals to offer testimonies before it. Among the distinguished presenters were the presidents of Lamar University, Prairie View A&M University, Texas Woman's University, and the Texas State University System; a former and current interim president to TSU; a congressman; a state senator; state representatives; and the TSU Faculty Senate assembly chair. Weighing and listening to these testimonies were members of the Blue Ribbon Committee: Glenn O. Lewis, chair (Fort Worth); Gary Bledsoe (Austin); Zinetta Burney (Houston); Larry Faulkner (Houston); Howard Jefferson (Houston); Richard Knight Jr. (Dallas); Albert Myers (Houston); Raymond A. Paredes (Austin); Richard Salwen (Austin); Cynthia A. Spooner (Houston); and Anthony Hall (Houston). In the Blue Ribbon Committee's hearing and deliberations, the independence of TSU and the fiscal controls were the key areas of concern. Following at a close second were the prospect of a new board of regents and a new mission for the university.[67]

On March 27, 2007, the committee submitted five recommendations to the governor, the lieutenant governor, the speaker of the house, and the board of regents: (1) TSU should remain an independent institution, but be held to the strictest financial oversight; (2) the governor should reconstitute the board of regents in order to bring about new directions and give a different character to the institution; (3) TSU should be placed under continuous financial audit by the state in the foreseeable future; (4) TSU's mission must be more clearly defined internally and externally so that the university can be held accountable to that mission; and (5) the Texas Legislature should provide emergency funding for TSU in order to allow it to complete the fiscal year 2007. The committee also recommended that TSU should be held in strict oversight following the stipulation in Rider 5. The law required that the state auditor play a role in TSU's finances, especially in emergency appropriations.[68]

At about the same time that Governor Perry established the Blue Ribbon Committee, he instructed TSU's board of regents to devise a plan to restore the institution to financial viability, but only two board members responded. Absent a report from the entire board, the governor argued that the board had failed to offer the specific recommendations needed to correct the current financial situation at the university, and that he was therefore calling on all of the regents to resign. According to Perry, "The systemic problem at TSU runs deep and now is the time to take swift and decisive action."[69] In lieu of having a board, Perry then decided to appoint a conservator over the university, one who would be responsible for spending, hiring, firing, and for making changes in the administrative structure. The governor announced his plans to do so on a Friday afternoon, April 13, 2007. The timing was designed to minimize the attention and uproar that he expected from the TSU family and from the black community. Perry's plan was to appoint an outsider as conservator, Kerney Laday. Laday was a retired Xerox executive, a retired army general, and a former administrator (for a brief time) at his alma mater, Southern University in Baton Rouge.[70]

The reactions to conservatorship were swift in the black community. There were rallies, protests, and letters written to the governor from students, faculty, alumni, friends, and supporters of the university. Representative Garnet F. Coleman said, "I'm very disappointed [that] Governor Perry has decided to put TSU into conservatorship, a decision that goes against the recommendation made by the TSU Blue Ribbon panel he appointed." Coleman went on to say he was further disappointed because "the current financial problems [were] caused by regents and other individuals Governor Perry appointed himself." A member of the committee, Gary Bledsoe, complained that "the Governor wanted more than what the Blue Ribbon [panel] gave him . . . [This is what] I'm reading between the lines." The chair of the Faculty Senate sent a letter of protest, while former president James Douglas said that "a conservatorship was tantamount to using a sledge hammer to kill a gnat." The sharpest criticism came from those who argued that conservatorship would jeopardize the university's accreditation with the Southern Association of Colleges and Schools and that such action would have a rippling effect on the accreditation of professional schools, a fact that was later confirmed by each agency.[71] Most troubled by the conservatorship issue were the black state legislators. When they met with Perry, they told him how drastic the impact of conservatorship would be on TSU. It would be like giving the university a death penalty. They further reminded the governor that conservatorship had never been used in Texas despite the problems that many other institutions had had in the past. After listening to their argument, Perry indicated that he would give some thought to a compromise.[72]

Whether real or imagined, the university faced a threat of conservatorship unless the governor changed his mind or new legislation was created to allow him to ensure accountability and to protect the university's accreditation. Since 1976, the state legislature had passed a bill to allow the governor to place a university or state agency in receivership.[73] What was now needed was a balancing act, any type of legislation that could be agreed on by the governor and the Black Caucus. To this end, Senator Rodney Ellis and Representatives Garnet Coleman and Sylvester Turner got together and drafted a bill, which consisted of three parts: (1) a reconstituted board; (2) a rehabilitation plan; and (3) a special legislative committee. With the power to reconstitute the board, the governor could force the current board members off and appoint five new members. The rehabilitation plan would deal with administrative and fiscal operations. The third element, a special legislative committee of five persons, would work in conjunction with the board of regents, the governor, the lieutenant governor, the speaker of the house, and the legislative audit committee to assist the university. On May 9, 2007, the Texas Senate passed the bill, and Ellis urged the governor to move quickly on it.[74]

By the time the bill was passed, most of the current TSU board members had stepped down, voluntarily or through term limitations and resignations. The three remaining board members, Belinda Griffin, David Diaz, and Robert Childress, refused to resign, stating that their resignations would mean an admission of guilt. After the governor called for conservatorship, Griffin wrote a letter to the governor stating that all the regents would resign once their replacements had been confirmed by the Texas Senate. While Diaz and Childress eventually resigned, Griffin, who in October 2006 became the first woman to chair TSU's board, scheduled a meeting in mid-May 2007. The purpose of the meeting was to decide whether to extend the contract of General Boddie, whose term as interim president had expired. In so doing, Griffin said she was not being defiant because the governor's office had told her to run the university until a new board was in place. Griffin stepped down reluctantly after the Texas Senate started impeachment proceedings against her.[75]

Now the way was clear for Perry to appoint new members to a new board. By September, 2007, Perry named the following to the board of regents: Glenn O. Lewis, chairman (Ft. Worth); Gary Bledsoe, president of Texas NAACP (Austin); Richard Salwen (Austin); Richard Holland (Plano); Tracey McDaniel (Houston); Samuel Bryant (Austin); Curtistene McCowan (DeSoto); Javier Hoya (Houston); and Richard Knight Jr. (Dallas). Meanwhile, before the naming of a new board, Boddie's contract expired, and Bobby Wilson was asked to serve in the position again. As soon as the new board was named, Boddie was reinstated as interim president. So within less than a year, both Wilson and Boddie had each served in the presidency twice. As soon as the new board was in place, both the board and the governor were receiving pressure from the general public to resolve the leadership and financial instabilities at the university. On November 28, 2007, the new board of regents submitted a reorganization plan to the Senate Finance Committee, but committee chair Steve Odgen responded by saying, "I do not believe the plan can succeed without a permanent president and his or her senior management team in place in the near future."[76] At that time, a search committee had already been established and had vetted a number of candidates.

It should be noted that in August 2007, SACS asked senior officials of the university to provide it with information about the university's financial stability by October. SACS's interest was sparked by the governor's office inquiring about the effect that conservatorship would have on TSU and about recent new accounts of financial problems at the university. After receiving and reading TSU's reply, and without even visiting the campus, SACS placed TSU on probation at its December 2007 meeting.[77] At about the same time (December 2007), the search committee named John M. Rudley as a finalist for the presidency.

Again, TSU was at a crossroads. The university was on probation and without a permanent president, and the former president was facing yet another trial. As previously stated, shortly after Slade's mistrial, prosecutors vowed to continue their efforts to prosecute her. A second trial was scheduled for March 2008 but was avoided when a deal was reached with the district attorney's office. Slade would pay back $127,672.18 to Texas Southern, make an apology to the court, perform four hundred hours of community service, and be given ten years deferred adjudication in exchange for a no-contest plea. This meant that, if she completed probation without incident, the finding of guilt would not be entered on her record.[78]

The End of an Era

Slade was selected as president in 1999 because the board members thought that that with her background in accounting, she could fix the financial problems at TSU and thus stave off the threat to take away TSU's independence. And for a while, she seemed the perfect fit. Under her watch, community support, grants, and private giving increased; enrollment and new construction expanded; student financial aid was paid; and audits went smoothly. The OCR settlement resulted in TSU receiving $12.5 million a year above the normal funding formula for at least six years. And as the school's enrollment increased, so did its revenue from students' tuition and fees, reaching $48 million in 2004. Slade and the university were on a roll. But her accomplishments took a back seat to a number of scandals.

Slade had the opportunity to become a good president, but she did not seize the moment. Even as TSU's image improved under her leadership, there were signs of accountability problems lurking just below the surface. In 2004, the TSU police chief was fired after reporting missing funds. He took his case to court and won in a whistle-blowing lawsuit. Shortly thereafter, a university audit revealed hundreds of thousands of dollars missing from the $2.7 million grant the university had received from the tobacco settlement. The university had to reimburse the state. Slade ostensibly had been appointed president to bring financial integrity to TSU. Instead she brought shame. Her apparent lapse in judgment concerning expenditures on her residence and her careless reading of state laws and policies concerning purchases that were allowable under her contract threatened the very existence of the university.

Although there was enough blame to go around with regard to the scandals that occurred, the board must bear some of the blame. Over the years, and even today, questions still linger over how much board members knew and whether they too were fiscally irresponsible. Houston's assistant district attorney shared the sentiments of many when she said, "There is no question that Dr. Slade made these purchases openly and that others knew about them." To what extent was the board monitoring the activities of the TSU president? Before the regents hired Slade in 1999, TSU had had three presidents in six years. With few exceptions, it appears that not much attention was given to the prior experience of individuals seeking the presidency of a financially troubled, urban, open-door institution. For example, Slade had a rather meteoric rise to the presidency in 1999 from graduate school in 1991. One could argue it took more than book learning and an accounting degree to deal with the challenges and opportunities that TSU faced in the political climate of the 2000s. But in large part, Slade was her own undoing. She forgot about or totally disregarded her fifth point of vision not only in terms of finance, but in her accountability to those students whose educations depended on keeping the doors of TSU open.

12

A New Beginning

The Rudley Era, 2008–2016

The year 2008 was a historic time for both the university and the country. In February of that year, the board of regents selected John Matthew Rudley as the eleventh president of Texas Southern University, and in November 2008, the United States elected Barack Hussein Obama as its first African American president. The presidential election of 2008 was shaped, in part, by a growing fear of recession brought on by a subprime mortgage crisis, a drop in oil prices, and plunging stock markets around the world. If unchecked, this global economic downturn could and would impact the fiscal well-being of the university. When Rudley assumed office in March 2008, TSU's economy, like that of the United States, was in a state of uncertainty. The university was suffering from a loss of accreditation, falling enrollment, low graduation rates, and the threat of merger or conservatorship. Any improvement in the situation would depend in large part on leadership. For both men, it would be a balancing act between continuity and change.

In selecting Rudley, Glenn Lewis, the chairman of TSU's board, said, "Rudley's prior experience set him apart from previous TSU presidents in that he [brings] a world of knowledge and [sees] a larger picture for TSU. . . . I think his resume speaks for itself."[1] Hailing from Benton Harbor, Michigan, Rudley, the second child born to Gus and Lottie Rudley, received his early education in the public schools of the city before matriculating at the University of Toledo, where he earned a bachelor's degree in business administration. Later, he received the master's and doctor of education (EdD) degrees in education administration and supervision from Tennessee State University. Almost immediately after receiving his undergraduate degree, Rudley became a certified public accountant and was employed by the firm of Coopers and Lybrand in Los Angeles and Seattle. After work-

John M. Rudley, 2008–2016. Courtesy of *TSU Archives.*

ing eight years at accounting firms, he took a job in 1981 at TSU as assistant to the vice president for fiscal affairs, and within three years, he rose to become the university's chief financial officer. In 1987, he left for a similar job at the University of Tennessee at Chattanooga. After a three-year stint at Chattanooga, Rudley accompanied former Tennessee Republican governor Lamar Alexander to the U.S. Department of Education and became special assistant and senior technical advisor for budget and management to the secretary of education. When the Democrats won the White House in 1992, Rudley returned to the University of Tennessee at Chattanooga. Two years later, he was appointed vice chancellor for business and finance for the Tennessee Board of Regents, the sixth largest higher education system in the nation. In 2002, he returned to Houston to become vice chancellor for administration and finance for the University of Houston System. From June 2007 to January 2008 he served in the interim positions as chancellor and president of the University of Houston System.[2]

Continuity and Change

In assuming the presidency, John M. Rudley declared himself as a dutiful executor who would restore TSU to its rightful place among institutions of higher learning. Having earlier served as vice president of finance at TSU,

Rudley was no stranger to the institution, but the problems he faced were now different. To assist him in solving some of these problems, he appointed former president James Douglas as interim provost and former community college executive Gloria Walker as interim fiscal officer. These two individuals were replaced by Sunny Ohia (and later James Ward) as provost and Jim McShan as vice president for fiscal affairs. Together, the Rudley team tackled the most pressing issues that called for immediate attention—finance, accreditation, and low graduation rates, which the state was threatening to tie to performance-based funding. A fiscal review revealed that the university had not balanced its books nor had a financial statement in five years. Rudley met this challenge by balancing the budget and producing acceptable audits within three years. Within the same time span, TSU had three upgrades from Moody Investor Bond Rating Services, resulting in a five-point increase in the university's rating. In getting TSU's fiscal house in order, Rudley also had to deal with the $13 million the university owed to the Department of Education (DOE). Using statistical sampling, he was able to prove that the way by which the Department of Education had calculated TSU's debt was wrong. After several conferences and negotiations between the two parties, the debt was reduced.[3]

In the interim between getting TSU's books balanced and dealing with the DOE, the university submitted a report to SACS requesting to be removed from probation for management and fiscal problems. Texas Southern's request was granted, but the university subsequently was again placed back on probation in 2009 for not submitting the proper documentation. Several months later, after coming into compliance, TSU received reaffirmation of accreditation.[4] Since that time, the university has undergone its regular reviews from SACS with positive results.

Another major problem facing the new president was low graduation and retention rates. Just as these rates had bedeviled past presidents, they also troubled Rudley. Two factors in particular contributed to these rates: an open-admissions policy that allowed anyone to enter the university regardless of grade point average; and TSU's status as a commuter school with a large number of older students who drop in and out of the university without having a timeline for degree completion. The university's open-door policy meant that a large number of students were not prepared for college work and thus had to take remedial courses. Because they lacked the necessary skills to preform successfully in college, many dropped out before completing the first year. For many years, the university's admissions policy had been viewed as a contributing factor to low graduation rates; and some of the past presidents had discussed the issue but got very little support from the board, faculty, or alumni. But by the time Rudley assumed the presidency, the Texas Higher Education Coordinating Board was calling for state-supported institutions of higher learning to adopt admissions standards. With this mandate, Rudley tackled the issue head-on. He met with faculty, alumni, the community, and friends of the university to discuss admissions, and although he faced some opposition, Rudley was able to sell his proposal to end the open-door policy by indicating that the university would institute a summer program to help remediate students who were not prepared for college work. Once the entrance requirements were met through the summer program, the students would then be formally admitted to the university. Shortly after this series of discussions, TSU's board approved a recommendation to change the university's admissions requirement for undergraduate programs. The policy changed the requirements from open-admissions (which had required only a GED or high school diploma) to having a grade point average of 2.0. It is instructive that about the same time this policy became effective in 2009, the board also approved a change in the university's mission statement from "a special purpose university for urban programing" to "a comprehensive metropolitan university."[5]

With regard to retention rates, Rudley revived and implemented the Urban Academic Village (UAV), an initiative started by former president James M. Douglas. This project, a freshman and sophomore enhancement program, was funded by a $2.7 million grant from the Houston Endowment and was designed as a student-centered community that focused on the students' academic performance, emotional stability, and professional growth. The mission of this program was to enable freshmen students to enter the university and become fully immersed in college life by living together in the same complex and taking classes together in order to maintain their academic focus through the sophomore year and beyond. To improve students' overall performance, the UAV program provided them with mentoring, personal and professional enrichment, cultural awareness experiences, and leadership development.[6] Despite what appeared to have been a great pilot program, it became too costly for the university to sustain and had to be suspended after three years.

Concomitant with the Urban Academic Village in helping improve graduation and retention rates was the Honors Program. Under Rudley's administration, the Honors Program expanded into a college with a new name—the Thomas F. Freeman Honors College. Not only was the name changed, but the basement of the library was renovated to house the college. The renovation included an auditorium, workrooms for the students, and administrative offices for the dean and staff. Along with this improvement came the Presidential Leadership Scholarships, which provide financial assistance to honor students as they progress through the university.[7]

Rudley's interest in students' success was not limited to the gifted; he was also concerned with other students, especially black males. The majority of black males, for one reason or another, never get to college. High school drop-out, homicide, and incarceration rates all have been cited as obstacles to black males not receiving degrees from institutions of higher learning. The president's interest in black male students peaked when a TSU student, Joshua McMackle, was shot and killed near campus. Moved by this incident, Rudley established the TIGER Project, a mentoring program designed to help male students graduate from college on time (preferably in four years), and to inspire them to achieve greater heights via careers. This project also hosted a speaker series and workshops on finances, résumé writing, career planning, and networking. One of the luminaries featured in this series was comedian Sinbad (David Atkins), a classmate of President Rudley from Benton Harbor, who performed a benefit comedy show to raise money for the TIGER Project.[8]

Along with restoring the fiscal health of the university, regaining accreditation, and implementing programs to improve graduation and retention rates, President Rudley oversaw an expansion of academic offerings. New program offerings included bachelor's degrees in maritime transportation management, aviation management, civil engineering, and computer engineering. Both engineering programs include a co-op engineering track that allows students the opportunity to gain work experience before graduating. At the master's level, there were new online programs, the executive MBA and the executive MPA, as well as the enhancement of the educational administration and school counseling programs. Also, the PhD program in urban planning, started under President Slade's administration, came to fruition.[9]

Under Rudley's administration, TSU expanded its influence via partnerships in the domestic and international communities. For example, Rudley reintroduced the Collegiate 100 Black Men and Collegiate 100 Black Women clubs to campus because of these young people's active involvements in their communities. In 2010, TSU entered into a partnership with the Houston Dynamo soccer organization to play its home football games in the BBVA Compass Stadium. For the use of this state-of-the-art facility, TSU agreed to a thirty-year partnership. In that same year (2010), TSU established a partnership with the Chinese government via the Confucius Institute, a center for the teaching of Chinese culture and language. In 2009,

TSU opened a satellite campus in northwest Houston, but because of cost and low enrollment the board of regents voted three years later to close the campus and put more resources on the main campus.[10]

Through a public relations campaign designed to bring everyone in the TSU family together under the slogan "One TSU," the Rudley administration sought to expose the hidden story of the university. One way this was done was through luminaries who visited the campus. In 2010, MSNBC, a cable television network, aired a program from the campus of TSU titled "Obama's America: 2010 and Beyond." This live television show was hosted by Chris Matthews of the Hardball Show and featured syndicated radio host Tom Joyner. It was broadcast to more than eight million viewers across the country and provided positive exposure for TSU. The following year, the president of South Africa visited the campus. Similarly, in 2015, Hillary Rodham Clinton, Democratic presidential nominee, came to TSU, where she was awarded the inaugural Barbara Jordan Leadership Award.[11]

Challenges and Changes

Rudley faced a number of challenges during his tenure. The first came in August 2008 with Hurricane Ike. This storm wreaked havoc on Houston. TSU was in the eye of the storm, and 90 percent of the university's buildings were damaged. Working with FEMA and insurance carriers, the university was able to make the necessary repairs. Out of this came an improved campus: new lighting, new benches, walkways, and a decorative fence defining the perimeter of the campus. A review of the campus facilities prior to and after Ike revealed there was a maintenance problem. Deferred maintenance had been neglected for years while new buildings came on line. Although it was estimated that it would take more than $80 million to catch up on the maintenance of existing structures, Rudley was able to rectify this problem, and along with his building, beautification, and landscaping programs came a transformed physical landscape.

The athletic program presented one of the greatest challenges to the Rudley administration. When Rudley arrived at TSU in March 2008, a number of sports programs had been on and off probation. Over the years, corrective action had been taken but not sustained. The new administration was, therefore, faced with some of the same old problems. Problems for Rudley's administration first surfaced after the hiring of a football and a basketball coach, both of whom had prior infractions with the NCAA. When asked by the news media about these infractions, Rudley's response was that

TSU was a university of "second chances." It should be noted that the football coach, TSU alumnus Johnnie Cole, was hired prior to Rudley's arrival. Most alumni were pleased with him, and he did not disappoint them. After two years on the job, Johnnie Cole won the Southwest Athletic Conference Championship, the first one in thirty-four years for TSU. Shortly after the championship game, the NCAA began an investigation of Johnnie Cole. The findings of this investigation revealed that among many other violations, Cole had used ineligible players. But the investigation did not stop with Cole. It was expanded to include basketball and its coach, Tony Harvey (who was hired during Rudley's tenure), as well as other sports. Violations in these areas included impermissible participation, academic improprieties, low scores on the NCAA's academic progress report, and a lack of institutional control from 2004 to 2011. During these years, TSU permitted 129 student athletes in thirteen programs to compete, to receive financial aid, and to travel when they were ineligible to do so. Consequently, TSU received the following sanctions: five years of probation; scholarship limitations in football and basketball; and vacating of all team records from 2006 to 2010 in all sports, as well as the 2010–11 records for football and women's sports.[12]

After the NCAA's investigation, TSU took corrective action to improve the situations in the athletic program. Newly hired athletic director Charles McClelland replaced both the basketball and football coaches. He also drew up a plan to help athletes meet academic standards for participation in their respective sports, as well as a plan to increase the graduation rates. A follow-through plan resulted in the men's basketball team being removed from probation, winning the SWAC Championship in 2015, and getting a chance to participate in the "big dance"—the NCAA Tournament. The plan also culminated in raising the academic progress report in all sports to 970 (the NCAA requirement is 930 or better) and winning the C. D. McKinney Award. The McKinney Award was given to TSU because the university won five SWAC championships in 2015—in basketball, indoor track and field, baseball, softball, and men's basketball. The girls' basketball team finished in first place in the SWAC for 2015 but did not participate in the championship game because of an altercation that the team had with an opposing team involving most of the first-string players.[13]

Rudley had come to the presidency not only to restore a broken system but to make changes to it. But changes and old habits die hard. Change for change's sake without an assessment often leads to chaos. For example, in an attempt to revitalize the physical appearance of the campus, Rudley took aim at the art murals in Hannah Hall. These murals were started by John Biggers, the renowned TSU artist and founder of the Department of Art.

They usually depict a certain aspect of the black experience and are created as art students' senior projects. Over the years, some of these murals had begun to deteriorate. Rudley saw these as eyesores and ordered one of them to be painted over. When asked about his decision, Rudley said, "When I bring dignitaries to campus, I cannot have them see this." This statement created a great deal of bad publicity for the president and the university. Art critics around the country railed against this action. But out of this unfortunate incident came some good. Many of the murals that were worn, scratched, or defaced are now being restored with the support and a budget from the president.[14]

Early into Rudley's administration, he seemed to have had a fairly good relationship with the students, but it turned sour over the years. The president's advocacy for change caused some to believe that he was not interested in black culture, and this notion helped give rise to a student movement called "Take TSU Back." For example, the students questioned the administration's logic and reason for a recruitment video that did not have any black students in it, although African Americans make up 85 percent of the student population. The rationale given by administration, but not accepted by the students, was that there were three videos, each presented to a different audience. Additionally, the homecoming parade, which had been held in the Third Ward area near TSU for years, was relocated to downtown. When asked about the change, the president argued that TSU is larger and its influence is greater than the Third Ward area, and that he wanted to expose TSU to business people in the larger community. The students' retort was that the parade is usually held on Saturday and that moving it to another venue prevented the community from witnessing a tradition that they had enjoyed for years. In other words, they envisioned a TSU and community relationship similar to the ones that had existed during Granville Sawyer's administration.[15]

Rudley, like past presidents, faced the problem of declining enrollment. This seemingly steady drop in enrollment was due to many factors, not the least of which were changes in the federal student grant and loan programs. A major change occurred in 2011 when the federal government limited students to twelve semesters total of Pell Grant eligibility during their lifetime. This change affected students who usually take longer to graduate, as well as institutions like TSU that depend on tuition revenue from these students. Recruitment, therefore, became extremely important to the TSU administration. In addition to the regular recruitment efforts, Rudley sponsored a recruitment bus tour that included a number of deans and other administrators going to cities within and outside of the state. These efforts brought newcomers to the university, but not enough to offset the decline in enrollment.[16]

Enrollment efforts were further stymied by the violence on campus. It is worth noting that TSU is located in a high crime area. In fact, between 2013 and 2015, there were several shootings on or near the campus, killing two individuals (one student) and wounding several others. The first incident of 2015 occurred in August, and a second incident, in September, led to a campus lockdown. The latter involved a dormitory resident and an off-campus person who got into an altercation over a basketball game. A week prior to the September shooting, students, in a meeting with the president, spoke about a lack of campus housing for some students, and pointed to the fact that security on campus was inadequate. By this time, the student movement to "Take TSU Back" had gained impetus, as these students had made their voices heard on social media, as well as in the board of regents' meetings. Keenly aware that it was incumbent on the administration to take steps to improve security on campus, the president replaced the police chief, put more lights on campus, and held security workshops for all involved. Yet, this gesture appeared to have been a little too late.[17]

Decentralization of academic areas, along with faculty issues, also posed problems for Rudley. The administration's emphasis on decentralization in some cases became chaotic as the line of authority was not always followed. As is the case in many colleges and universities, the faculty complained of a top-heavy administration, whereas the hiring of new faculty was virtually miniscule. Another faculty complaint was that while the majority had not received a merit raise in five years, a few selected individual faculty members had. Not only did Rudley have an adversarial relationship with the chair of the Faculty Senate, but he subsequently barred him from the president's meetings, causing some faculty to question whether such action was a violation of SACS' policy of shared governance. It should be noted, however, that despite the disagreement between the president and the Faculty Senate chair, Rudley did heighten awareness of faculty achievements by increasing the dollar value of the annual faculty awards and by creating a Presidential Achievement Award in the amount of $5,000.00. This award is given annually to a faculty member who has been at the university over twenty years and who has excelled in teaching, research, publications, and community services.[18]

As Rudley entered the eighth year of his presidency in 2016, Governor Gregory Wayne Abbott appointed three new board members and reappointed another. At the October board meeting of that year, Derrick Mitchell was elected as the new chair of the board of regents. Mitchell was elected at time when the university had begun to receive increasingly negative

press, when student protests were growing louder, and when money anticipated from the legislature did not materialize. Consequently, the board of
regents held three meetings between October and December, 2015. When a
second meeting was scheduled one week from the first one, rumors became
rife that changes in the administration were imminent. At the Commencement Day Exercises on December 11, 2015, Rudley announced that his resignation would become effective August 31, 2016.[19]

The Exit

To sum up, it can be said that Rudley restored the fiscal health of the university during a great financial crisis and helped get TSU reaccredited by
SACS. Under his auspices, several discipline-specific accreditations were
reaffirmed, while others were acquired for the first time. Arguably, Rudley's
greatest accomplishment is in the area of physical landscape. His improvement of the university mall, the Tiger Walk, the newly created walkway
between Cleburne and Tierwester, and the facelift to the Sterling Student
Life Center all give the campus the ambience of a modern urban university
with an exterior environment conducive to learning. The university mall has
been graced with a new sprinkler system, flowers, newly planted trees, and
a new lawn. The same applies throughout the campus. The completion of
the Mickey Leland/Barbara Jordan Building and the Spearman Technology
Building, as well as the renovation of the Human Services and Consumer
Sciences Building, became evident. The OIT computing system, as well as
two parking garages (constructed under Slade), were enhanced. Rudley also
joined forces with the city of Houston and the Fifth Ward Redevelopment
Authority Corporation to revitalize the Deluxe Theatre on Lyons Avenue.
Moreover, an eight-hundred-bed freshman dormitory came on line in fall
2016; and at its last session, the state legislature appropriated $62 million for
the construction of a new library.[20]

But Rudley's accomplishments came with a price. Texas's funding
system for colleges and universities is tied to enrollment, the fluctuations
of which are more pronounced at smaller institutions like TSU with fewer
than ten thousand students. In other words, any drop in enrollment often
leads to budget cuts. Since 2010, the flow of state funding to TSU shrunk
by 15 percent. In 2011, the state cut a quarter of the $25 million that was
previously granted to TSU under the state's 1996 agreement with the U.S.
Department of Education's Office for Civil Rights. In order to get the
money fully restored, Rudley had to get a letter from the Department of

"All Roads Lead to TSU." The Tiger Walk Mall—a physically improved landscape of the campus. Courtesy of *TSU Yearbook,* 2010.

Education stating otherwise. Even so, it took two legislative sessions—four years—to get the money fully restored. It is worth noting that the state in previous years often approved budget items for institutions facing declining enrollment. For example, in 2012–13, the state gave TSU $10.5 million to make up for an enrollment shortfall, but this fund was eliminated at the next biennium even though the enrollment continued to drop. During the 2015 legislative session, the state of Texas increased its higher education budget by $329 million, but the funding formula was still tied largely to enrollment. The result of the funding formula's impact was that TSU lost $3.5 million—more than any other state institution in the state.[21]

Undaunted, Rudley used ingenuity and looked elsewhere for money to accomplish his goal. To rebuild those parts of the campus damaged by Hurricane Ike, Rudley turned to the Federal Emergency Management Agency. Likewise, he sought and received monies from the $1.1 billion federal fund dedicated to providing low-cost capital to finance improvement at black colleges. This money helped fund a $41.5 million eight-hundred-bed dormitory. This assistance notwithstanding, Rudley leaned heavily on tuition fees, which have risen 150 percent at TSU since 2003. TSU's high tuition fee is one of the reason for a drop in enrollment. Many students who would probably come to TSU go instead to community colleges where the tuition fee is lower.[22]

Despite Rudley's accomplishments, to some he did not have the best relationship with some of the Faculty Senate and was even called by some a divisive figure. Rudley never meshed well with the elected faculty representatives, often branding the leadership as "malcontents who opposed his efforts to make changes at the university," and who in his opinion "did not accurately represent the 520 faculty members." The faculty members, however, were given an opportunity to vote via a democratic process; and however small or large their voting numbers were, they were representatives of the faculty and were a force to be reckoned with. In a contentious relationship, the Faculty Senate often accused the president of violating provisions in the *Faculty Manual*, approving faculty merit raises for some faculty without going through the evaluation process, and increasing the administrative budget at the time when enrollment was falling. The situation between the two parties got so bad that even after Rudley tendered his resignation, the Faculty Senate gave him a vote of no confidence and moved to censure him. Among other things the Senate cited were decreased enrollment and resistance to shared governance.[23]

As Rudley approached his departure from office, there appeared to have been tension between him and some members of the board. This became

Austin Lane, 2016. Courtesy of *TSU Archives.*

evident at the March 2016 board of regents meeting. At that time, the president accused Derrick Mitchell, the board chairman, of micromanagement, saying "There are days when I come to work, I am not sure who is in charge." Rudley also made references to conversations that the chair had had with faculty, staff, or students. Mitchell's retort was that he was simply listening to complaints from these individuals. Their differences aside, at its April meeting, the board made amends with Rudley by passing a resolution to present him with the Medal of Honor for his contributions to the university at the commencement exercises on May 14, 2016. The board went even further in heaping praise on Rudley by naming him as president emeritus at the May board meeting. Despite the appearance of consensus, it appears that the board that would select Rudley's successor was divided and would remain so, barring some changes in politics and philosophy at identifying a direction for the university. On May 17, 2016, the board selected a community college president, Austin L. Lane, as the twelfth president of Texas Southern University.[24] A native of New Jersey, Lane received a bachelor's degree in psychology from Langston University, a master's in human relations from the University of Oklahoma, and a doctorate in higher education administration from the University of Alabama.

Epilogue

Historically Black Colleges and Universities have played a vital and unique role in the history of higher education in this country. The collective contributions of students, faculty, and administrators have effectively challenged and helped transform the nation's social, political, and economic landscape. Texas Southern University is no exception. TSU, like other HBCUs, has struggled for effective education via self-reliant and empowering strategies. From the request for a "colored" junior college to the argument for a segregated university, African Americans in general, and black Texans in particular, have used self-determined strategies to overcome Jim Crow laws and practices in education. Such behavior is consistent with the African American cultural value of self-determination, which stems from an ethos of service that calls on those who acquire literacy to transfer this information to others in the black community, whether it comes via sacrifice, trial, tribulation, or triumph.

The desire of African Americans to establish a state supported institution of higher learning with a liberal arts curriculum began after the Civil War, but their efforts were stymied along the way. The major obstacle to establishing such an institution for African Americans was overcome by a legislative act that was bolstered by products of the human spirit—determination, stamina, and ingenuity. Established "in a hurry" in 1947, the fate and development of TSU centered on political and philosophical conflicts involving segregation and integration. In 1951, the Texas Legislature removed the one-race designation from the university, but segregation in treatment and funding did not go away, nor did integration remove all the vestiges of segregation. It is noteworthy that even though the institution has had to operate with meager resources and has suffered the trials and tribulations of negligence, racism, and internal conflicts, Texas Southern has done remarkably well. The variables and constancies that have contributed most to the vitality and success of the university are presidential leadership, the faculty, and the students.

As has already been delineated in this work, for the most part, the presidents of TSU have gone to great lengths to maintain the existence of the university. Although each manifested and articulated his or her policies, aspirations, and philosophies differently, some exerted more powerful influence on certain aspects of the university than did others. For example, Samuel Nabrit and William Harris were considered by many as the academic presidents; Leonard Spearman and John Rudley did a great deal to build the infrastructure of the university. Granville Sawyer and James Douglas were student-focused and community relations presidents. Lanier was a courageous visionary, whereas Slade was a leader in fundraising. The mere web of multiple constituencies that these chief executives have had to work with and often overcome to gain acceptance and favor for the university often placed them in precarious positions. Many times, the actions of these presidents clashed with policies and procedures of the university or changes that they initiated, thereby precipitating their departure from the university. Whereas older HBCUs had stability in leadership for twenty to thirty years, this has not been the case during TSU's existence. Yet, the diversity of leadership roles in this study points to the diversity of viewpoints and approaches to maintaining and promoting the mission of the university. As this study shows, this diversity is important in understanding the complexities of the university—from the limitations and restrictions that circumscribed opportunities during Jim Crow to approaches that got mixed up with politics and egos, and from attempts to respond to the current trends in higher education to the responses to TSU's history as an HBCU.

The second variable in the success of TSU was and still is the faculty. The faculty embodied a meaningful collective sacrifice in salary and service. Despite having wages far below the national average, and even further below their white counterparts, these professors taught with dignity, influence, and discipline, serving as role models for their students. Examples of a few are therefore instructive. When John Biggers started the Department of Art, there was no special art building or equipment. Absent a place for the students to draw and paint, Biggers instructed his students to draw murals on the walls of Hannah Hall, the only classroom building during the early years. Today, these walls remain as a showcase and testimony for anyone to view. Thomas Freeman—Barbara Jordan's debate coach—served for fifty years coaching and mentoring the students in the art of debating. Llayron

Clarkson, the first black person to receive a PhD degree in mathematics from the University of Texas, was known throughout campus for helping students academically and financially to stay enrolled. Earl Carl served as the dean of the law school and kept it alive during its darkest hours. Henry Bullock, a sociologist noted for his seminal work on black education, produced many students who followed in his footsteps. Alvin Wardlaw served the university for over fifty years in several capacities—as budget director, as summer school director, and as a member of the mathematics department. Robert Bullard, another sociologist and known as the father of environmental justice, started working in this area along with his students while teaching at the university. Deanna Burrell, one of the leaders of the student sit-in demonstrations in the early 1960s, went on to earn a terminal degree in social work from the University of California at Berkley and returned to TSU to start the Department of Social Work. Alvia Wardlaw, curator of John Biggers's art works, has been instrumental in getting the university to establish a museum and procuring internships for her students at the national African American Museum. Cary D. Wintz and Merline Pitre, along with other colleagues in the field of history, have produced more African American students who earned a PhD degree in history than any other university in the state of Texas. Likewise, the science faculty, with less than state-of-the-art laboratories, sent a number of students to medical school. J. Marie McCleary (English), John Reuben Sheeler (History), and Hortense Dixon (Home Economics) were all role models who molded and shaped students in their respective disciplines. These are only a few such examples among the countless unsung heroes and heroines of TSU.

As has already been pointed out, women have played an important role in the history of TSU. Unlike white women, who at most coeducational institutions were shut out of faculty positions except in traditional female disciplines, women at TSU were on the faculty and staff from its inception. The need was so great for educated black faculty members that barring women would have been difficult. In the past, men commanded more earning power in comparable positions, and some still do. Even so, despite their heavy teaching loads and low salaries, these women showed the same dedication and commitment to the students as did the men.

The students also played a leading role in the institutional life of TSU. They dynamically and creatively occupied the space between their era's relevant social movements and the significant educational, curricular, and administrative ambiguities of higher education. The students' efforts to bring change and to increase their involvement in the functioning of the university were due in part to the *Zeitgeist*. As a result, their protests usually

Barbara Jordan peruses her alma mater's yearbook as she serves in the Texas legislature. Courtesy of *TSU Yearbook,* 1970.

(Below) Nationally known debate coach Thomas F. Freeman and students enjoying the success of winning first place at a forensic tournament. Since the 1950s, the debate team has won first place in at least one of its invited tournaments every year. Dr. Freeman also coached Denzel Washington for his role in *The Great Debaters.* Freeman and the debate team are now featured in the African American Museum in Washington, D.C. Courtesy of *TSU Archives.*

Llayron Clarkson, a faculty member who served the university over forty years in several capacities—instructor, vice president of academic affairs, and director of institutional advancement. Courtesy of *TSU Archives*.

Alvin Wardlaw, a member of the Mathematics Department who served the university over fifty years. Courtesy of *TSU Archives*.

had the support of the majority of the students. They were determined to increase their influence in deciding educational policies and to discard obsolete social regulations, but few were willing to tear down the university to do so. In addition to helping bring about reform in education, they joined the drive for social justice. They also fought against institutional racism in the city of Houston and carved a niche for themselves in the black liberation struggle.

Through all of its years of trials and missteps, TSU has provided an invaluable good. Nowhere is this idea more evident than in the more than forty thousand graduates it has produced. Among these are teachers, college professors, medical doctors, lawyers, scientists, legislators, professional athletes, television personalities, and social workers, to name but a few occupations. Three of its most noted graduates are Barbara Charlene Jordan, the first black female from the South to be elected to the United States Congress; George Thomas "Mickey" Leland, a former United States Congressman, whose advocacy to alleviate hunger did more than anyone else to make this country and the international community aware of this issue; and Michael

Strahan, media personality, football Hall of Famer, and co-anchor of ABC's "Good Morning America." In addition, the university has produced a large number of the teachers in the Houston Independent School District and a high percentage of the pharmacists and lawyers in Houston. In countless other ways, TSU has added to the workforce in this country. It has produced both a middle class and a professional class of individuals who hold important positions in the city, state, and nation. Most of them are black, but a sizeable number came from other ethnicities. Equally important, TSU has served as a bulwark against poverty for countless families. Although TSU has often had high-achieving students over the years, it has also developed unrecognized black potential and provided students with a second chance. For seventy years as a state supported institution it has educated the poor and disadvantaged individuals and has earned a remarkable reputation for motivating students to strive for excellence. The essence of TSU's story will not likely be found in majority newspapers, but rather in the works of its alumni—in books on library shelves; in legislative journals; in research studies published in professional journals and periodicals; in newsletters in social services organizations, churches, sororities, and fraternities; and in professional sports.

Currently, TSU is a comprehensive, metropolitan institution providing academic and research programs that address critical urban issues. It prepares its diverse student body population to become a force for positive change in a global society. With ten schools and colleges sitting on a 150-acre campus, the university offers more than one hundred undergraduate and graduate programs and awards bachelor's, master's, doctoral, and professional degrees.

Like many HBCUs, TSU faces many problems as it serves its different constituents today: cuts to government financial aid; low graduation rates; and performance-based funding. Despite the concerns and tensions of the present, the university remains as a beacon on a hill. The university's birth was in response to an unmet need for the education of black citizens of the state of Texas. It served then—and continues to serve now—as an educational access point for minorities and other ethnic groups throughout the nation and the world. As John Lash put it, "The university [which] could have become a perpetual monument to racial separation in America, is still alive and thriving, but significantly as an enterprise in collective pluralism." "Born to serve" the African American citizens of Texas, TSU has since become inclusive over the years. And it continues its core function of service, meeting the needs of students of all ethnicities, from all states, and from various countries of the world.

Chronology of Texas Southern University History

1927 Houston Colored Junior College was established and placed under the control of HISD.

1932 Houston Colored Junior College received its first accreditation from the Southern Association of Colleges and Schools.

1934 Houston College for Negroes was established after Houston Colored Junior College was removed from the control of HISD.

1936 First four-year graduating class of Houston College for Negroes received degrees.

1944 Houston College for Negroes' Vocational School opened at 1227 Dart Street.

Fifty-three acres of land were acquired for Houston College for Negroes in the Third Ward.

1945 Construction began on the Thornton McNair Fairchild Memorial Building, the first building on Houston College for Negroes' campus. It was not completed until 1947.

1947 On March 4, Texas State University for Negroes is created by an act of the Fiftieth Texas Legislature after the state purchased the Houston College for Negroes.

On September 14, Texas State University for Negroes opened its doors with an enrollment of 2,303 students in the College of Arts and Sciences, the School of Vocational and Industrial Education, the School of Law, and the Graduate School.

1948 Raphael O'Hara Lanier selected as the first president of Texas State University for Negroes.

1948 School of Pharmacy is established.

1950 Mack H. Hannah Hall Classroom and Administration Building opened.

1951 Texas State University for Negroes is redesignated Texas Southern University.

1952 Spurgeon E. Gray Hall (School of Pharmacy) opened.

1955 Samuel M. Nabrit is selected as second president of Texas Southern University. The School of Business became a separate university unit.

1956 The first Student Union is erected.

1957 University Library Building is erected.

1958 Charles Rhinehart Music Auditorium and the Science Building are opened.

1960 Edward H. Adams Gymnasium and Physical Education Building are opened.

1962 Industrial Education Building is opened.

      Ina A. Bolton junior and senior residence halls for women are opened.

1963 Fine Arts Building and Child Development Laboratory are opened.

1965 Bruce Hall and student-faculty apartments are opened.

1966 Joseph A. Pierce is appointed acting president of Texas Southern University. He is named the third president after he retires.

1967 The TSU "riot" occurred.

1968 Granville M. Sawyer is selected as fourth president of Texas Southern University.

      George Allen School of Business Building is opened.

      Martin Luther King Humanities Center is opened.

1970 School of Vocational Education is renamed School of Technology.

Rollin-Stewart Music Building is opened.

Lane Home Economic Building is opened.

1971 School of Education is established as a separate academic unit.

1972 Urban Resources Center is established.

1973 TSU is designated by the Sixty-Third Texas Legislature as a "special-purpose institution for urban programming."

Weekend College program begins as a pilot in the spring and assumes regular operations status in the fall of 1973.

Radio station KTSU-FM became operational.

1974 School of Communication is approved by coordinating board in October, but becomes operative in the fall of 1975.

School of Public Affairs is approved by coordinating board in July, but becomes operative in the fall of 1975.

TSU offered its first doctoral degree—the doctorate degree in education.

1976 TSU's School of Law is renamed the Thurgood Marshall School of Law.

Earnest Sterling Student Life Center is opened.

1977 The College of Education Building is completed.

1979 Ex-Congresswoman Barbara Jordan deposited her official papers with Texas Southern University.

198 Everett O. Bell served as interim president of Texas Southern in 1980 and was retroactively named the fifth president of the university in 1981.

Leonard H. O. Spearman became the sixth president of Texas Southern University.

1982 Patricia R. Williams became the first female academic dean at the university. She was Dean of the College of Arts and Sciences.

1985 The General Services Building is completed.

The Health and Physical Education Building (Gymnasium) is opened.

1986   Robert Terry is named interim president.

The School of Technology Building is opened.

1987   Robert Terry dies in a train wreck, September 12, 1987.

1988   William H. Harris is named the seventh president of TSU, December 1987, but did not assume office until June 1988.

1989   George Thomas "Mickey" Leland dies in a plane crash in Ethiopia. The Leland Center on Hunger, Poverty, and World Peace is established.

1993   Joann Horton is named as the first female and eighth president of the university.

1995   James M. Douglas is named ninth president.

The Art Center is designated the John Biggers Art Center.

1998   The Jesse J. Jones School of Business Building is opened.

2000   Priscilla D. Slade is named as the tenth president.

2005   KTSU moved to a new renovated building.

2006   New Science Center is completed.

2008   John M. Rudley is named as the eleventh president of TSU.

2009   The Barbara Jordan/Mickey Leland Building is opened.

2010   TSU wins the SWAC Football Championship for the first time in thirty-four years.

2011   TSU entered into a thirty-year agreement with the Dynamo Soccer organization to play its home football games in the BBVA Compass Stadium.

2014   The new Technology Building is opened.

2015   Hillary Rodham Clinton receives the Barbara Jordan Freedom Award at TSU.

2016   Austin E. Lane is named the twelfth president of Texas Southern University.

New Freshman Dormitory is opened.

Schools and Colleges of Instruction and Dates Established

Schools and Colleges	Dates
Graduate School	1947
College of Arts and Sciences	1947–83; 1987–2001
School of Vocational and Industrial Education	1947–70
School of Law	1948
School of Pharmacy	1948–83
School of Business	1955–83; 1987–present
School of Technology	1970–83
College of Education	1971–83; 1987–present
School of Public Affairs	1974–83; 2006–present
School of Communication	1974–83; 2006–present
College of Humanities and Communications	1983–87
College of Science and Technology	1983–87; 2001–present
School of Management	1983–87
School of Education and Behavioral Sciences	1983–87
College of Pharmacy and Health Sciences	1983–present
College of Liberal Arts and Behavioral Sciences	2001–present

Academic Degrees Conferred
and Dates of First Conferral

Type of Degree	Date
Bachelor of Science	1948
Bachelor of Arts	1949
Bachelor of Laws	1950*
Juris Doctor	1969
Master of Science	1949
Master of Arts	1950
Doctor of Education	1974
Doctor of Pharmacy	1984
Doctor of Philosophy	1994**

*No longer awarded.

**Since awarding the first Doctor of Philosophy degree in environmental sciences in 1994, TSU has awarded the degree in three other areas: urban planning and environmental policy (2003), pharmaceutical sciences (2004), and administration of justice (2009).

Distinguished Alumni

Following is only a sample of the university's many distinguished alumni.

Yolanda Adams, American Grammy Award winner, Gospel singer and producer.

Bruce Austin, former president of Houston Community College System Board of Directors.

Llayron L. Clarkson, first black to receive a PhD in mathematics from the University of Texas.

James M. Douglas, ninth president of TSU and president of NAACP.

Harold V. Dutton Jr., Texas State Representative.

Albert "Al" Edwards, State Representative and author of the bill that made Juneteenth a state holiday.

Rodney Ellis, former Houston City Councilman, State Representative, State Senator and currently Harris County Commissioner.

Sylvia Garcia, Texas State Senator.

Jodie Giles, former chairman of the Greater Houston Partnership.

Alexander N. "Al" Green, United States Representative for Texas's 9th congressional district.

Isaac Hampton, quartermaster historian, U. S. Army, Fort Lee, Virginia.

Kenneth Holt, second African American to serve as a federal judge in Texas.

Mack Jones, professor emeritus and founder of the PhD program in political science at Atlanta University.

Barbara C. Jordan, first black person elected to the Texas Senate and first black female elected from the South to the U.S. Congress.

Leslie King, Mississippi Supreme Court Justice.

Kase L. Lawal, chairman and CEO of CAMAC International Corporation, chairman and CEO of Erin Energy Corporation, and chairman of Allied Energy Corporation in Houston, Texas.

El Franco Lee, first African American commissioner of Harris County.

George T. "Mickey" Leland, former United States congressman who advocated eradicating world hunger.

Thomas Melancon, nationally renowned playwright.

George McElroy, first black person to receive a master's degree in journalism from the University of Missouri, the first black writer of the *Houston Chronicle*, and the first black journalist there to have his own column.

Bernadine Oliphant, world renowned operatic soprano whose image was placed on a postage stamp in Germany.

Morris L. Overstreet, first African American elected to a statewide office in the history of the State of Texas. He also served on the Texas Court of Criminal Appeals from 1990 to 1998.

Belvin Perry, former chief judge of Florida's Ninth Judicial Circuit who presided over the high-profile Casey Anthony murder trial.

James Race Jr., medical doctor.

Michael Strahan, football Hall of Famer and television personality.

Carrol A. "Butch" Thomas, former superintendent of Beaumont Independent School District.

Senfronia Thompson, Texas state representative, dean of the Women's Caucus of the Texas legislature.

Kirt Whalum, renowned jazz saxophonist.

Tony Wyllie, senior vice president of Washington Redskins.

Athletic Championships

National Championship NAIA

Men's Basketball	1977

Conference: Midwestern Athletic Association

Men's Football	1952
Men's Basketball	1952, 1954

Conference: Southwestern Athletic Association—Men's Sports

Men's Football	Men's Basketball (Reg. Season)	Men's Basketball Tournament
1956 (tied with Wiley)	1956–57	
	1957–58	
1966 (tied with Grambling, Southern)		
1968 (tied with Alcorn, Grambling)		
	1976–77	
	1982–83	
	1988–89 (tied with Grambling, Southern)	
		1990
	1991–92 (tied with Mississippi Valley	
	1993–94	1994
	1994–95	1995
	1997–98	
	2003	
2010 (vacated by NCAA)	2010–11	
	2012–13	
		2014
	2014–15	2015

Conference: Southwestern Athletic Association
—Men's Sports (cont'd.)

Indoor Track and Field (inaugural year 1976)	1979, 1980, 1981, 1984, 1985, 1987, 1988, 1994, 2014, 2015
Cross Country	1978, 1982, 1987, 1992, 1993
Tennis	2006
Golf	2007
Baseball	2004, 2008

Conference: Southwestern Athletic Association
—Women's Sports

Women's Tennis	2006
Women's Basketball (Regular Seasons)	2012–13, 2014–15
Women's Softball	2000, 2014–15
Women's Volleyball	1989, 1990, 1991, 1994
Women's Bowling	2000, 2001, 2005, 2006
Women's Indoor Track and Field	1981, 1982, 1988, 1990, 1991, 1992
Women's Outdoor Track	1981, 1989, 1990, 1991, 1992

Notes

Chapter 1

1. Tex. Const. of 1876, art. VII, § 14.

2. Hornsby, "Colored Branch University." See also Woolfolk, *Prairie View*; Pitre, *Through Many Dangers*, 75; William H. Holland to Oran M. Roberts, September 28, 1882, in Oran M. Roberts Papers, Texas State Archives, Austin.

3. Texas Legislature, *House Journal of the 19th Legislature, Regular Session* (Austin, 1983), 43; *Galveston Daily News*, January 23, 1888; Texas Legislature, *House Journal of the 23rd Legislature, Regular Session* (Austin, 1893), 275, 422; *Galveston Daily News*, March 17, 1893; Texas Legislature, *House Journal of the 25th Legislature, First Session* (Austin, 1897), 62, 11, 153, 428.

4. *Texas School Journal* 14 (May 1896): 191; *Texas School Journal* 15 (February 1897): 75.

5. Texas Legislature, *House Journal of the 25th Legislature, First Session* (Austin, 1897), 62, 111, 153, 428.

6. Texas Legislature, *House Journal of 26th Legislature, First Regular Session* (Austin, 1899), 336; *Hogue v. Baker*, 92 Tex. 58 (1899).

7. Anderson, *Education of Blacks*, 111–47. In 1885, Jack Yates and other blacks established the Houston Baptist Academy and later reorganized it into what was called a Houston College. Despite this title, this college offered only primary and secondary school courses. See Aulbach, *Buffalo Bayou*.

8. Hine, *Black Victory*, 16–19.

9. Bryant, *Texas Southern University*, 1–3.

10. Ibid.

11. Ibid.; Nicholson, *In Time*, 10.

12. Bryant, *Texas Southern University*, 1–3.

13. Bryant, *Texas Southern University*, 5. Nicholson, *In Time*, 10–12.

14. Nicholson, *In Time*, 5. See also "Proposed Faculty Salary" in Texas Southern University History Files, TSU Heartman Collection, Houston (hereafter all information from this file will be cited as TSUH); see also Minutes of the Houston School Board of Education for May 14, July 12, and August 6, 1927, in Houston Independent School District Education Archives. Unless otherwise specified, all minutes from Houston Board of Education come from this source.

15. Minutes of the Houston School Board of Education Meeting, September 14, 1927. See also Minutes for March 7, 1927, April 11, 1927; June 13, 1927, May 14, 1927.

16. Minutes of the Houston School Board of Education Meeting, September 14, 1927; Bryant, *Texas Southern University*, 5–6.

17. Hine, *Black Victory*, 26, 235.

18. Minutes of the Houston School Board of Education Meeting, September 14, 1927; Bryant, *Texas Southern University*, 7.

19. Bryant, *Texas Southern University*, 7.

20. The 1933–34 Catalog of the Houston Colored Junior College, TSU Heartman Collection, Houston; Terry, *Origin and Development of Texas Southern University*.

21. Bryant, *Texas Southern University*, 9.

22. Raphael O' Hara Lanier's biography in Raphael O'Hara Lanier's Papers, TSU Heartman Collection, Houston; Bryant, *Texas Southern University*, 9; see also "College for Negroes," 8 *Herald (1934)* University of Houston Archives; Minutes of the Houston Board of Education Meeting, September 8, 1931.

23. Bryant, *Texas Southern University*, 9–10.

24. Texas Legislature, *General and Special Laws Passed in the 44th Legislature, Regular Session*, H.B. 194 (Austin, 1935). See also the 1932, 1933, and 1934 catalogs of the Houston College for Negroes; Minutes of Houston Board of Education Meeting, August 18, 1932.

25. Pitre, *In Struggle*, 28.

26. Bryant, *Texas Southern University*, 12. Minutes of the Houston Board of Education Meeting, August 22, 1938.

27. Bryant, *Texas Southern University*, 12.

28. Bryant, *Texas Southern University*, 13; see also the 1934, 1935, 1936, 1937, 1938, 1939, 1940, 1941, 1942, and 1943 catalogs of the Houston College for Negroes, TSU Heartman Collection, Houston.

29. Allen E. Norton to Edwin R. Embree, October 28, 1944, in TSUH Files, TSU Heartman Collection, Houston. The Graduate courses were held at Houston College for Negroes in 1943. See the 1943 catalog of the Houston College for Negroes.

30. See flyers *Building Fund Campaign* and *Donors to the Houston College for Negroes* in the TSUH Files.

31. Texas Legislature, *Senate Journal of the 49th Legislature, Regular Session*, S.B. 207 (Austin, 1945); Nicholson, *In Time*, 224.

32. *Smith v. Allwright*, 321 U.S. 657, 64 Sup. Ct. 757 (1944).

33. *Missouri ex rel Gaines v. Canada*, 305 U.S. 337 (1938).

34. *Dallas Express*, October 15, 22, 23, 29, 1938.

35. Lulu B. White to Gloster Current, December 5, 1944, NAACP Papers, Manuscript Collection, Library of Congress (MCLC). All letters to and from Lulu B. White [LBW], Thurgood Marshall, Walter White, A. Maceo Smith, and R. L. Carter are taken from the NAACP files. See also *Dallas Morning News*, March 28, April 25, May 2, and June 6, 1945.

36. Texas Legislature, *General and Special Laws Passed in the 49th Legislature, Regular Session*, S.B. 228 (Austin, 1945), 506.

37. Pitre, *In Struggle*, 92.

38. LBW to Walter White, January 2, 1947; LBW to Marshall, January 14, 1947; LBW to Gloster Current, January 20, 1945.

39. LBW to Marshall, October 10, 1945; A. Maceo Smith to LBW, November 19, 1945; William Durham to Marshall, January 28, 1946.

40. Theophilus Painter to Grover Sellers, February 26, 1946. This letter was leaked by the *Houston Informer*, March 2, 1946. See the Texas Attorney General Opinion, Texas, No. 0–7126, March 16, 1946. See also Texas Legislature, *General and Special Laws Passed in the 49th Legislature, Regular Session*, S.B. 228 (Austin, 1945), 506

41. A. Maceo Smith to Carter Wesley, March 21, 1946; Wesley to Smith, March 30, 1946; Carter Wesley to William Durham, March 22, 1946.

42. Dudley K. Woodward to Gibb Gilchrist, June 20, 1946, in General Files, Negroes in College 1939–54, University of Texas President's Records (UTPOR), Dolph Briscoe History Center at the University Texas at Austin.

43. A. Maceo Smith to R. L. Carter, August 9, 1946; Mack Magee to Coke Stevenson, December 6, 1946; Bi-Racial Commission Report, December 17, 1946, both in General Files, Negroes in College 1939–54 (UTPOR); *Houston Chronicle*, May 17, 1946; LBW to Marshall July 30, 1946.

44. A. Maceo Smith to R. L. Carter, August 9, 1946; *Houston Post*, August 9, 1946.

45. A. Maceo Smith to R. L. Carter, August 9, 1946; "Resolution of the Texas Council of Negro Organizations to the Governor's Biracial Commission," August 8, 1940, in NAACP files (MDLC).

46. *Houston Post*, August 9, 1946; LBW to Marshall, July 30, 1946.

47. Pitre, *In Struggle*, 97–98; Mark Magee to Coke Stevenson, December 17, 1946; Bi-Racial Commission Report, December 9, 1946 in General File, Negroes in College 1939–1954 (UTPOR); *Houston Informer*, December 7, 1946; *Houston Informer*, March 15, 1947; *Houston Post*, February 25, 1947.

48. Texas Legislature, *General and Special Laws Passed in the 50th Legislature, Regular Session*, S.B. 140 and H.B. 780 (Austin, 1947), 36–40.

Chapter 2

1. Texas Legislature, *General and Special Laws Passed in the 50th Legislature, Regular Session*, S.B. 140 and H.B. 780 (Austin, 1947), 36–40.

2. Ibid.; "Texas State University for Negroes (TSUN) Report to the Legislature," in Raphael O'Hara Lanier's Papers. See also Bullock, "Availability of Education," 425–32; Thompson, "Separate, but Equal," 105–12; Shabazz, *Advancing Democracy*; Lee, ed., *TSU Meets the Press*; Lavergne, *Before Brown*.

3. "Second Draft: Report to the Governor by TSUN Board of Directors," 1949, in Raphael O'Hara Lanier's Papers.

4. *Houston Chronicle*, April 1, 1947. See Lulu B. White to Gloster Current, May 9, 1947, NAACP Files; Bryant, *Texas Southern University*, 51–53.

5. *Houston Chronicle*, April 1, 1947; Price Daniel to Alan Shivers, May 9, 1950, in TSUH Files; Beauford Jester's Address at Texas Southern University Commencement Exercise, May 30, 1949, in TSUH Files and in Raphael O'Hara Lanier's Papers.

6. Willette Banks to Lanier, May 21, 1949 in Raphael O'Hara Lanier's Papers; Bryant, *Texas Southern University*, 52.

7. *Page v. The Board of Education*, City of Dallas, 1943; *Dallas Express*, March 6, 1943; See Camille Davis, "Thelma Elizabeth Page Richardson," *Texas State Historical Association*, accessed June 31, 2013, https://www.tshaonline.org/handbook/

online/articles/fri65; Minutes of Administrative Committee Meeting of Houston College for Negroes, March 1, 1946; W. W. Kemmerer to Allen Norton, December 1, 1947; Norton to William Bell, November 4, 1947, all in TSUH Files.

8. The 1947–48 catalog of Texas State University for Negroes (TSUN) TSU Heartman Collection, Houston. See also Minutes of the TSUN Board of Directors Meeting, August 5–8, 1947, in TSUH Files TSU Heartman Collection, Houston.

9. Allen E. Norton to Edison E. Oberholtzer December 5, 1946, in TSUH Files; the 1947–48 catalog of *Texas State University for Negroes.*

10. Edison Oberholtzer to Oscar Holcombe January 23, December 24, 1947; W. W. Kemmerer to W. R. Shipping, September 24, 1947, in TSUH Files; see also Senate Bill 140.

11. William H. Bell to Allen E. Norton, February 20, 1948, in TSUH Files; Biography of Raphael O'Hara Lanier in Raphael O'Hara Lanier's Papers; Minutes of the TSUN Administrative Committee Meeting, March 1, 1948, in TSUH Files. See also Presidential Report in the Minutes of the Regular Board Meeting, July 13, 1948, in TSUH Files. In May 1950, when Mack Hannah served as chairman of the board, he wrote Governor Shivers and suggested the nomination of Connie Carney "if it's not out of place to nominate a woman." Mack Hannah to Alan Shivers, May 23, 1950, in Raphael O'Hara Lanier's Papers.

12. *Houston Informer,* August 18, 1951; *Dallas Post,* February 16, 1952; *Houston Defender,* August 11, 1953. See also Minutes of the Houston College for Negroes Board of Directors Meeting, September 8, 1931, TSUN Files. Lanier became president in 1948 but was not formally inaugurated until November 4, 1951. He earned a doctorate of education after leaving TSU. His dissertation was titled "The History of Higher Education for Negroes in Texas, 1930–1955, with particular Reference to Texas Southern University."

13. Presidential Report to the Board, July 13, 1948, Texas State University for Negroes (TSUN) in Lanier's Paper; Minutes of the Board of Directors Regular Meeting, July 13, 1948, TSU Heartman Collection, Houston.

14. Bryant, *Texas Southern University,* 54–56. See also Willette Banks to Lanier, May 2, 1948; Fred McCuster to John H. Robertson, February 24, 1948; John H. Robertson to Lanier, October 11, 1961, all in TSUH Files.

15. Raphael O'Hara Lanier to State Board of Education, November 8, 1948, in Raphael O'Hara Lanier's Papers.

16. Ibid.

17. Craig F. Cullinan to Governor Beauford H. Jester, June 29, 1949 in Raphael O'Hara Lanier's Papers; Texas Legislature, *General and Special Laws Passed in the 51st Legislature, Regular Session,* S.B. 253 and H.B. 379 (Austin, 1949); William A. Miller Jr. to John H. Robertson, July 9 1949; John H. Robertson to Major T. Bell, July 6, 1949; all correspondences in TSUH Files.

18. Johnson, *Price of Freedom,* 55–65.

19. Minutes of the Regular Board Meeting, August 8, 1948, TSUH Files. See also Finance Committee Report of Board Meeting, August 8, 1948, TSUH Files.

20. Minutes of the Regular Board of Directors Meeting, November 16, 1948; Lanier's Memo to Members of the Business Committee, October 14, 1949; John H. Robertson to Lanier, October 11, 1949; John H. Robertson to Lanier April 17, 1950; John H. Robertson to Willette Banks, May 1950; John H. Robertson to Cullinan,

October 19, 1949. See also Budget Recommendations 1948–49. All of the above items in TSUH Files and also in Raphael O'Hara Lanier's Papers.

21. Johnson, *Price of Freedom,* 55–65.

22. John E. Henry to Lanier December 9, 1948, in TSUH Files; Sapper, "Rise and Fall of the NAACP," 59–60.

23. John E. Henry to Lanier, December 9, 1948, TSUH Files; Major T. Bell to Lanier, December 9, 1948, TSUH Files; John H. Robertson to Willette Banks, April 17, 1950, TSUH Files; Johnson, *Price of Freedom,* 70–71.

24. Johnson, *Price of Freedom,* 70–71.

25. Ibid., 55–65. Minutes of TSUN Regular Board of Directors Meeting, February 11, 1949; in TSUH Files, TSU Heartman Collection, Houston. Ozie Johnson to Craig Cullinan, February 11, 1948 in Johnson, *Price of Freedom,* 70–71.

26. Johnson, *Price of Freedom,* 105.

27. Pitre, *In Struggle,* 101; John H. Robertson to Major T. Bell, July 6, 1949, TSUH Files; Minutes of the Regular Board of Directors Meeting, August 9, 1949, TSUH Files; William A. Miller Jr. to John H. Robertson, June 29, 1949, TSUH Files.

28. Pitre, *In Struggle,* 101–2; Painter to I. M. Maddox, Sept 1, 1949, Negroes in College, 1939–45); Craig F. Cullinan to Theophilus Painter, July 13, 1949, all items found in the General Subject Files Negroes in College 1939–54, University of Texas President Office Records (UTPOR), Dolph Briscoe History Center at the University of Texas at Austin.

29. Pitre, *In Struggle,* 102. See also Gillette, "Blacks Challenge the White University," 336; Sapper, "Rise and Fall," 61–62.

30. *Sweatt v. Painter,* 339 U.S. 629, 70 848–51 (1950); "Texas Southern University Five-Year Report, 1948–1953" (Houston, 1953), TSU Heartman Collection, Houston. Pitre, *In Struggle,* 103.

31. Pitre, *In Struggle,* 98. See Texas Legislature, *General and Special Laws Passed in the 50th Legislature, Regular Session,* S.B. 140 (Austin, 1947).

32. Texas Legislature, *General and Special Laws Passed in the 52nd Legislature, Regular Session,* H.B. 82 (Austin, 1951); *Houston Informer,* February 17, 11, 1951; Bryant, *Texas Southern University,* 86.

33. See Texas Legislature, *General and Special Laws Passed in the 50th Legislature, Regular Session,* S.B. 140 and H.B. 780 (Austin, 1947), 36–40.

34. Alan Shivers's speech at Nabrit's inauguration, March 19, 1956, in Samuel M. Nabrit's Papers, TSU Heartman Collection, Houston.

35. "Texas Southern University: Five-Year Report, 1948–1953," 9. See also Minutes of the Regular Board of Directors Meeting, 1953, in Raphael O'Hara Lanier's Papers.

36. "Texas Southern University: Five-Year Report, 1948–1953," 9–11.

37. Ibid.

38. Ibid., 12–13.

39. Ibid., 15–18.

40. Ibid.; see also Minutes of Regular Board of Directors Meeting, September 12, 1955 and December 12, 1955, TSU Heartman Collection, Houston.

41. "Texas Southern University: Five-Year Report, 1948–1953," 23–24.

42. Minutes of Regular Board of Directors Meeting, February 11, 1949, TSUH Files; *Houston Chronicle,* February 12, 1949; Edmund Coston to Alan Shivers, December 26, 1949, TSUH Files; Alan Shivers to Edmund Coston, January 6, 1950,

in Bryant, *Texas Southern University*, 67–72.

43. Edmund Coston to Alan Shivers, April 22, 1953, TSUH Files. See also "TSU Board Press Release in Lanier's Files" in Bryant, *Texas Southern University*, 69–79.

44. See "Citizen Report" in Bryant, *Texas Southern University*, 69–72.

45. Minutes of Regular of Board of Directors Meeting, September 23, 1951, TSUH Files. "Texas Southern University: Five-Year Report, 1948–1953." Bryant, *Texas Southern University*, 69–79.

46. Minutes of Regular of Board of Directors Meeting, September 23, 1951, TSUH Files; "Texas Southern University: Five-Year Report, 1948–1953."

47. *Houston Informer*, August 12, 1953; Bryant, *Texas Southern University*, 88; *Houston Informer*, August 27, 1953.

48. Bryant, *Texas Southern University*, 88.

Chapter 3

1. *Houston Post*, October 3, 1955; *Houston Informer*, May 12, 1956; Pitre, "Samuel Milton Nabrit," *BlackPast.org*; Pitre, "Samuel Milton Nabrit," Texas State Historical Association website. Nabrit died December 30, 2003, at age 98.

2. *Houston Post*, October 3, 1955.

3. *Houston Informer*, March 27, 1956; *Houston Informer*, September 2, 1956.

4. *Houston Post*, October 3, 1955; *Houston Informer*, March 16, 1961.

5. Samuel Milton Nabrit, interviewed by Merline Pitre, March 6, 1997, in the possession of Merline Pitre.

6. Ibid.

7. *TSU Herald*, January 19, February 15, 1956.

8. Nabrit, interview; Minutes of the Board of Directors Meeting, September 25, 1957, in TSU Heartman Collection, Houston.

9. *Houston Informer*, September 15, 1956; *TSU Herald*, March 29, 1956.

10. *Houston Chronicle*, March 19, 1956.

11. *Houston Chronicle*, March 19, 1956; *TSU Herald*, March 29, 1956; *Houston Informer* March 17, 29, 1956.

12. *Houston Informer*, March 17, 24, 1956. See Allan Shivers's speech at TSU, March 19, 1956, in Samuel M. Nabrit's Papers; *TSU Herald*, March 18, 29, 1956. See Nabrit's Inaugural Address, *Houston Chronicle*, March 19, 1956; *Houston Informer*, March 17, 24, 1956.

13. *Atlanta Daily World*, February 10, 1956; *TSU Herald*, March 29, 1956; *Houston Post*, March 19, 1956; *Houston Chronicle*, March 19, 1956; *Houston Informer*, September 16, 1956.

14. *TSU Herald*, March 29, 1956. See also *Dallas Star Post*, October 16, 1956; *Houston Informer*, March 19, 1956; *Houston Post*, March 19, 1956.

15. *Houston Informer*, March 29, 1956; *Houston Post*, March 19, 1956.

16. *Houston Informer*, September 2, 1956; Administrators Conference Program, February 4, 1956, TSU Heartman Collection, Houston.

17. *TSU Herald*, February 4, 1956; *TSU Herald*, February 10, 1962; Administrators Conference Program, February 4, 1956.

18. *TSU Herald*, February 4, 1956.

19. Nabrit, interview.

20. Ibid.

21. Minutes of Board of Directors Meeting, September 27, 1960, TSU Heartman Collection, Houston. See Bryant, *Texas Southern University*, 104.

22. Minutes of Board of Directors Meeting, September 27, 1960, TSU Heartman Collection, Houston.

23. *Houston Chronicle*, November 1, 17, 1963; *Houston Post*, September 27, 1963.

24. *Houston Chronicle*, March 13, 1963, July 28, 1964; *Houston Post*, July 28, 1964. See also *Houston Post*, July 5, 1962; *Houston Post*, July 25, 1965.

25. From the Nabrit File at the University of Houston Archives, see Samuel Nabrit to Donald C. Agnew et al., April 14, 1964; Nabrit to Phillip G. Hoffman and Kenneth Pitzer, April 14, 1964; Agnew to John Lash, June 17, 1964; John Lash to Donald Agnew, June 23,1964; and Kenneth Pitzer to Samuel Nabrit, June 4, 1965. See also John Lash to Kenneth S. Pitzer, February 13, 1964, in Samuel M. Nabrit's Files, University of Houston Archives; *Houston Post*, March 1, 1964.

26. Lash, Dixon, and Freeman, *Texas Southern University*.

27. *Houston Chronicle*, July 25, 1964; *Houston Chronicle*, June 27, 1965.

28. *Houston Chronicle*, March 13, 1965; *Houston Chronicle*, July 28, 1966.

29. *Houston Chronicle*, July 28, 1966.

30. Ashworth, "Texas Higher Education Coordination Board."

31. *Houston Post*, June 6, 1962; *Houston Chronicle*, July 25, 1962.

32. In Samuel M. Nabrit's Papers, see Mack Hannah to George L. Allen and Everett H. Givens, June 11, 1962, and Mack Hannah to Everett H. Givens, July 6 and 9, 1962, Nabrit Files, TSU Heartman Collection, Houston; see also *Houston Chronicle*, July 6, 1962. Nabrit also established the first honors program at the university.

33. *Houston Chronicle*, April 29, 1962.

34. Nabrit's speech at Texas Commission of Higher Education (TCHE) on July 6, 1962, in Samuel M. Nabrit's Papers; *Houston Post*, October 12, 1964; *Houston Post*, January 11, 1965; *Houston Chronicle*, October 12, 1965. See also *Houston Post*, February 5, 1965; *Houston Post*, March 31, 1966; Kenneth Tollette's speech before the American Bar Association, April 23, 1962, in Samuel M. Nabrit's Papers.

35. Kenneth Tollette to the Texas Commissioner of Higher Education, October 12, 1964, in Samuel M. Nabrit's Papers. See also *Houston Informer*, October 24, December 24, 1964.

36. *Houston Informer*, December 24, 1964; Nabrit, interview; *Houston Family Newspages*, October 10, 1964. See also *Houston Chronicle*, May 1, 1966;

37. Minutes of the Regular Board of Directors Meeting, January 10, 1956, TSU Heartman Collection, Houston; *Houston Chronicle*, September 12, 1956; Ralph Lee to the Board of Directors, July 1, 1955, cited in *TSU Herald*, June 19, September 12, 1956.

38. *Houston Family Newspages*, November 3, 1963; Nabrit, "Desegregation and the Future," 414–18.

39. Samuel Nabit to Ira Bryant, March 12, 1974. This letter contains President Nabrit's "Assembly Speech to TSU Students and Faculty" on the student sit-in demonstration, cited in Bryant, *Texas Southern University*, 103–4.

40. Holly Hogrobrooks, interview by Jean Schwartz, Houston, Texas, October 27, 1988, Oral History Collection, Houston Metropolitan Research Center, Houston Public Library. See also Cole, *No Color*, 25–26.

41. Cole, *No Color*, 25–26; *Houston Chronicle*, March 5, 1960; Jensen, "Houston Sit-in," 214; *Houston Informer*, March 19, July 30, 1960.

42. Nabrit's "Assembly Speech to the TSU Students and Faculty," in Bryant, *Texas Southern University*, 104; *Houston Informer*, March 1, 1961.

43. Cole, *No Color*, 40.

44. Ibid., 37; *Houston Informer*, March 1, 1961.

45. Bryant, *Texas Southern University*, 104.

46. Cole, *No Color*, 36.

47. Ibid., 46–47.

48. Ibid., 46.

49. Jensen, "Houston Sit-in," 214; *Houston Chronicle*, June 13, 1963; *Houston Chronicle*, April 26, 1964.

50. Mack Jones to Franklin Jones, April 10, 2012, in Franklin Jones's personal archives (Houston, Texas); *Houston Chronicle*, June 20, 21, 1961, June 13, 1963; April 26, 1964.

51. *Houston Chronicle*, June 19, 1966, July 27, 1966; *Houston Informer*, July 27, 1966

52. *Houston Chronicle*, June 19, 1966.

Chapter 4

1. Joseph Alphonso Pierce's biography in Joseph A. Pierce's Papers, TSU Heartman Collection, Houston. Minutes of the Regular Board of Directors Meeting, June 22, 23, 1966, TSU Heartman Collection, Houston; *Houston Chronicle*, June 23, 1966 and August 7, 1966.

2. Terry H. Anderson, *The Sixties* (New York: Pearson, 2011), 33.

3. A flyer titled *Friends of Student Non-Violent Coordinating Committee Calls for New Members at TSU*, Fall 1966, in TSU Riot File, TSU Heartman Collection, Houston; *Houston Post*, October 5, 1966; *Houston Chronicle* October 4, 5, 1966. See also Cole, *No Color*; Watson, *Race and the Houston Police*, 48. See also Carson, *In Struggle*.

4. James B. Jones to Friends of SNCC, January 20, 1967, in Mack Jones's personal archives, Atlanta, Georgia.

5. See Mack Jones to Franklin Jones, "The 1967 Police Riot on TSU Campus: My Reflections," April 10, 2012, in Mack Jones's personal archives (Atlanta Georgia); Bryson, "Born in Sin." See also Friedberg, "Houston and the TSU Riot," 131–42; Bullard, *Invisible Houston*.

6. See the memo "Police Brutality Throughout the State of Texas," circa March 5, 1967, in TSU Riot File, TSU Heartman Collection, Houston. The memo is also found in Mack Jones's personal archives.

7. Ibid.

8. James B. Jones to Friends of SNCC, March 11, 1967, in Mack Jones's personal archives,

9. Henry Bullock to Mack Jones, March, 15, 1967, in Mack Jones's personal archives and also cited in Watson, *Race and the Houston Police Department*, 48–52; Mack Jones to Henry Bullock, circa March 15, 1967, cited in Bryson, "Born in Sin."

10. See the flyer titled *Attention Students, Faculty and Other Citizens of Texas*, no date, but circa March or April, 1967, in TSU Riot Files; John Biggers to President

Joseph A. Pierce, April, 8, 1967, in Joseph A. Pierce's Papers and in the TSU Riot File. *Houston Post,* March 29, April 4, 5, 6, 7, 1967; *Houston Chronicle,* April 5, 1967. See also the following letters from John B. Connally's Papers, Houston Riot File, 60–30–14, Lyndon Baines Johnson Library, Austin; Mane D. Park to Joseph Pierce, April 4, 1967; and Louie Welch to Helen Elmwood, March 9, 1967. See also Connally, "Proclamation," in John B. Connally's Papers. See also Phelps, *People's War,* 96–103.

11. *Houston Post,* April 4, 5, 6, 7; May 18, 1967; *Houston Chronicle,* May 4, 5, 1967.

12. *Houston Post,* April 4, 5, 6, 7; May 18, 1967.

13. *Arizona Republic,* March 30, 1967; *Houston Chronicle,* May 9, 1967; G. L. Nance to John B. Connally, April 4, 1967, in John B. Connally's Papers; Louie Welch to Helen Elwood, May 9, 1967, in John B. Connally's Papers.

14. *Houston Chronicle,* April 14, 1967.

15. *Forward Times,* May, 20, 27, 1967.

16. *Houston Chronicle,* April 6, 1967. Pierce wanted to discuss the issues with the students and to drop charges based on conduct. See Joseph Pierce's "Memo: Re: Organization of a Student Advisory Committee," April 10, 1967 in Joseph A. Pierce's Papers.

17. *Houston Post,* April 15, 1967. Stokley Carmichael was on his way to the University of Houston when he stopped by TSU and gave a noontime speech on April 13, 1967.

18. *Houston Post,* May 18, 1967.

19. *Forward Times,* May 20, 1967; *Houston Chronicle,* May 16, 17, 1967.

20. *Forward Times,* May 20, 1967.

21. *Houston Chronicle,* May 17, 1967; *Houston Post,* May 17, 1967; *Forward Times,* May 27, 1967; Nelson Godfrey to Connally, May 19, 1967, in John B. Connally's Papers.

22. *Houston Post,* May 17, 1967. See Homer Garrison Jr. to John B. Connally, "A Memo: Racial Problems in Houston," Department of Public Safety Interoffice Memorandum, May 24, 1967, File 60–30–14, in John B. Connally's Papers.

23. *Houston Post,* May 17, 1967; *Houston Chronicle,* May 19, 1997; *Forward Times,* May 20, 1967.

24. *Forward Times,* May 20, 1967. See also Connally, "Proclamation," May 17, 1967, in John B. Connally's Papers.

25. *Forward Times,* May 27, 1967; *Houston Chronicle,* 17, 1967.

26. *Forward Times,* May 27, 1967.

27. Ibid.

28. Ibid.

29. Ibid.

30. Ibid. See also Nelson Godfrey to Connally, May 19, 1967, in John B. Connally's Papers.

31. Minutes of the Regular Board of Directors Meetings, May 18, 1967, and June 19, 1967, TSU Heartman Collection, Houston; *Forward Times,* June 10, 1967; *Houston Post,* June 19, 1967; Regular Meeting of the Board of Directors Meeting, August 9, 1967, TSU Heartman Collection, Houston; *Houston Chronicle,* August 10, 1967.

32. Jimmie Hick to Governor John B. Connally, May 18, 1967; Lewis Bud Smith to Connally, May 23, 1967; James Martin Hill, Jr., to Connally, May 27, 1967; A. H.

Benney Jr., to Connally, May 24, 1967. All letters found in John B. Connally's Papers.

33. Lewis "Bud" Smith to John B. Connally, May 23, 1967, in John B. Connally's Papers.

34. W. N. Oates to Connally, May 19, 1967, in John B. Connally's Papers.

35. M. W. Webb to John B. Connally, May 19, 1967, in John B. Connally's Papers.

36. Richard C. Riley, May 19, 1967; see also Loy Golden to John B. Connally, April 4, 1967, in John B. Connally's Papers.

37. Jesse E. Gloster to John B. Connally, May 19, 1967, and John B. Connally to Jesse E. Gloster, June 7, 1967, in John B. Connally's Papers. See KHOU TV 11 Daily Broadcast Editorial #957, May 18, 1967, Houston, Texas.

38. Alice M. Bell to John B. Connally, May 20, 1967, in John B. Connally's Papers.

39. Hunter H. White to John B. Connally, May 25, 1967, In John B. Connally's Papers.

40. *Forward Times,* May 27, 1967. See "Department of Public Safety Interoffice Memo: Homer Garrison Jr. to John Connally," May 24, 1967, in John B. Connally's Papers. Garrison also informed the governor that "all was quiet at Prairie View after a fire setting incident on campus."

41. Memo from Chaplain Penrose W. Hirst to John B. Connally on June 5, 1967, "The Riot at TSU," in John B. Connally's Papers. See also "Presbyterian Church Petition to Expunge Records of the Students," May 20, 1967, in John B. Connally's Papers.

42. Granville V. Peaks Jr. and William F. Romelke (United Ministers) to John B. Connally, May 25, 1967, in John B. Connally's Papers.

43. See Connally, "Proclamation," May 17, 1967, in John B. Connally's Papers. Connally was ready to activate the national guard but refrained from using them, saying that "in my opinion, the city of Houston has the situation under control [and I see] no reason for the state to take action." See Carol Vance to John B. Connally, May 17, 1967, in John B. Connally's Papers; Homer Garrison to John B. Connally, May 24, 1967, in John B. Connally's Papers.

44. Regular Board of Directors Meeting, August 9, 1967; Stanley Wright, William Richard, Trazawell Franklin Jr., Douglas Wayne Waller, Charles Freeman Jr. John Parkers and Floyd Nicholas v. TSU, Civil Action #67-H-694, U.S. District Court, Southern District of Texas, September 15, 1967; *TSU Herald,* March 1, 1968; *Houston Chronicle,* September 15, 1967; *Houston Chronicle,* June 2, 3, 6, 10; July 25; August 1, 1967; *Houston Post,* June 7, 1967. TSU students sponsored a fundraiser to help fellow students who were on trial and to help others attend the trial via bus.

45. *Houston Post,* August 1, 1967, 2, 3.

46. Mrs. John Donnelly to John B. Connally, February 25, 1968, in John B. Connally's Papers; Harold R. Fray to John Connally, March 1, 1965, in John B. Connally's Papers; Ed. Boltz to John Connally March 2, 1968, in John B. Connally's Papers; *Houston Post,* November 5, 1970; *Houston Informer,* November 14, 1970.

47. "Riot, Civil and Criminal Disorder: Part 3, A Hearing before the United States Committee on Government Operations: Permanent Subcommittee, An Investigation," *United States Congress, Senate Journal, 90th Congress, First Session* (November 29–30, 1967); *Forward Times,* November 11, 21, 1967.

48. *TSU Herald,* March 1, 1968; *Houston Post,* November 9, 1968; *Houston Chronicle,* November 9, 14, 1968.

49. John Biggers (faculty assembly liaison) to Senator John L. McClellan, Novem-

ber 7, 1967, and Kenneth Tollette to John L. McClellan, November 10, 1967, TSU
Riot File, TSU Heartman Collection. See *Houston Post,* November 5, 7, 14, 1967. See
also "Students' Concerns to Senate Committee," *Houston Chronicle* November 4, 9,
1967, and in John B. Connally's Papers; *TSU Herald,* March 1, 1968.

50. See the "Findings of President's Commission on Civil Disorder," *Houston
Chronicle,* November 30, 1967.

51. *Houston Chronicle,* November 21, 1967; Minutes of the Regular Meeting of the
Board of Directors, March 1968, TSU Heartman Collection, Houston.

Chapter 5

1. Biography of Granville Sawyer from his obituary program, in Granville M.
Sawyer's Papers, TSU Heartman Collection, Houston. Sawyer died April 12, 2008.
A memorial was held for him on June 7, 2008.

2. Granville Sawyer, "The Challenge of the Negro University," 1964, Mimeograph 5, in Granville M. Sawyer's Papers.

3. Ibid.

4. Ibid.

5. Granville Sawyer, "Remarks to Administrative Officers," July 1968, in Granville M. Sawyer's Papers. See also Sawyer's "Remarks to the Faculty," September 9,
1968, in Granville M. Sawyer's Papers.

6. Sawyer, "Remarks to Administrative Officers," July 1968.

7. Ibid.

8. *Forward Times,* August 8, 1968.

9. Granville Sawyer, "Address at Opening Fall Convocation," October 3, 1968, in
Granville M. Sawyer's Papers.

10. *Houston Post,* March 8, 1969; *Houston Chronicle,* March 8, 1969. See also Sawyer's "Statement to the President's Commission on Campus Unrest (Washington,
DC)," July 17, 1970, in Granville M. Sawyer's Papers.

11. *Houston Chronicle,* December 20, 1969. See TSU *Student Code of Conduct
Handbook,* 1968, in Granville M. Sawyer's Papers.

12. *Houston Post,* March 8, 1969; *Houston Chronicle,* March 8, 1969; *TSU Herald,*
March 12, 1971; *Houston Post,* April 15, 1971.

13. *Forward Times,* December 27, 1969; Sawyer, "Challenge of the Negro University," in Granville M. Sawyer's Papers. See also Sawyer's "Statement to the President's Commission," in Granville M. Sawyer's Papers.

14. *Mid-Winter Planning Conference Proceedings of the First Annual Conference,*
December 26–28, 1968, in Granville M. Sawyer's Papers. See also Sawyer's "Challenge of the Negro University," in Granville M. Sawyer's Papers. This speech was
given at the Texas Southern University Fall Convocation, September 19, 1974.

15. *Mid-Winter Planning Conference Proceedings,* 1968, 38, in Granville M. Sawyer's Papers.

16. Ibid.; see also Sawyer, "Reshaping the University: A Plan for Relevancy," no
date, mimeograph, in Granville M. Sawyer's Papers.

17. Sawyer, "Reshaping the University."

18. Texas Southern University's 1970 *Self Study Report,* in TSU Heartman
Collection, Houston.

19. Ibid. See also the 1970 *TSU Catalog.*

20. "Goals for TSU: Discussion and Design," May 1969, mimeograph, in Granville M. Sawyer's Papers.

21. Ibid.

22. *The Second Mid-Winter Planning Conference Proceedings*, 1970, in Granville M. Sawyer's Papers. Sawyer, "Toward an Urban Institution, 1970"; Sawyer, "Texas Southern University, A Special Purpose University: A Source of Pride," no date, in Granville M. Sawyer's Papers.

23. See the following in Granville M. Sawyer's Papers: "An Agreement Between HUD and TSU, March 22, 1972"; Hortense Dixon and Naomi Lede, "The Role of TSU in Community Development," *HUD Challenge* 5, No.5 (May 1974): 12; Dixon and Lede, "Urban Minority Groups in Houston: Problems, Progress and Prospects," mimeograph, 1973, Houston; Sawyer's Commencement Address, "Toward an Urban University: A Position Statement, TSU: A Special Purpose University," May 12, 1972, both in Granville Sawyer Papers, TSU Heartman Collection. See also *Forward Times*, May 15, 1972, and "Model City," *Success* 5, January 23, 1973, Office of Advancement for Public Negro Colleges, University of Houston Archives.

24. Sawyer, "Toward an Urban University: A Position Statement, TSU: A Special Purpose University," in Granville M. Sawyer's Papers.

25. *The Third Mid-Winter Planning Conference Proceedings*, 1972, in Granville M. Sawyer's Papers. The theme for 1972 was "Excellence in Achievement." See also "Agreement Between HUD and TSU," in Granville M. Sawyer's Papers; Sawyer, "Toward an Urban University: A Position Statement, TSU: A Special Purpose University," in Granville M. Sawyer's Papers.

26. *Third Mid-Winter Planning Conference Proceedings*, 1972.

27. Granville Sawyer, "Texas Southern University: An Overview—The Urban Commitment," 1972, in Granville M. Sawyer's Papers; *The Fourth Mid-Winter Planning Conference Proceedings*, 1973, in Granville M. Sawyer's Papers. See also Sawyer, "A Special Purpose University: Program Profile," in Granville M. Sawyer's Papers.

28. Sawyer, "Toward an Urban Institution: A Design for TSU 1972." See also "Agreement Between HUD and TSU," in Granville M. Sawyer's Papers.

29. Sawyer, "A Prospectus for an Urban Resources Center at TSU," June 2, 1972, in Granville M. Sawyer's Papers. The center was approved May 11, 1972, by the board of directors and by the Texas State Coordinating Board, July 1972. See Sawyer, "Texas Southern University: An Overview—The Urban Commitment," in Granville M. Sawyer's Papers.

30. See the pamphlet *A Decade of Decisions 1968–1978: A Report—Ten Years of the Administration of President Granville Sawyer* (Houston: Texas Southern University Press, 1978), TSU Heartman Collection, Houston.

31. Minutes of the Board of Directors Meeting, March 1, 1973 TSU Heartman Collection, Houston. See "Resolution on the Need for Official Legislative Recognition of a New Dimension in the Role of TSU as an Institution of Higher Education Under Public Support," 1973, in Granville M. Sawyer's Papers; and Sawyer, "Texas Southern University, A Special Purpose Institution: A Source of Community Pride, 1972," in Granville M. Sawyer's Papers.

32. Texas Legislature, *General and Special Laws Passed in the 63rd Legislature, Regular Session*, S.B. 823 (Austin, 1973); and Tex. Ed. Code § 106.02 (1973). See also

Sawyer, "TSU, A Special Purpose Institution of Higher Education: What Does It Mean?" June 19, 1973, in Granville M. Sawyer's Papers. Sawyer also used this paper to deliver his speech at TSU's summer commencement in August of 1973. See also Sawyer, "One University's Urban Commitment," *Journal of Extension* 11, no. 1 (Spring, 1973): 41–48; Lash, Dixon, and Freeman, *Texas Southern University*.

33. *Decade of Decisions*, 1–39; Sawyer, "One University's Urban Commitment," *Journal of Extension* (Spring 1973): 9–12. See also Sawyer, "Black College and Community Development," *Journal of Black Studies* 6, no. 7 (September 1975): 77–99.

34. *Decade of Decisions*; Sawyer, "A Special Purpose University: Program Profile," in Granville M. Sawyer's Papers; Sawyer, "Texas Southern University: An Overview—The Urban Commitment," in Granville M. Sawyer's Papers. See also "Prospectus for An Urban Resources Center at TSU," June 2, 1972, in Granville M. Sawyer's Papers; H. Hadley Hartshorn to James R. Nolan, February 14, 1968, in Granville M. Sawyer's Papers.

35. Naomi Lede and Hortense W. Dixon, "Minority Groups in Houston: Problem, Progress and Prospect," 1973, in Granville M. Sawyer's Papers.

36. Ibid.; Sawyer, "A Special Purpose University: Program Profile," in Granville M. Sawyer's Papers.

37. A brief history of KTSU Radio can be found at http://ktsuradion.com/about.

38. Ibid.; *Houston Post,* December 6, 1974. See also "A Prospectus for Urban Resources Center at TSU," June 2, 1972, in Granville M. Sawyer's Papers.

39. *Ralph Bunche Journal* in TSU Heartman Collection, Houston; *Texas Southern Law School Journal* in TSU Law Library. See also *Decade of Decisions*.

40. *Mid-Winter Planning Conference Proceedings*, 1968.

41. Ibid. See Sawyer's "Remarks to the Faculty," September 8, 1968, in Granville M. Sawyer's Papers; *TACT Newsletter*, May 1974, in TSU Heartman Collection, Houston.

42. *TACT Newsletter*, May 1972, TSU Heartman Collection, Houston.

43. Ibid.

44. Robert J. Terry to Sawyer, October 2, 1972; Robert J. Terry, "Memo to Faculty Assembly," September 23, 1972; Terry to Sawyer, May 1974; Timothy Cotton to Sawyer, April 12, 1973. All correspondences are found in the May 1974 issue of *TACT Newsletter*, TSU Heartman Collection, Houston.

45. *TACT Newsletter*, May, 1974, TSU Heartman Collection, Houston.

46. Ibid.

47. Ibid.

48. *TACT Newsletter*, October 1977, TSU Heartman Collection, Houston.

49. Ibid.

50. Granville Sawyer to TSU Faculty, October 5, 1977, *TACT Newsletter*, October 1977, TSU Heartman Collection, Houston.

51. Robert Terry et al., *Faculty Manual: Policies Regulations, Procedures* (Revised 1974), TSU Heartman Collection, Houston; *TACT Newsletter*, October 1977, TSU Heartman Collection, Houston.

52. Authur W. Danner, *Procedures and Internal Control* (Houston, mimeographed), May 12, 1979, in Granville M. Sawyer's Papers; *Houston Post,* March 29, 1970, December 1, 1971, October 29, 1974, December 12, 1974, September 6, 1975, December 14, 1976; *Houston Chronicle*, December 11, 1974, March 29, 1976, August 31, 1980.

53. Senate Bill 2031, An Act Relating to the Governance of Certain State Agencies, Sec. 1.01 involving subchapter G 51 Ed. Code amended by addition Sec. 51.358 and 51.359 (1976); *Houston Post,* December 14, 15, 16, 1976. See also *Houston Chronicle,* December 14, 15, 16, 1976.

54. *Houston Post,* December 12, 28, 1979; *Houston Chronicle,* January 1, 4, 10, 11, 15, 16, 1979.

55. John Westberry to Granville Sawyer, February 16, 1978, in Granville M. Sawyer's Papers; *TSU Staff Conference Proceedings,* September 8, 1977, in Granville M. Sawyer's Papers; *Houston Chronicle,* November 4 and 17, 1979; *Houston Chronicle,* December 11, 1979; Minutes of the Regular Board of Regents Meeting, December 4, 1979 and August 31, 1980. TSU, Heartman Collection, Houston.

56. *Decades of Decisions,* 39.

Chapter 6

1. Everett O. Bell's biography and obituary program in Everett O. Bell's Papers, TSU Heartman Collection, Houston; Minutes of the Board of Regents Meeting, August 15, 1980, TSU Heartman Collection, Houston.

2. Nebraska Mays to Everett O. Bell, May 7, 1980, in Everett O. Bell's Papers; Joseph Jones to Nebraska May 22, 1980, in Everett O. Bell's Papers. See also "TSU 1980 Self-Study Report," in Everett O. Bell's Papers; *Houston Post,* November 8, 1980. A student services building was named in Bell's honor on May 13, 1983.

3. Leonard Hall O'Connell Spearman's biography and obituary program, January 25, 2008, in Leonard H. O. Spearman's Papers, TSU Heartman Collection, Houston; Pitre, "Leonard H. O. Spearman"; *Transition,* September 7, 2008; *Houston Chronicle,* June 4, 1980. Spearman died January 16, 2008 and was funeralized January 25, 2008.

4. Spearman, "Excellence—Key to A New Decade at TSU," *TSU Today,* September 7, 1980, a publication of TSU Office of Development, in Leonard H. O. Spearman's Papers.

5. Ibid. "The President's Management Memorandum to Faculty," June 15, July 27, 1981, in Leonard H. O. Spearman's Papers.

6. See "Amendment Granting Texas Southern University Authority to Use Undelegated 247 Funds to Liquidate Certain Liabilities," in Leonard H. O. Spearman's Papers. See also *Houston Chronicle,* November 6, 1980; *Houston Post,* August 29, 1988.

7. *Adams v Richardson,* 351 F Supp. 636; *Adams v. Bell,* 711 F2 & lll, 1983. See *Kenneth Adams et al. Appellate v. Terrell Bell et al.,* 711 F, 2d 161 (D.C. cen 1983). This case was originally brought against the secretary of HEW, John Richardson, but later changed to the current secretary of education, Terrell Bell.

8. "Texas Plan for Equal Educational Opportunity: A Brief History," Texas Higher Education Coordinating Board Report (Austin, November 1999); TSU HEW Compliance Review, 1981, both in Priscilla D. Slade's Papers, TSU Heartman Collection, Houston; "President's Management Memo, March 9, June 15, 1981, in Leonard H. O. Spearman's Papers. See also "Texas Southern University: The Stepchild of the Texas Higher Education System," *Journal of Blacks in Higher Education* 25 (Autumn, 1999).

9. Texas Legislature, *General and Special Laws Passed in the 67th Legislature, Regular Session* (Austin: 1981). In Leonard H. O. Spearman's Papers, see the following: "TSU Mission Study: President's Management Memo," July 15, 1984; Kenneth Ashworth to Leonard Spearman, March 11, 1983; *TSU Mission Study Journal* 1, no. 6, June 1983.

10. *Houston Chronicle*, April 12, 1983; "President's Management Memo," August 10, 1983, in Leonard H. O. Spearman's Papers.

11. "TSU Mission and Enhancement Study," Summer 1982, in Leonard H. O. Spearman's Papers.

12. Spearman to Charles E. Bishop, February 18, 1982. All letters to and from Spearman are taken from Leonard H. O. Spearman's Papers.

13. Spearman to Kenneth Ashworth, March 4, 1982. See also Spearman, "Education in America: Whose Needs Are Being Served?" *Issue Magazine* 1, no. 1 (January 1982): 4–7.

14. Bishop to Ashworth, June 3, 1982, in Leonard H. O. Spearman's Papers.

15. Spearman to Wilhelmina Delco, September 8, 1982. See also Spearman, "Minority Rights to Post-Secondary Education," given at the National Negro Scholarship Fund Meeting, Atlanta Georgia, October 27, 1987.

16. "A Bill to be Entitled: An Act Relating to the Creation of the Texas Southern University System Sec.1, Chapter 106, Texas Education Code is amended by adding Sec. 106.7 See 106.91 68R 540 5RC-D," in Leonard H. O. Spearman's Papers.

17. Mission and Enhancement Study for TSU, 1982. See also Spearman to Kathy Whitmire, August 16, 1983, both in Leonard H. O. Spearman's Papers.

18. Spearman to Mrs. Woodward, August 20, 1982.

19. Bob Bullock to Spearman, January 10, 1983; Spearman's remarks at opening faculty and staff meeting, August 26, 1983, in Spearman Papers.

20. *TSU Today*, September 15, 1984; Minutes of the Board of Regents Meeting, July 6, 1984, TSU Heartman Collection, Houston; *Houston Chronicle*, July 7, 1984.

21. "The Texas Plan: A Draft," mimeograph, 64, 133–35, in Leonard H. O. Spearman's Papers; *Houston Chronicle*, September 24, 1985.

22. "Texas Plan," 64.

23. Ibid.; *Houston Post*, March 13, 1983; *Houston Chronicle*, March 10, 1983.

24. *Houston Post*, April 12, 1983. See also "TSU's HEW Compliance Review," no date, in Leonard H. O. Spearman's Papers.

25. Harry W. Singleton to Mark White, June 14, 1983; Spearman to Mark White, June 16, 28, 1983; "Texas Plan," 28–29, 64, 133–35; *Houston Chronicle*, August 21, 1982. See also John W. Fainter to Spearman, March 4, 1983. All of the above in Leonard H. O. Spearman's Papers.

26. *Houston Chronicle*, June 28, 1983. See also TSU Press Release, June 28, 1983, in Leonard H. O. Spearman's Papers.

27. *Houston Chronicle*, June 28, 1983.

28. Ibid.

29. *Houston Defender*, July 27, August 4, 1983.

30. Pamela Bradshaw to Mark White, July 26, 1983; James Lang to Mark White, August 1, 1983; Mark White to Wyman Barnett, August 4, 1983. All in Leonard H. O. Spearman's Papers.

31. Mike Petrizzo to Mark White, October 29, 1983; White to Petrizzo, October

31, 1983. Both in Leonard H. O. Spearman's Papers.

32. *Houston Chronicle*, December 23, 1983; *Houston Post*, December 22, 1983. Bob Slager to Dr. & Mrs. Spearman, January 11, 1983; and Spearman to Mark White, January 10, 1983.

33. *Houston Defender*, July 27, 1984, *Forward Times*, January 14, 17, 23, 1984.

34. Spearman to David F. Johnson, August 10, 1984.

35. Spearman to Kenneth Ashworth, March 1, 1985.

36. *TSU Chat and Talk Newsletter* 7 (March 13, 1986), in Leonard H. O. Spearman's Papers; Minutes of the Board of Regents Meeting, March 13, 1986, TSU Heartman Collection, Houston.

37. *TSU Herald*, July 1986; "People-to-People Campaign," *TSU Today*, July 19, 1983, in Leonard H. O. Spearman's Papers; *Houston Defender*, February 6, 1986.

38. See "National Conference on Excellence and Economic Growth, Program," *TSU Today*, April 24, 1984, TSU Heartman Collection, Houston.

39. Larry Temple to Howard D. Kervin et al., February 15, 1985, in Leonard H. O. Spearman's Papers.

40. Minutes of Regular Board of Regents Meeting, November 1985; *Houston Chronicle*, November 2, 1985.

41. Spearman to Ashworth, February 5, 1986. See also Spearman to Ashworth, July 29, 1982; Spearman to William P. Hobby, September 1982.

42. *Houston Chronicle*, June 6, 1986; *Houston Post*, June 6, 1986; Spearman to Milton Carroll, June 6, 1986; Minutes of the Board of Regents Meeting, June 6, 1986, TSU Heartman Collection, Houston. See also Earnest Sterling to Mark White, April 11, 1983, in Leonard H. O. Spearman's Papers. In Sterling's letter, he asks White to remain on the TSU board.

Chapter 7

1. Biography of Robert J. Terry, in Robert J. Terry's Papers, TSU Heartman Collection, Houston; *Houston Chronicle*, June 18, 1986; *Forward Times*, June 28, 1986.

2. *Forward Times*, June 28, 1986.

3. *Forward Times*, September 26, 1986. See also the record of enrollment in the Registrar's Office. Robert Terry to Mark White, July 22, 1986, in Robert J. Terry's Papers; *Houston Chronicle*, February 17, 1987.

4. *Houston Informer*, October 8, 1986. See Chuck Smith's press release, October 8, 1986. See also Kenneth Ashworth to Robert Terry, August 6, 1986, in Robert J. Terry's Papers.

5. *Houston Post*, June 6, 1962. See *Houston Chronicle*, June 6, 9, 1962.

6. *Family Newspages*, October 13, 1964; *Houston Post*, July 14, October 8, 10, 13, 1964.

7. *Houston Chronicle*, July 9, 1962; *Houston Post*, June 6, 1962.

8. *Houston Family Newspages*, October 13, 1964; *Houston Chronicle*, October 13, 1964.

9. *Houston Chronicle*, January 7, 11, 1965.

10. Minutes of the Regular Board of Regents Meeting, January 6, 1965, TSU Heartman Collection, Houston; *Houston Chronicle*, January 7, 11, 31, 1965.

11. *Houston Post*, March 31, 1965.

12. *Houston Chronicle,* May 1, 1966. See also *Houston Chronicle,* April 5, 12, 18, 1966.

13. *Houston Chronicle,* April 2, 11, 14, 1969. See also *Houston Post,* April 2, 13, 1969. See also *Houston Post,* April 14, 1965.

14. *Houston Chronicle,* April 2, 11, 14, 1969.

15. *Houston Post,* March 5, 21, 23, 1975.

16. *Houston Post,* March 5, 21, 23, 14, 1975.

17. *Houston Post,* March 5, 11, 1975.

18. *Houston Chronicle,* February 21, 1982; *Houston Chronicle,* November 25, 1983; *Houston Chronicle,* June 14, November 22, 25, 1986.

19. *Houston Chronicle,* November 22, 25, 1986.

20. Minutes of the Regular Board of Regents Meeting, November 11, 1985, TSU Heartman Collection, Houston; Larry Temple to Board of Regents June 3, 1986; Larry Temple to Vic Arnold, June 2, 1986. See also Larry Temple to Winston Webster, February 15, 1985, in Robert J. Terry's Papers, TSU Heartman Collection.

21. *Houston Chronicle,* October 11, 13, 14, 1986.

22. *Houston Chronicle,* October 11, 1986.

23. *Houston Chronicle,* November 18, 20 1986; *Houston Post,* November 14, 18, 19, 20, 1980; *Houston Chronicle,* November 18, 1986.

24. "A Bill to Be Entitled: An Act Relating in the Creation of a Texas Southern University System, Sec. 1, Chapter 106, Texas Educational Code Amended by Adding 106.7." See copy in Leonard H. O. Spearman's Papers. See also *Houston Chronicle,* December 3, 1986.

25. *Houston Chronicle,* November 22, 1986.

26. *Houston Chronicle,* November 21, 1986. Joe L. McCormick to Larry Temple, December 2, 1986. See also Hershel Meriwhether et al. to Mark White, November 20, 1986. Leland spoke off the cuff at the meeting, but he had a prepared statement. See "Mickey Leland Opposes TSU-UH Merger," Press Release, November 13, 1986. See also his handwritten statement on merger; all items are in Robert J. Terry's Papers.

27. Robert Terry's speech on "TSU Response to the Merger Proposal," November 21, 1986, in Robert J. Terry's Papers.

28. Ibid.

29. Ibid.

30. Mark White to Larry Temple, November 20, 1986, in Robert J. Terry's Papers; *Houston Chronicle,* November 26, 1986. See also *Houston Chronicle,* November 29, December 3, 10, 12, 1986.

31. *Houston Chronicle,* November 10, 1987; *Houston Chronicle,* January 11, 1987, February 8, 17, 21, 1987, and August 30, 1987. See Minutes of the Meeting of the President's Council, September 1, 1987, in Leonard H. O. Spearman's Papers.

32. *Houston Chronicle,* September 13, 14, 15, 17, 1987; Minutes of Regular Board Meetings, September and October, 1987. TSU Heartman Collection, Houston. After his death, the TSU library was named in Terry's honor. See *Inside Edition Library Newsletter* 1, no. 1 (September 28, 1989) and also "TSU Library Program Honoring Terry," in Robert J. Terry's Papers; *Houston Chronicle,* September 28, 1989.

Chapter 8

1. Biography of William H. Harris in William H. Harris's Papers, TSU Heartman Collection, Houston; Harris, *Keeping the Faith*; Harris, *Harder We Run*; *Houston Post*, December 9, 1987, May 25, 1988. In a *Houston Post* Op-Ed piece (May 25, 1988), Harris gives an extensive coverage of his background.

2. See the website for the Texas Higher Education Coordinating Board, https://www.thecb.state.tx.us; see also "Texas College and University System Co-coordinating Board," Scrapbook, Dolph Briscoe Center for American History, University of Texas at Austin; Ashworth, "Texas Higher Education Coordinating Board."

3. *Developing Partnerships and Building Futures: TSU 2020 Conference,* Proceedings and Conference Program, November 9, 1990, in William H. Harris's Papers.

4. Minutes of Board of Regents Meeting, July 15, 1988, TSU Heartman Collection, Houston; TSU press release, July 15, 1988, in William H. Harris's Papers.

5. Minutes of TSU Academic Council Meeting, July 19, 1988, in William H. Harris's Papers.

6. Ibid., *Houston Newspages,* September 24, 1988, in William H. Harris's Papers.

7. *Houston Newspages,* September 24, 1988, in William H. Harris's Papers.

8. Ibid.

9. Harris's "Speech to TSU Faculty," September 27, 1988; *TSU Today,* September 27, 1988; *Houston Post*, September 28, 1988. All items can be found in William H. Harris's Papers.

10. Harris's "Speech to TSU Faculty," September 27, 1988.

11. Ibid.

12. Minutes of the Regular Board of Regents Meeting, February 3, 1989, TSU Heartman Collection, Houston; William Harris to Wilhelminia Delco, February 27, 1989. All correspondences to and from Harris are taken from William H. Harris's Papers. See also Harris's speech on accomplishments, September 20, 1989, in William H. Harris's Papers.

13. *Houston Post,* October 27, 1988; William Harris's letter to the editor in the *Houston Post*, March 10, 1989.

14. *Houston Post,* October 27, 1988; March 10, 1989; William Harris to Gilbert "Gib" Lewis and William P. Hobby, November 13, 1989; *Houston Chronicle,* November 16, 1989.

15. William Harris to Ann Richards, March 25, 1991; *Houston Chronicle,* November 16, 1989; William Harris to William Clements, William P. Hobby, and Gib Lewis, April 4, 1990.

16. Minutes of the Board of Regents Meeting, February 3, 1989, TSU Heartman Collection, Houston; William Harris to Irma Malloy, January 3, 1990. See Harris's speech at the opening faculty meeting, January, 12, 1990. See also the TSU budget statement presented to the Legislative Budget Board, February 28, 1989, both in William H. Harris's Papers.

17. Harris's speech at opening faculty meeting, January 12, 1990.

18. Ibid.

19. William Harris to Wilhelmina Delco, February 27, 1989; William Harris to Larry Evans, February 1, 1989; Larry Evans to William Clements, June 26, 1989; Harris to William P. Hobby, May 1, 1989; TSU's press release on the Center on the

Family and the Black Male Initiative, September 23, 1988. See also "TSU Response to Rider." All items are in William H. Harris's Papers.

20. Harris's speech on accomplishments, January 12, 1990; William Harris to Craig Washington October 23, 1991. See "Faculty Evaluation Instrument 1990"; all items in William H. Harris's Papers.

21. Harris's speech on accomplishments, January 12, 1990; TSU's press release on the center on the black male initiative, September 23, 1988; Harris's speech at the open faculty meeting, September 2, 1990; all in William H. Harris's Papers. Harris to the Board of Regents, Minutes of Board of Regents Meetings, September 16, 1992; October 13, 1992, TSU Heartman Collection, Houston.

22. See the Mickey Leland Center proposal and TSU press release, December 4, 1989 in William H. Harris's Papers; *Houston Chronicle*, March 6, 1993.

23. Harris's speech on accomplishments, September 20, 1989. See also TSU press release, July 17, 1989; both items in William H. Harris's Papers. *Houston Chronicle*, October 13, 1992.

24. Harris's speech on accomplishments, January 5, 1991; Larry Evans to William Clements, June 26, 1989; Harris to Evans July 7, 1989. All items in William H. Harris's Papers. See also Op-Ed, *Houston Chronicle*, March 6, 1991.

25. See *Developing Partnerships and Building Futures: TSU 2020 Conference*, in William H. Harris's Papers.

26. Harris's speech, "Toward a Bold New Vision for Texas Southern University," was delivered November 9, 1990, at the *Developing Partnerships and Building Futures: TSU 2020 Conference*. The speech can be found in William H. Harris's Papers.

27. Minutes of the Board of Regents Meetings, April 3, 1991, and January 5, 1991, TSU Heartman Collection, Houston; Harris to Advisory Committee, September 3, 1991, in William H. Harris's Papers.

28. Minutes of the Board of Regents Meetings October 4, 1991; November 1, 1991, TSU Heartman Collection, Houston.

29. Minutes of the Board of Regents Meeting, June 5, 1992, TSU Heartman Collection, Houston; *Houston Chronicle*, June 6, 1992; *Houston Post*, June 18, 1992. See also a draft of Harris's "Evolving Thoughts on Admission Policy and TSU Evolving Success Story," in William H. Harris's Papers.

30. *Houston Post*, June 13, 1992. See also Harris's Op-Ed piece, "If Our Children Are Going to Learn More, We Must Demand More," *Houston Chronicle*, June 6, 1992. See also *Houston Chronicle*, June 13, 1992, November 30, 1992, and December 1, 1993.

31. Minutes of the Board of Regents Meeting, December 4, 1992, TSU Heartman Collection, Houston

32. Ibid. See also "Message from President Harris to TSU Alumni," September 5, 1990, in William H. Harris's Papers.

33. *Houston Post*, December 16, 18, 19, 20, 1992; *Houston Chronicle, December* 1, 6, 20, 22, 31, 1992; January 12, 13, 17, 26; and February 13, 1993.

34. *Houston Chronicle*, March 1, 1993; *Houston Post*, March 1, 6, 1993; *Houston Post*, December 16, 1992; *TSU Herald*, March 5, 1993; *Houston Chronicle*, February 7, 13, 19, 1993; Minutes of the Board of Regents Meeting, February 19, 1993, TSU Heartman Collection, Houston. See also *Houston Post*, January 5, 14, 17, 27, and February 7 and 13, 1993.

35. William Harris to Board of Regents, February 19, 1993, in William H. Harris's Papers; *TSU Herald,* February 25, 1933; *Houston Chronicle,* February 25, 1993.

Chapter 9

1. *Houston Chronicle,* June 25, 1993.
2. Joann Horton's biography in Joann Horton's Papers, TSU Heartman Collection, Houston; *Houston Chronicle,* August 7, 1993; *Houston Post,* August 6, 1993.
3. Mark S. Smock to William Harris, July 9, 1993, in William H. Harris's Papers.
4. William Harrell to Board of Regents in Minutes of the Board of Regents Meeting, June 1, 1993, TSU Heartman Collection, Houston. See *Faculty Voice,* June 1997.
5. Joann Horton's presentation to board of regents, in the Minutes of Board of Regents Meeting, December 1994, TSU Heartman Collection, Houston.
6. *Houston Newspages,* August 23, September 3, 1993.
7. Rufus Cormier to TSU administrators, faculty, and staff, August 18, 1993; audio recording of TSU's opening faculty meeting, August 25, 1993. Both items are in Joann Horton's Papers, TSU Heartman Collection.
8. *TSU Herald,* September 13, 1993.
9. Ibid.
10. Minutes of Board of Regents Meetings, November 30, 1993; October 7, 1994; December 4, 1993, TSU Heartman Collection, Houston.
11. Horton's inaugural address, "For the 21st Century and Beyond: A Revitalization of our Tradition of Excellence in Achievement," December 10, 1993; TSU press release, December 14, 1994. See also Horton's "Proposed Performance Goals and Objectives, Fiscal Year 1994–1995," presented to the board of regents, Minutes of Board of Regents Meetings, December 3, 1993, in Joann Horton's Papers. See also Minutes for the Board of Regents Meetings, February 4, 1994, April 8, 1994, June 3, 1994, TSU Heartman Collection, Houston. See also *Houston Newspages,* September 26, 1994.
12 Horton's inaugural address, December 14, 1994, in Joann Horton's Papers.
13. Minutes of Board of Regents Meetings, December 3, 1993; February 7, 1994; April 8, 1994, June 3, 1994, TSU Heartman Collection, Houston; *Houston Chronicle,* June 12, 1994.
14. *Houston Chronicle,* June 2, 1994. See also Michael Berryhill, "The Terminator," *Houston Press,* October 6, 1994; *Faculty Voice,* January 1997; *Houston Sun,* June 2, 1994.
15. *Houston Chronicle,* June 21, 1994; William A. Lawson to Rufus Cormier, July 21, 1994, in Joann Horton's Papers.
16. *TSU Herald,* August 23, 1994, and September 3, 1994; *Houston Newspages,* August 23, 1994.
17. Berryhill, "The Terminator," *Houston Press,* October 6, 1994; Kenneth Jackson to Horton on Strategic Plan, October 25, 1994, in Joann Horton's Papers.
18. Horton's speech to the board of regents, October 7, 1994; Minutes of the Board of Regents Meeting, October 7, 1994, TSU Heartman Collection, Houston.
19. *Faculty Voice,* January 1997.
20. Mark S. Smock (Auditor) to William. H. Harris, July 7, 1993, Harris and Hor-

ton Papers; *Houston Chronicle,* July 15, 16, 1994, and September 6, 1994; *Houston Post,* July 16, 1994. See also the 1993 financial compliance (audit) SAO report # 94–105, April 1994, 1994, in William H. Harris's Papers. See also athletic operation and follow up audit (internal audit report) #94–07, released June 4, 1994, in Joann Horton's Papers

21. Joann Horton, "State of the University," in *TSU Fall Quarterly,* 1994, TSU Heartman Collection, Houston.

22. *Houston Chronicle,* September 25, 1994.

23. Smock to Harris, July 9, 1993, in Joann Horton's Papers and William H. Harris's Papers.

24. *Houston Chronicle,* July 16, 1994; Rufus Cormier to Joann Horton, September 1, 1994, and James Ward to Joann Horton, Houston, September 1, 1994; TSU press release, September 2, 1994. All items are in Joann Horton's Papers.

25. *Houston Chronicle,* July 16, 1994. Rufus Cormier to Joann Horton, September 1, 1994, and James Ward to Joann Horton, September 1, 1994, in Joann Horton's Papers. Smock to Harris, July 7, 1993.

26. *Houston Chronicle,* September 25, 1994; Berryhill, "The Terminator," *Houston Press,* October 6, 1994.

27. Minutes Regular Board of Regents Meeting, October 7, 1994, TSU Heartman Collection, Houston; Smock to Harris, July 7, 1993, in William H. Harris's Papers; *Houston Chronicle,* September 1, 1994; February 15, 16; March 9; November 11; December14, 1994; April 11, 1995; June 6, 1995.

28. *Houston Chronicle,* January 30, 1995; April 2, 16, 1995.

29. *Houston Chronicle,* March 11, 1995; April 29, 1995.

30 *Faculty Voice,* June 1997. See flyer *Faculty, Staff, Students, Take a Stand. Send a vote of no confidence in Joann Horton to our Regents,* circa March 1995, in Joann Horton's Papers.

31. See *Faculty Voice,* June 1997; *Houston Chronicle,* April 29, 1995.

32. Jenard Gross to Al Edward, May 10, 1997 printed in *Faculty Voice,* June 1997.

33. Minutes of the Regular Board of Regents Meeting, June 2, 1995, TSU Heartman Collection, Houston. See Horton's "Open Letter to the TSU Family," circa June 2, 1955. See also "Some Notes and Observations," circa June 1995, no author, no date, in Joann Horton's Papers.

34. Minutes of the Regular Board of Regents Meeting, August 2, 1995, TSU Heartman Collection, Houston; *Houston Chronicle,* August 7, 1995.

35. "An Agreement between Horton and the TSU Board of Regents," September 1995, in Joann Horton's Papers.

Chapter 10

1. *Houston Chronicle,* October 7, 1995. Minutes of the Regular Board of Regents Meeting, October 1995.

2. James M. Douglas's biography in the "50th Anniversary Charter Day and the Inauguration Program" of James M. Douglas, March 7, 1997. See also "Presidential Inaugural Symposium Program," March 6, 1997, in James M. Douglas's Papers, TSU Heartman Collection, Houston.

3. *Houston Chronicle,* December 14, 18, 21, 1995.

4. See the 1993 financial compliance (audit) SAO report # 94–105, April 1994; the management central audit SAO report, June 1994; and also the athletic operation and follow up audit (internal audit report) # 94–07, released June 4, 1994. All items are in Joann Horton's Papers.

5. See the 1993 financial compliance (audit) SAO report # 94–105, April 1994.

6. "1995 Financial and Compliance Audit Results of Texas Southern University," in James M. Douglas's Papers; President Douglas's press release, February 15, 1996, in James M. Douglas's Papers; Michael Berryhill, "No Problem Man," *Houston Press,* January 28, 1997.

7. An "Open Letter from the President" [to the faculty], February 3, 1996, in James M. Douglas's Papers. See also president's press release of the 1995 financial aid compliance audit results, February 15, 1996, in James M. Douglas's Papers.

8. *Houston Chronicle,* March 27, April 2, 1996. See also *Faculty Voice,* December 1997.

9. *Houston Forward Times,* November 20–26, 1996.

10. "President's Management Mission Statement," December 13, 1996, in James M. Douglas's Papers.

11. Douglas, "Memo to University Faculty and Staff," April 26, 1996, in James M. Douglas's Papers.

12. TSU Legislative Request to 75th Legislation, 1997 (Houston: TSU Press, 1997), in James M. Douglas's Papers.

13. Douglas's inaugural address, March 7, 1997, in James M. Douglas's Papers; *Houston Chronicle,* March 8, 1997; *Forward Times* March 15, 1997. See also Douglas's "Memo to University Family," April 24, 1998, in James M. Douglas's Papers.

14. The President's Inaugural Symposium Program, "21st Century Challenges Impacting Texas Southern University," March 6, 1997, in James M. Douglas's Papers; *The Houston Chronicle,* March 8, 1997.

15. *Houston Chronicle,* March 9, 1997; *Houston Newspages,* March 13–19, 1997; *Forward Times, March,* 13–19, 1997.

16. *Houston Chronicle,* May 28, 1997.

17. See "An Open Letter from the President to Faculty," February 3, 1996, in James M. Douglas's Papers. See also "President's Press Release of the 1995 Financial and Compliance Audit Result," February 15, 1996, in James M. Douglas's Papers.

18. Minutes of the Board of Regents Meeting, August 29, 1997, TSU Heartman Collection, Houston; *Houston Chronicle,* August 30, 1999.

19. *Houston Chronicle,* August 30, 1999.

20. *Houston Chronicle,* September 8, 1997.

21. Willard Jackson to James Douglas, November 14, 1997, and Douglas to Jackson November 17, 1997, in Priscilla D. Slade's Papers; *Faculty Voice,* November 1997; Minutes of Regular Board of Regents Meeting, October 10, 1997, TSU Heartman Collection, Houston; *Houston Chronicle,* October 10, 11, 20, 1997.

22. Minutes of Regular Board of Regents Meeting, November 21, 1997, TSU Heartman Collection, Houston.

23. *The Faculty Voice,* November 1997.

24. Ibid.

25. Minutes of Regular Board of Regents Meeting, December 1, 1997, TSU Heartman Collection, Houston.

26. *Houston Chronicle*, December 1, 1997, and March 7, 8, 9, 1998.

27. *Houston Chronicle*, December 1, 1997.

28. Douglas, "An Open Letter from the President to the Faculty," February 3, 1996; Douglas, "Memo to Faculty and Staff," April 26, 1996; Douglas, "President's Management System," December 12, 1996, in James M. Douglas's Papers.

29. *Houston Chronicle*, 23, 1998. See the flyer *Students Taking Over the Negotiations of the Contract for President Douglas,* April 21, 1998. See also the United Front press release, "Hands Off TSU: Hands Off Douglas," April 21, 1998; both items are in James M. Douglas's Papers.

30. Minutes of the Regular Board of Regents Meeting, April 21, 1998, TSU Heartman Collection, Houston.

31. Anthony Lyons to Willard Jackson, April 27, 1998, and Jackson to Lyons, April 27, 1998; both cited in the *Houston Chronicle*, April 27, 1998. See also *TSU Voice*, May 1998.

32. Flyer "TSU on the Move: A Press Statement from a Coalition to Save Douglas," May 14, 1998, in James M. Douglas's Papers; *Houston Chronicle*, May 14, 19, 29, 1998.

33. *Houston Forward Times*, May 20–26, 1998. See also *Houston Chronicle*, May, 20, 30, 1998.

34. *Houston Chronicle*, May 18, 1998.

35. Minutes of Regular Board of Regents Meeting, May 22, 1998, TSU Heartman Collection, Houston; *Houston Chronicle*, May 23, June 9, 1998.

36. *Houston Chronicle*, May 30, 1998, and June 9, 1998.

37. *Houston Chronicle*, May 30, 1998 and June 9, 1998; *Faculty Voice*, May 1998.

38. *Faculty Voice*, May 1998; Minutes of the Regular Board of Regent Meetings, May 22, 1998, TSU Heartman Collection, Houston.

39. Douglas, memo to members of the TSU Board of Regents, June 9, 1998, in James M. Douglas's Papers; *Houston Chronicle*, May 30, 1998, and June 9, 1998.

40. Minutes of Regular Board of Regents Meeting, July 11, 1998, TSU Heartman Collection, Houston; *Houston Chronicle*, July 11, 1998.

41. *Houston Chronicle*, July 11, 1998.

42. Minutes of the Regular Board of Regents Meeting, October 3, 1998, TSU Heartman Collection, Houston.

43. David Morgan to Douglas, April 3, 1998; Douglas to Morgan, April 6, 1998, cited in *Faculty Voice*, May 1998.

44. *Houston Chronicle*, October 3, 1998. See Douglas's "Memo to University Family," April 24, 1998, in James M. Douglas's Papers.

45. Minutes of Regular Board Meeting, November 8, 1998, TSU Heartman Collection, Houston; *Houston Chronicle*, November 9, 1998.

46. *Houston Chronicle*, November 9, 1998.

47. *Houston Chronicle*, November 12, 1998.

48. Willard Jackson's Op-Ed, "TSU Addressing Concerns," *Houston Chronicle*, November 16, 1998.

49. Op-Ed, "Warning, TSU–A Harrowing Place to Seek College Education," *Houston Chronicle*, November 20, 1998. See also *Houston Chronicle*, November 21, 22, 24, 1998.

50. Robert Junell and William Ratliff to the TSU Board of Regents, December 4,

1998, cited in *Houston Chronicle,* January 5, 1999.

51. Minutes of the Regular Board of Regents Meeting, January 5, 1999, TSU Heartman Collection, Houston; *Houston Chronicle,* January 6, 9, 22, 23, 1999.

52. Minutes of a Special Board of Regents Meeting, January 22, 1999, TSU Heartman Collection, Houston; *Faculty Voice,* January 1999.

53. Minutes of Regular Board of Regents Meeting, February 6, 1999, TSU Heartman Collection, Houston.

Chapter 11

1. Priscilla Dean Slade's biography in "Inaugural Program of Priscilla Slade, April 26, 2000," in Priscilla D. Slade's Papers, TSU Heartman Collection, Houston. Slade was part of Governor Perry's transition team, December 14, 2000.

2. Minutes of Regular Board of Regents Meeting, February 5, 1999, TSU Heartman Collection, Houston.

3. Lawrence F. Alwin to Legislative Audit Committee, "Follow up Audit, Texas Southern University," February 12, 1999 (Austin, Texas), in Priscilla D. Slade's Papers; *Houston Chronicle,* March 5, 1999.

4. *Houston Chronicle,* March 2, 3, 5, 1999

5. "Whither Bound?" Slade's address to the faculty, March 4, 2000, in Priscilla D. Slade's Papers. A tape recording of this speech is also in the TSU Heartman Collection, Houston.

6. *Houston Chronicle,* March 9, 17, 19, 1999.

7. *Houston Chronicle,* March 17, 19, 1999; Minutes of Regular Board of Regents Meeting, March 17, 1999, TSU Heartman Collection, Houston.

8. Audio tape recording of Priscilla Slade's presentation to the Legislative Budget Board, March 2, 1999, in Priscilla D. Slade's Papers.

9. Ibid.

10. Lawrence F. Alwin, "Follow up Audits," February 5, June 1999, in Priscilla D. Slade's Papers; *Houston Chronicle,* April 11, 1999; April 5, 6, 7, 8, 1999; May 1, 1999.

11. Rick Perry to Willard Jackson, August 13, 1999; Willard Jackson to Priscilla D. Slade, August 30, 1999; both in Priscilla D. Slade's Papers.

12. Minutes of Regular Board of Regents Meeting, October 26, 27 1999, TSU Heartman Collection, Houston; *Houston Chronicle,* October 28, 1999.

13. See Slade's inaugural speech, April 26, 2000, or listen to the audio version of this speech. Both sources in the Heartman Collection; *Houston Chronicle,* April 28, 2000.

14. Slade's inaugural speech, April 26, 2000; TSU's Opening Faculty Meeting Programs 2001, 2003, 2004, 2005, in TSU Heartman Collection, Houston.

15. TSU's Opening Faculty Meeting Program, 2001.

16. *TSU Quarterly Magazine* 8, no. 12 (Summer/Fall 1999), in Priscilla D. Slade's Papers. See "Image Campaign–Billboard," *Houston Chronicle,* August 9, 2002. See "President's Report 2004," http://www.tsu.edu/pdffiles/academic /business/hjlayout.pdf. See also article on "Open Doors," in *President's 2002 End of Year Report,* 1, in Priscilla D. Slade's Papers.

17. Texas Plan, OCR Report online, http://www.PVAMU.eduprint 1665.255. See "Office for Civil Rights Plan Update, Texas Southern University," May 25, 2006,

in Priscilla D. Slade's Papers; Minutes of THECB Meeting, November 1999, http://
pages.prodigy.net/gmoses/tcrr/history.htm. See also "The Texas Plan for Equal
Educational Opportunity: A Brief History: Texas Coordinating Board (Austin),"
November 1999, in Priscilla D. Slade's Papers.

18. "Office for Civil Rights Plan Update, Texas Southern University," May 25,
2006, in Priscilla D. Slade's Papers.

19. See Judith Craven to Priscilla Slade, December 22, 1999, in Priscilla D. Slade's
Papers.

20. See "TSU Recommendations for Texas Plan," in Priscilla D. Slade's Papers, no
date.

21. Ibid. See "Office for Civil Rights Plan Update, Texas Southern University,"
May 25, 2006, in Priscilla D. Slade's Papers.

22. "Office for Civil Rights Plan Update, Texas Southern University," May 25,
2006, in Priscilla D. Slade's Papers.

23. Slade's inaugural address, April 26, 2000, in Priscilla D. Slade's Papers; *Houston Chronicle,* April 28, 2000.

24. Slade to Reginna Giovanni and Willard Jackson, May 1, 2001, in Priscilla D.
Slade's Papers.

25. Slade's "Accomplishments Fact Sheet," 2001. See also image campaign literature in Priscilla D. Slade's Papers; *Houston Chronicle,* August 8, 2002.

26. "State Auditor's Report, Follow Up Report on Rider 5," March 29, 2002; "A
Financial Review of Texas Southern University SAO Report," March 29, 2002.
See "Audit Statement 2003, Rider 5: TSU Accountability System," June 26, 2002;
"Accomplishment Facts Sheet," 2001. All items are found in Priscilla D. Slade's
Papers; *Houston Chronicle,* April 4, 2003, and May 28, 2003.

27. TSU's Opening Faculty Meeting Program, January 9, 2003; TSU enrollment
data for 2000, 2001, 2002, and 2003 can be found in TSU's Office of the Registrar
and also in Priscilla D. Slade's Papers. See also *The Texas Almanac,* 2000–2001,
2002–2003; *Houston Chronicle,* July 26, 2000.

28. Slade's "Accomplishments Fact Sheets," 2001, in Priscilla D. Slade's Papers.

29. Ibid.

30. Slade's "Accomplishments Fact Sheets," 2001–2005, in Priscilla D. Slade's
Papers.

31. Ibid.

32. *Houston Chronicle,* December 4, 5, 6, 7, 14, 2004. Asquith, "Trouble at Texas
Southern," in Priscilla D. Slade's Papers.

33. *Houston Chronicle,* December 4, 5, 6, 7, 2004, and June 27, 2005.

34. *Houston Chronicle,* June 27, 2005.

35. See Justin Jordan, Oliver Brown, and William Hudson, "Special Crisis
Report," no date, in Priscilla D. Slade's Papers.

36. *African American Issues and News,* March 30–April 5, 2005.

37. Ibid.; *Houston Chronicle,* October 29, 2005.

38. Williams G. Hudson, Justin R. Jordan and Oliver Brown v. Board of Regents
et al., September 21, 2005, case no. 05-3297; *Houston Chronicle,* October 29, 2005.
"The TSU Three Report" may have played a role in the district attorney's decision
to prosecute Slade. The students eventually won their case in an out-of-court settlement in November 2010.

39. *Houston Chronicle,* February 4, 2006; *Houston Chronicle,* April 12, 2006.

40. *Houston Chronicle,* April 12, 2006; April 17, 2010.

41. Minutes of Regular Board of Regents Meeting, January 30, 2006, TSU Heartman Collection, Houston; *Houston Chronicle,* January 28; February 2, 3, 4, 7, 2006.

42. *Houston Chronicle,* February 2, 3, 4, 2006.

43. Minutes of Special Called Meeting of the Board of Regents, February 3, 2006, TSU Heartman Collection, Houston; *Houston Chronicle,* February 4, 2006.

44. Minutes of Regular Board of Regents Meeting, March 16, 2006, TSU Heartman Collection, Houston; *Houston Chronicle,* March 17, 19, 2006. See *Houston Defender,* March 12–18, 2000.

45. Paul Johnson, interview by Merline Pitre, April 17, 2010; *Houston Chronicle,* March 17, 2006.

46. *Houston Chronicle,* April 12, 2006. A tape recording of Slade's appearance on KCOH AM Radio on April 14, 2006, can be found in Priscilla D. Slade's Papers.

47. "Bracewell and Giuliani Audit Report to TSU Board of Regents," in Minutes of the Board of Regents Meeting, April 17, 2006, TSU Heartman Collection, Houston; *Houston Chronicle,* April 18, 2006.

48. "Bracewell and Giuliani Audit Report to TSU Board of Regents," in Minutes of the Board of Regents Meeting, April 17, 2006, TSU Heartman Collection, Houston; *Houston Chronicle,* April 18, 2006.

49. *Houston Chronicle,* April 19, 2006.

50. Minutes of the Board of Regents Meeting, June 2006, TSU Heartman Collection, Houston. See also J. Paul Johnson to Faculty and Staff, March 28, 2006, in Priscilla D. Slade's Papers; *Houston Chronicle,* April 19, 2006.

51. *Houston Chronicle,* April 23, 2006.

52. *Houston Chronicle,* April 18, 2006.

53. *Houston Chronicle,* January 31, 2007.

54. *Houston Chronicle,* August 6, 2006.

55. *Houston Chronicle,* August 2, 2006; *Houston Defender,* August 6–12, 2006. See *State of Texas v. Priscilla Dean Slade,* # 1078832, Harris County District Court #338, Charge: Misapplication of Fiduciary Property, vol. 276.97. Grand jury filed August 11, 2006.

56. See *State of Texas v. Quintin Wiggins,* 2007 Tex. App. LEXIS 5739 Tex. App-Houston [1st] 2007 September, August; *Houston Chronicle,* September 8, 2006. See also *TSU Faculty Manual,* 2002.

57. Richard Pitre to Bobby Wilson, September 8, 2006; Bobby Wilson to Priscilla D. Slade, September 8, 2006, in Priscilla D. Slade's Papers.

58. *Texas Southern University Faculty Manual,* 2004, TSU Heartman Collection, Houston.

59. Audit report on Slade's spending from Bracewell and Giuliani, April 17, 2006, in Priscilla D. Slade's Papers; Houston *Chronicle,* October 13, 2007; *Dallas Morning News,* October 10, 2007.

60. *Houston Chronicle,* September 7, 2007.

61. *Houston Chronicle,* October 14, 2007.

62. *Houston Chronicle,* October 13, 14, 2007.

63. Bobby Wilson to TSU Faculty, June 13, 2006, Priscilla D. Slade's Papers.

64. Ibid.

65. Minutes of Regular Board Meeting, November 27, 2006, TSU Heartman Collection, Houston. J. Paul Johnson to Timothy Boddie, November 27, 2006, in Timothy Boddie's Papers, TSU Heartman Collection, Houston.

66. Timothy Boddie's biography in Timothy Boddie's Papers; "Memo: J. Paul Johnson to Faculty and Staff," November 29, 2006, in Timothy Boddie's Papers.

67. Minutes of the Advisory Committee, May 2007, in Priscilla D. Slade's Papers; *Houston Defender*, January 30, 2007.

68. "Texas Southern Advisory [Blue Ribbon] Committee: A Report to the Governor, Lt. Governor, Speaker of the House and TSU Board of Regents," March 26, 2007, in Priscilla D. Slade's Papers; *Houston Defender*, April 1–7, 2007; *Houston Chronicle*, May 9, 2007.

69. *Houston Defender*, April 22–28, 2007.

70. *Houston Chronicle*, April 13, 2007, May 4, 2007; *Houston Defender*, April 22–29, 2007; May 29, 2007.

71. *Houston Defender*, April 22–28, 2007. *Houston Chronicle*, April 13, 2007.

72. *Houston Defender*, April 22–28, 2007; *Houston Chronicle*, April 13, 2007.

73. *Houston Chronicle*, April 28, 2007.

74. "An Act Relating to the Governance of certain state agencies, Sec. 1.01, subchapter G, Chapter 51, Ed. code is amended by adding Sec. 51.358 and 51.359." See also Texas Legislature, *General and Special Laws Passed in the 80th Legislature, Regular Session*, S.B. 2039 (Austin, 2007); *Houston Defender*, May 5, 2007; *Houston Chronicle*, May 9, 10, 2009.

75. *Texas Legislature, General and Special Laws Passed in the 80th Legislature Regular Session (Austin 2007)*; *Houston Chronicle*, April 28, 2007, May 9, 2007. Press release from My Fox Houston, April 13, 2001, in Timothy Boddie's Papers; Belinda Griffin to TSU Faculty, February 19, 2007, in Timothy Boddie's Papers.

76. *Houston Chronicle*, July 30, 2007; Steven Ogden to Glenn Lewis, November 28, 2007, in Priscilla D. Slade's Papers.

77. *Houston Chronicle*, August 23, 2007.

78. *Houston Chronicle*, March 26, 2008; *Dallas Morning News*, October 24, 2009.

Chapter 12

1. Minutes of the Regular Board of Regents Meeting, January 11, 2008, TSU Heartman Collection, Houston; *Houston Chronicle*, January 11, 12, 2008.

2. John M. Rudley's biography in John M. Rudley's Papers, TSU Heartman Collection, Houston. See also "Legacy Now: The Inauguration Program of John M. Rudley, 11th President of Texas Southern University," September 6, 2008, in John M. Rudley's Papers; *Houston Chronicle*, December 19, 2011.

3. John Rudley to faculty and staff, January 31, 2012, in John M. Rudley's Papers; *Houston Chronicle*, February 12, 2012, April 27, 2014.

4. Belle Wheelan to John M. Rudley, January 5, 2010, and Rudley to faculty and staff, February 15, 2011; both are in John M. Rudley's Papers. *Houston Chronicle*, February 15, 2011.

5. Minutes of the Regular Board of Regents Meeting, June 29, 2008, January 29 and July 29, 2009, TSU Heartman Collection, Houston; *Houston Chronicle*, February 24, 2008. See also "Admission Requirements" in *Texas Southern University*

Catalog, 2012-2015, in TSU Heartman Collection, Houston. When the university changed from its open-door policy, it also made provision for students who were deficient in reading, mathematics, and English. These individuals can attend a summer camp designed to help them reach college standards before being admitted to the university. The university has since raised its entrance requirement to a 2.5 grade point average.

6. See TSU's Urban Academic Village website at http://www.mystudentvillage. com/us/urban-academic-village/. See also Rudley to faculty and staff, September 2013, in John M. Rudley's Papers.

7. *Houston Defender,* July 14, 2012.

8. Rudley to faculty and staff, no date, in John M. Rudley's Papers.

9. *Texas Southern University Catalog, 2014–2015; Inside TSU Magazine,* 2015; both items are in the TSU Heartman Collection, Houston.

10. *Houston Chronicle,* May 6, 2012; Minutes of the Regular Board of Regents Meeting, August 2014, TSU Heartman Collection, Houston.

11. *Houston Chronicle,* January 17, 2010; *Houston Chronicle,* September 24, 2011; June 4, 5, 2015.

12. Texas Southern University Public Infraction Report, October 9, 2012; in John M. Rudley's Papers; *Houston Chronicle,* April 1, 2001.

13. *Forward Times,* July 4, 2015.

14. *Houston Chronicle,* January 7, September 6, 15, 2010; *Houston Press,* September 13, 15, 2010; Rudley to faculty and staff, September 10, 2010, in John M. Rudley's Papers.

15. See *TakeBackTxSU Demands,* circa 2015, in John M. Rudley's Papers.

16. Rivard, "Fighting for Survival."

17. *Houston Chronicle,* October 9, 10, 12, 2015; KHOU Broadcast, "Campus on Lock Down," October 25, 2015; Marshall Khambrel KPRC Broadcast, "TSU President with Kambrel," October 25, 2015.

18. Sunny Ohia to Academic Deans, August 2014; Rasoul Sandifer to TSU Faculty, August 10, 2014. Later, Sandifer told the faculty that he was barred from the president's meetings; in Faculty Senate Archives in the TSU Heartman Collection, Houston and in the possession of Sandifer. See also Faculty Awards Day Programs, April 2012, 2013, 2015, TSU Heartman Collection, Houston.

19. Minutes of the Regular Board of Regents Meeting, October 16, 2016; Minutes of Special Board Teleconference Meeting, October 24, 2016; *Houston Chronicle,* December 12, 2015.

20. Earl Carl Institute, *Our Story,* 128–37; *Inside TSU Magazine,* 2012–2013, 2014. See Rudley to faculty and staff, September 18, 2015; *Houston Chronicle,* January 11, 2016.

21. *Houston Chronicle,* April 24, 2016; June 21, 2015.

22. Earl Carl Institute, *Our Story,* 128–37; *Houston Defender,* January 21, 2016.

23. See "Notice of Censure and Vote of No Confidence," Faculty Senate to the Honorable Regents of Texas Southern University, April 7, 2016 Faculty Senate Archives.

24. Regular Board of Regents Meetings, March 24, April 24, and May 7, 2016.

Bibliography

Manuscript and Archival Sources

African American Library at the Gregory School, Houston.
Everett O. Bell's Papers, TSU Heartman Collection, Houston.
General Files, Negroes in College 1934–1954, University of Texas, President Office Records, Dolph Briscoe History Center, the University of Texas at Austin.
Granville M. Sawyer's Papers, TSU Heartman Collection, Houston.
Gregory Lincoln African American Museum, Houston.
Houston Independent School District Education Archives, Houston.
Houston Metropolitan Research Center, Houston.
James M. Douglas's Papers, TSU Heartman Collection, Houston.
Joann Horton's Papers, TSU Heartman Collection, Houston.
John B. Connally's Papers, Houston Riot File, 60-30-14, Lyndon Baines Johnson Library, Austin.
John M. Rudley's Papers, TSU Heartman Collection, Houston.
Joseph A. Pierce's Papers, TSU Heartman Collection, Houston.
Leonard H. O. Spearman's Papers, TSU Heartman Collection, Houston.
NAACP Papers, Manuscript Collection, Library of Congress.
Oral History Collection, Houston Metropolitan Research Center, Houston Public Library.
Oran M. Roberts's Papers, Texas State Archives, Austin.
Priscilla D. Slade's Papers, TSU Heartman Collection, Houston.
Raphael O'Hara Lanier's Papers, TSU Heartman Collection, Houston.
Robert J. Terry's Papers, TSU Heartman Collection, Houston.
Samuel M. Nabrit's Papers, TSU Heartman Collection, Houston.
Texas Southern University History Files, TSU Heartman Collection, Houston.
Timothy Boddie's Papers, TSU Heartman Collection, Houston.
TSU Riot File, TSU Heartman Collection, Houston.
University of Houston Archives.
William H. Harris's Papers, TSU Heartman Collection, Houston.

Books and Articles

Anderson, James. *The Education of Blacks in the South, 1860–1935.* Chapel Hill: University of North Carolina Press, 1988.

Anderson, Terry H. *The Sixties.* New York: Pearson, 2011.

Ashworth, Kenneth. "Texas Higher Education Coordination Board." Texas State Historical Association website. https://tshaonline.org/handbook/online/articles/mdtpx.

Asquith, Christina. "Trouble at Texas Southern." *Diverse Issues in Higher Education* (December 14, 2006), http://diverseeducation.com/article/6764/.

Aulbach, Louis F. *Buffalo Bayou: An Echo of the Houston Wilderness Beginnings.* Houston: CreateSpace Independent Publishing Platform, 2011.

Beeth, Howard, and Cary Wintz, eds. *Black Dixie: Afro-Texans History and Culture in Houston.* College Station: Texas A&M University Press, 1992.

Bryant, Ira B. *Texas Southern University: Its Antecedents, Political Origin and Future.* Houston: Armstrong, 1975.

Bryson, William C. "Born in Sin: A College Finally Makes Houston Listen." *Harvard Crimson Magazine,* May 22, 1967.

Bullard, Robert D. *Invisible Houston: The Black Experience in Boom and Bust.* College Station: Texas A&M University Press, 1987.

Bullock, Henry Allen. "The Availability of Education in the Texas Negro Separate School." *Journal of Negro Education* 16, no. 3 (Summer, 1947): 425–32.

Carson, Clayborne. *In Struggle: SNCC and the Black Awakening of the 1960's.* Cambridge: Harvard University Press, 1996.

Cole, Thomas. *No Color Is My Kind: The Life of Eldrewey Stearns and the Integration of Houston.* Austin: University of Texas Press, 2001.

Earl Carl Institute. *Our Story: A History of the Presidents of Texas Southern University.* Houston: Earl Carl Institute, 2012.

Friedberg, Bernard. "Houston and the TSU Riot." In *Anti-Black Violence in Twentieth-Century Texas,* edited by Bruce Glasrud, 131–42. College Station: Texas A&M University Press, 2015.

Gillette, Michael. "Blacks Challenge the White University." *Southwestern Historical Quarterly* 86 (Oct 1983): 321–44.

Harris, Williams H. *The Harder We Run: Black Workers since the Civil War.* New York: Oxford University Press, 1982.

———. *Keeping the Faith: A. Philip Randolph, Milton P. Webster, and the Brotherhood of Sleeping Car Porters, 1925–1937.* Urbana: University of Illinois Press, 1977.

Hine, Darlene C. *Black Victory: The Rise and Fall of the White Primary in Texas.* Columbia: University of Missouri Press, 2003.

Hornsby, Alton Jr. "The 'Colored Branch University' Issue in Texas—Prelude to Sweatt v. Painter." *Journal of Negro History* 61, no. 1 (January, 1976): 51–60.

Jensen, Kenneth. "The Houston Sit-In Movement, 1960–1961." In *Black Dixie: Afro-Texan History and Culture in Houston*, edited by Howard Beeth and Cary Wintz, 211–22. College Station: Texas A&M University Press, 1992.

Johnson, Ozie Harold. *The Price of Freedom*. Houston: Armstrong, 1954.

Lanier, Raphael O'Hara. "The History of Higher Education for Negroes in Texas with Particular Reference to Texas Southern University." EdD diss., New York University, 1957.

Lash, John, Hortense Dixon, and Thomas Freeman. *Texas Southern University: From Separation to Special Designation*. Houston: Texas Southern University Press, 1992.

Lavergne, Gary. *Before* Brown: *Heman Marion Sweatt, Thurgood Marshall, and the Long Road to Justice*. Austin: University of Texas Press, 2010.

Lee, E. Bun, ed. *TSU Meets the Press: White Newspaper Coverage of a Black University in Houston, Texas, 1947–2006*. Houston: Prestige Printers, 2007.

Nabrit, Samuel M. "Desegregation and the Future of Graduate and Professional Education in Negro Institutions." *Journal of Negro Education* 27, no. 3 (Spring, 1988): 414–18.

Nicholson, Patrick J. *In Time: An Anecdotal History of the First Fifty Years of the University of Houston*. Houston: Pacesetter Press, 1977.

Phelps, Wesley G. *A People's War on Poverty: Urban Politics and Grassroots Activists in Houston*. Athens: University of Georgia Press, 2014.

Pitre, Merline. "Black Houstonians and the Separate but Equal Doctrine: Carter W. Wesley versus Lulu B. White." *Houston Review* 12, no. 1 (1990): 23–36.

———. "The Establishment of Texas Southern University, 1947." In *Eavesdropping on Texas History*, edited by Mary Scheer, 240–65. Denton: University of North Texas Press, 2016.

———. "Leonard H. O. Spearman." Texas State Historical Association website. https://tshaonline.org/handbook/online/articles/fsp34.

———. "Samuel Milton Nabrit." *BlackPast.org*. http://www.blackpast.org/aaw/nabrit-samuel-milton-1905-2003.

———. "Samuel Milton Nabrit," Texas State Historical Association website. https://tshaonline.org/handbook/online/articles/fna31.

———. *In Struggle against Jim Crow: Lulu B. White and the NAACP, 1900–1957*. College Station: Texas A&M University Press, 2010.

———. *Through Many Dangers, Toils, and Snares: Black Leadership in Texas 1868–1898*. College Station: Texas A&M University Press, 2016.

Rivard, Ry. "Fighting for Survival." *Inside Higher Ed*. June 24, 2014. https://www.insidehighered.com/news/2014/06/24/public-hbcus-facing-tests-many-fronts-fight-survival.

Sapper, Neil. "The Rise and Fall of the NAACP in Texas." *The Houston Review* 7 (1985): 53–68.

Sawyer, Granville. "Black College and Community Development." *Journal of Black Studies* 6, no.7 (September 1975): 77–99.

———. "The Image of the Negro College: Basis in Fact?" *College and University Journal* 5, no. 3 (Summer, 1966): 36–41.

———. "One University's Urban Commitment." *Journal of Extension* 11, no. 1 (Spring, 1973): 41–48.

Shabazz, Amilcar. *Advancing Democracy: African Americans and the Struggle for Access and Equity in Higher Education in Texas*. Chapel Hill: University of North Carolina Press, 2004.

Spearman, Leonard H. O. "Education in America: Whose Needs Are Being Served?" *Issue Magazine* 1, no. 1 (January, 1982): 4–7.

Terry, William E. *Origin and Development of Texas Southern University*. Houston: privately printed, 1978.

"Texas Southern University: The Stepchild of the Texas Higher Education System." *Journal of Black Higher Education* 25 (Autumn, 1999): 64–66.

Thompson, Charles Henry. "Separate, but Equal: The Sweatt Case." *Southwest Review* 33, no. 3 (Spring 1948): 105–12.

Watson, Dwight. *Race and the Houston Police Department, 1930–1990: A Change Did Come*. College Station: Texas A&M University Press, 2005.

Williams, David A. "The History of Higher Education for Black Texans, 1872–1977." PhD diss., Baylor University, 1978.

Woolfolk, George R. *Prairie View: A Study in Public Conscience, 1878–1946*. New York: Pageant, 1962.

Index

References to illustrations appear in italic type.

conference, 138–39; and Douglas
inauguration, 162; and financial
hurdle, 133; "good teaching"
mantra of, 136; and leadership
team, 133; legacy of, 143, 210; major
problems confronting, 140, 159;
and major renovations, 138; named
seventh president, 129, 130; and
Ocean of Soul scandal, 142–43, 145;
priorities of, 131–33; resignation of,
143–44; and TASP, 133, 134, 135, 136;
and Texas Plan continued, 135; and
visions of, 139–40
Harris County Council of
Organizations, 57
Harris era (1988–93), 130–44;
achievements of, 143–44; challenge
and discovery, 132–38; change and
implementation, 138–43; Harris
named seventh president, 129,
131–32
Hartshorn, H. Hadley: and Committee
of Three, 74; and firebomb in
home of, 77; new post for, 85; on
reorganization of TSU, 95; riots
blamed on police brutality by, 76
Harvey, Tony, 202
Hawkins, Erskine, 116
Hayes, Leonard, 145
Head Start programs, 50, 60, 93
Heartman, Charles Fred, 28
Heatly, William S., 122
Henry, John E., 29
HEW (Department of Health,
Education, and Welfare), 107, 110
Higher Education Assistance Funds,
138
Hill, Joshua, 133
Hobby, William P., 136, 161
Hogrobrooks, Ted and Holly, 54
Hogue v. Baker (1898), 4
Holcombe, Oscar, 24
Holderman, Terry, 174
Holland, Richard, 193
Honors Program, 115, 136, 199

Hopkins, Roy Lee, 11
Horton, Joann (1993–95), *146*, *155*; and
administrative shake-up, 149; and
audits, 152–53; background of, 145–
46; and firings and resignations,
149–51; goals of, 147–48, 152, 153;
inaugural of, 148–49; legacy of,
156; management skills of, 146, 148;
named eighth president, 145–46,
159; ouster of, 155–56, 157; problems
facing, 146–47; resignation called
for, 154; response to criticisms,
151–52
Horton era (1993–95), 145–56;
administrators removed, 149–51;
agenda of, 153–54; criticisms of,
151–53; honeymoon period, 147–49;
Horton removal, 154–56; Horton
selection, 145–47
Houston, Tex., as boomtown, 4–5
Houston Area Urban League, 187
Houston Chronicle, 37, 117, 153, 187,
240n42
Houston College for Negroes
(HCN; 1927–47), 5; and contract
arrangements, 21–23; establishment
of, 10–11; expansion of, 12, 236n29;
and Fairchild Building, 13–14, *14*;
and HISD problems, 13; proposed
as nucleus, 18–19; purchase of by
state, 20. See also Lanier, Raphael
O'Hara (1947–55); *Missouri ex rel.
Gaines v. Canada* (1938); *Smith v.
Allwright* (1944); *Sweatt v. Painter*
(1950)
Houston Colored Junior College:
establishment of, 6–8; and Fox
administration progress, 9; and
Lanier, 10–11; and name change,
11–12; and political climate, 8–9;
purpose of, 8; and salaries, 7, 9,
225n14; site of (1926–47), 5. *See
also* Houston College for Negroes
(HCN; 1927–47); Lanier, Raphael
O'Hara (1947–55)

Strickland, Don (judge), 184
Student Nonviolent Coordinating
    Committee. *See* SNCC (Student
    Nonviolent Coordinating
    Committee)
subprime mortgage crisis, 197
Sweatt, Heman Marion, 16, *17*, 127. See
    also *under Sweatt v. Painter* (1950)
Sweatt v. Painter (1950): impact of,
    17, 32, 35, 40, 53; state's reaction to
    ruling, 32–34; Sweatt as plaintiff,
    16–20

"Take TSU Back" movement, 203, 204
TASP (Texas Academic Skills
    Program). *See under* Harris,
    William Hamilton (1988–93)
Taylor, B. E., 25
TCHE (Texas Commission of Higher
    Education), 51–52
Teacher Corps Program, 93
Temple, Larry, 126–28
Terry, Robert J. (1986–87), *120*, *125*;
    background of, 85, 96, 119; and
    budget, 128; and commission
    proposals, 126–27; death of, 128;
    goals of, 119–20; merger as major
    issue, 120–21; and merger failure,
    128; and Select Committee hearing,
    124, 126–28
Terry's interim years (1986–87), 119–29;
    and budget after merger failure,
    128; issues faced by Terry, 119–21;
    and merger failure, 126–28; and
    merger history, 121–24; and search
    for new president, 128–29
Texas, as one-party state, 8–9
Texas A&M System, 15, 18, 27, 123
Texas Association of Colleges and
    Universities, 154
Texas Commission of Higher
    Education (TCHE), 51–52
Texas Constitution (1876), 3, 16, 19
Texas Coordinating Board, 177

Texas Council of Negro
    Organizations, 17–18
Texas Education Agency, 38
Texas Higher Education Coordinating
    Board (THECB), 89, 109
Texas Plan: acceptance by OCR
    (1983), 112–13; approval of (2000),
    177; continuation of, 135; final
    phase of, 176–77; history of, 107;
    as milestone, 113; mission and
    enhancement study (1981), 107–9;
    negotiation of, 123; provisions of,
    111–12; submission to HEW (1982),
    109–10; and TSU requirements,
    177–78. *See also* Slade, Priscilla
    Dean (1999–2006); Spearman,
    Leonard Hall O'Connell (1980–86)
Texas Southern University. *See* TSU
    (Texas Southern University)
Texas State Board of Law Examiners,
    29, 30
Texas State University for Negroes
    (later TSU). *See* TSUN (Texas State
    University for Negroes; later TSU)
THECB (Texas Higher Education
    Coordinating Board), 89, 109
Third Ward, Houston, 166
Thomas, Gayla, 173, 176
Thomas F. Freeman Honors College,
    199
"Three of Us Dinner Dance," 106
Thurgood Marshall School of Law, 101,
    111, 128, 158, 217
TIGER Project, 200
Tiger Walk Mall, 205–6
Title III, Higher Education Act, 50–51,
    137
Title VI, Civil Rights Act of 1964, 107,
    176
Tobacco Center, 180
Tollette, Kenneth S., 52, 76
"Toward an Urban University"
    (circulars), 88–89
Trinity Methodist Church, 5–6

CPSIA information can be obtained
at www.ICGtesting.com
Printed in the USA
LVHW042015010623
748605LV00014B/412/J

9 780806 160023